Dear Mendl, Dear Reyzl

Dear Mendl, Dear Reyzl

YIDDISH LETTER MANUALS
FROM RUSSIA AND
AMERICA

Alice Nakhimovsky & Roberta Newman

INDIANA UNIVERSITY PRESS

Bloomington and Indianapolis

This book is a publication of

INDIANA UNIVERSITY PRESS
Office of Scholarly Publishing
Herman B Wells Library 350
1320 East 10th Street
Bloomington, Indiana 47405 USA

iupress.indiana.edu

Telephone orders 800-842-6796
Fax orders 812-855-7931

♾The paper used in this publication
meets the minimum requirements of
the American National Standard for
Information Sciences–Permanence of
Paper for Printed Library Materials,
ANSI Z39.48–1992.

*Manufactured in the
United States of America*

*Library of Congress Cataloging-in-
Publication Data*

Nakhimovsky, Alice S., author.
  Dear Mendl, dear Reyzl : Yiddish letter
manuals from Russia and America /
Alice Nakhimovsky and Roberta
Newman.
      pages cm
  Includes bibliographical references and
index.
  ISBN 978-0-253-01199-2 (cl : alk. paper)
— ISBN 978-0-253-01203-6 (pb : alk.
paper) — ISBN 978-0-253-01207-4 (eb)
1. Letter writing, Yiddish. 2. Yiddish
letters—Translations into English. I.
Newman, Roberta, 1958- author. II. Title.
PJ5118.N35 2014
839'.16308—dc23

                              2013039248

1 2 3 4 5   19 18 17 16 15 14

publication of these templates
was made possible by a grant
Jewish Federation of Greater Hartford

CONTENTS

PREFACE

In 1913, Sonia Lubelski, a young woman living in the Lithuanian shtetl of Baltrumants, wrote a letter to her fiancé in America. The two young people were trying to negotiate a present and a future through the mail, and Sonia was still uncertain about whether to join Morris—the former Meyshe Abba—in Lynn, Massachusetts. "I too want to put an end to the paper life," she writes, hopefully. But her next words are more resigned: "As the women say, 'They take people and they exchange them for paper.'"[1]

Sonia and Meyshe Abba were hardly the only young couple who were living through the mail. A paper life—a life of correspondence—ran parallel to the real lives of East European Jews at the turn of the twentieth century. People wrote letters of all kinds: family letters, business letters, courtship letters. For a highly migratory people, letters were a necessity. Even within the Russian Empire, sons left home to study, or to make a living, or to board with in-laws, or because they had been drafted. Daughters left with husbands or went alone to seek a better life in big cities. Men traveled to seek business opportunities. And few families were unaffected by emigration.

Letters presented all sorts of opportunities beyond satisfying the desire to maintain contact with loved ones. Write the right kind of letter, and you present yourself as you want to be seen; use good arguments, and you impel others, for example, your grownup children, to act in ways that match your expectations. But to take advantage of these opportunities, lower-middle-class Jews needed skills they might not have had a chance to acquire. Jews in Russia and Poland needed help in writing correct Yiddish, and sometimes, Hebrew and Russian (in America, they needed English). They needed examples of how to express feelings in a formal or classy or modern way, and models for constructing effective arguments. For all these purposes, people turned to the *brivnshteler,* an anthology of letters for business and private correspondence.

The idea of correspondence to copy—the occasional letter-writing manual actually leaves blanks to fill in—is by nature a little comical: letters, especially of the family and romantic variety, are supposed to be spontaneous and sincere. People were aware of the paradox. The heroine of Isaac Bashevis Singer's story "A Crown of Feathers" dismisses an unattractive suitor with the comment that he talks like a brivnshteler.[2] Sometimes, brivnshtelers even poked fun at themselves, as in this joke from a manual of 1900:

The Convenient Brifshteller

A not too bright young man wanted to write a letter to a girlfriend but didn't know how to begin. So he bought a *brifshteller* and immediately found the sort of letter he wanted. He wrote it down exactly the way he found it and sent it on its way. The girlfriend also had the exact same *brifshteller* and when she found the letter there, she answered him on the spot: "*Mein herr!* I have received your letter," adding the page number on which his reply to her letter could be found.[3]

The mockery was widespread—this was not a genre that commanded respect. And yet these cheaply printed handbooks provided thousands of readers with formulas for turning private, often highly emotional, real-life situations into expressions on paper. A standard brivnshteler had sections for love letters, business letters, letters asking for a loan, and letters between parents and children that were linked to particularly Jewish dilemmas. If a reader wanted to know how to write to a son who had been drafted into the Russian Army, if a wife needed help writing to her husband who had emigrated to America years before, there was a brivnshteler that had anticipated the situation. In short, the brivnshteler taught its readers how to live a paper life.

The specificity and emotional intensity of the brivnshteler allowed it to function as a kind of cheap literature. The sensationalist letters that appear in some brivnshtelers—letters, for example, from abandoned wives—served the same Jewish audience that, in Yiddish-speaking America, read *shund* (lowbrow) literature and pored over the confessions in the advice column of the *Forverts* newspaper. But however indispensable this entertainment aspect might have been, the core of the brivnshteler was pedagogical.

Aside from letters, brivnshtelers featured varieties of lists and guides, some useful for business (information on postage, place names, forms of address, even lessons on bookkeeping); and others helpful to the composer of any kind of letter (lists of how to spell men's and women's names; names of months and days of the week in different languages). Jewish men, whose base-level traditional education did not include instruction in secular practicalities like writing in their native language, turned to the brivnshteler for self-instruction. In it, they found not only a guide to writing good, educated Yiddish, but also the meaning and spelling of Hebrew phrases that were standard for openings and closings in the correspondence of more highly educated elites.

Teachers of handwriting and spelling—*shraybers*—also made use of brivnshtelers, either in the *kheyder* (traditional elementary school), or in private lessons at home. The target learners in a home setting were often girls. Proficiency in secular skills like business correspondence and foreign languages would boost their worth as brides without challenging the male sphere of religious learning.

Another pedagogical function of the brivnshteler was foreign-language instruction. Bilingual brivnshtelers served not only as textbooks of foreign languages, but also as manuals of foreign behavior. Yiddish-speakers who wanted to assimilate Russian manners and attitudes could learn from Yiddish-Russian brivnshtelers how to write a passionate (as opposed to decorous) love letter or how to write a letter of friendship between men. Readers of Harkavy's 1902 American manual, *Amerikanisher briefen-shteler un speller* (American brivnshteler and speller), could study the American approach to courtship and friendship, presented in American English with a complete Yiddish gloss.

The focus of this book is on the ways that brivnshtelers portray and reflect Jewish life in both Eastern Europe and America during the latter part of the nineteenth century, and the first decade or so of the twentieth. We approach the letters as social history documents and also as literary texts, but with the acknowledgment that unlike prose that aspires to art, these texts are distinguished by their unapologetic pursuit of banality. Unlike today's off-the-shelf texts—for example, *outré* birthday cards—brivnshtelers rarely try to push the envelope of the genre.

What they were after was fluent banality, the kind that would enable users to fit in as people who understood acceptable modern patterns of discourse and behavior. The scope of instruction was extremely broad. It ranged, on the personal end, from the composition of love letters to the crafting of a moralistic or impatient letter to your adult child—and on the business end, from how to properly announce the opening of an import-export business to how to mollify someone to whom you owe a rather large debt.

The pursuit of banality was probably not conscious, and involved some contradictions. On the one hand, authors and publishers pursuing time-honored clichés plagiarized shamelessly from earlier sources. On the other, they often trumpeted their superiority by stressing how much better they were at meeting the needs of modern times. Their books, they claimed in their prefaces, were more up-to-date in language and content, simply more relevant than the competition.

It is the very banality of brivnshtelers that makes them fascinating. In pursuing what they thought ordinary people needed and wanted, authors captured and packaged the notions, keywords, and aspirations of everyday life.[4] Studying these texts now, we can read them as reflections of some of the emotional realities and concerns that underlay East European Jewish society. The mirror is of course imperfect. On the one hand, as a commercial genre, brivnshtelers had to respond to market needs. But their authors had their own agendas, which come through quite clearly, though not always consistently.

Letter manuals were not a Jewish invention. Yiddish brivnshtelers in Eastern Europe borrowed from Hebrew, Russian, and German sources, sometimes Judaizing what they took from German and Russian and sometimes not. Throughout the lifespan of the genre, the books both repeat one other and strike out on their own. Most East European Jewish letter manuals published before the middle of the nineteenth century were not written in Yiddish, despite the fact that they might have the word "brivnshteler" in their titles. Such books were meant for the more educated male elite, and often used combinations of three high-status languages: Hebrew, Russian, and German written in Hebrew characters (Judeo-German). The set of manuals that feature a Hebrew/Russian/Judeo-German trifecta have no love letters at all and few, if any, letters written by women.[5] By the end of the century, though, all newly published brivnshtelers feature colloquial Yiddish and clearly cater to female as well as male readers. Love letters—along with family letters in general—are front and center.

Change over time is matched by diversity among manuals written at around the same time: one is distinctly playful; another few are assimilation-oriented; still others focus on youth and modern life.[6] More surprising are the contradictions within individual manuals. A brivnshteler of 1904 features two letters in which seekers of secular entertainment get their just deserts when the theater they are attending catches fire (one letter concludes: "Dear Son! Keep the Sabbath laws and you will spare yourself such punishment").[7] Yet the very same book features a letter in which a young man, drawn to secular subjects, pours out his rebellious heart to his brother-in-law.[8] Exactly what is behind this inconsistency is hard to determine: perhaps the marketplace—it makes sense to have something for everybody—or perhaps merely carelessness in a genre on which nobody wasted much effort.

Brivnshtelers were, in fact, ephemeral and cheap. They were printed on poor-quality paper. Typesetting was often sloppy, resulting in poorly printed text and occasional errors; and pagination was haphazard. When books were cobbled together from different brivnshtelers, compilers often made no effort to insert new page numbers, leading to editions in which, for instance, page 17 follows page 147, and there is a jump from page 21 to page 81.[9]

Our book begins with a history: how brivnshtelers fit into the Jewish Enlightenment and the rise of Yiddish and Yiddish literature; how they filled gaps in Jewish education; and how they reflected the rapid cultural, social, and economic changes of the turn of the twentieth century. Examining what made brivnshtelers specifically Jewish, we compare their worldview to that of non-Jewish letter manuals from Russia, America, and German-speaking Europe. In the second part of the book, we explore characteristic brivnshteler themes: encounters with modernity; the image of America in East European manuals and the discovery of America in American ones; courtship; parents and children; business; and finally, Judaism and Jewish identity. For each section, we present half a dozen or so letters in translation—most because they are representative of the genre, and others for precisely the opposite reason: because they are quirky and unusual.

At the end of the book is a sampling of the sorts of non-letter materials that were almost always included in brivnshtelers. Some of these items—like the lists of names and honorifics mentioned earlier—are directly related to letter writing. But there are also templates for the mundane needs of everyday life, like laundry lists (to accompany the clothes sent to a laundress), or shopping lists (sent along with the servant who is doing your shopping). One brivnshteler, published in Vilna in 1910, has an etiquette guide. Others include poems, children's games, or—aiming at the pedagogical high end—introductions to arithmetic or bookkeeping.

The brivnshtelers in this book all appeared in print between the early nineteenth century and the 1920s, when the genre finally died out. They range from the brivnshtelers of Avrom Lion Dor and his son Hirsh, first published as early as 1826, but frequently reprinted well into the twentieth century, to the last edition of *Shaykevitsh'es nayer brivnshteler* (Shaykevitsh's new brivnshteler), published in New York by the Hebrew Publishing Company in 1928.[10] The books we look at fall into several categories. Some are original works and present never-before-published content. Others, despite their new titles and authors, merely recycle tried-and-true material from earlier books. A third category mixes pirated letters with new ones.

The recycling often involves letters of obviously archaic content. Some good examples come from *Eyn nayer brifenshteler* (A new brivnshteler), an anonymously authored manual published in Vilna in 1900. One of its letters concerns a boy being sent to Prague to continue his Jewish education—a life event that would not have been unheard of in the eighteenth to mid-nineteenth century, but would have been unusual at the time the book was published.[11] Business letters in the same book refer to *Reichsthalers,* a form of currency in German lands that became obsolete in 1857.

There is no way to judge how readers reacted to archaic material, and indeed no clear way to assess the popularity of different books. We have no information on print runs. But looking at individual copies of books, which sometimes have penned-in marginal notes, home and business addresses, and even—in the case of bilingual texts—corrections, we can see that they were read and used. And the many reprints of these books tells us that they were considered profitable enough to sell. The title page of the 1890 *Yudish-daytsher morall brifenshteller* (Yiddish-German ethical brivnshteler) is a good example: it claims that ten thousand copies of the book have been printed and that the book is in its third edition.[12]

One unsolved mystery is the word *brivnshteler*.[13] The plural of "letter" (*briv*) in modern Yiddish is *briv* and not *brivn*. In German, the word for letter manual is *Brief Steller*. Historian Elisheva Carlebach points out that Brief Steller came into use only in the eighteenth century. Prior to that German letter manuals were called by other names, such as *Formelsammlungen* and *Rhetorik*.[14] *Brivn* is an example of an old weak genitive, an archaic form of a word that has survived in a compound word even as it has disappeared from any other usage.[15] It is one clue that the brivnshteler may be a very old genre, far predating its short run in print, which spanned less than two hundred years, and only a century in Eastern Europe.

The brivnshteler was a transitional genre in Yiddish literature, rendered obsolete after World War I by the availability of superior educational options and a new abundance of reading material in Yiddish. And yet, in the words of David Barton and Nigel Hall, letter writing is "one of the most pervasive literate activities in human societies."[16] Letters are just about the only written texts generated by non-elites and thus provide a rare chance to gain insight into the lives of ordinary people and the ways in which cultural, social, and economic change manifested itself in everyday life.

Real letters represent one type of evidence. The more mediated, fictional world of the brivnshteler represents another. In all of its hodgepodge of language and content, the brivnshteler reflects the fluidity and instability of Jewish life of its era. Its not always coherent pages jumble together the new and the old, the Jewish and the non-Jewish, Yiddish and other linguistic influences. This modest, messy genre provides a perspective on Jewish life not offered by more carefully crafted and self-conscious literary products, such as memoirs, novels, and feuilletons.

Our approach has been influenced by the many theorists (Erving Goffman, Michel de Certeau, Henri Lefebvre, Iurii Lotman) who have uncovered the meaning-laden systems underpinning everyday life. The Tartu School is of particular relevance here, not only because its main subject is the Russian Empire, the home territory of our Yiddish-speakers, but because a lot of Russian structuralist work is concerned with the past, and integrates the ideas of the intelligentsia with the practice of everyday life. We have paid close attention to the work of scholars such as Jeffrey Brooks, Catriona Kelly, and Anna Shternshis, who use Russian or Russian-Jewish popular texts as a way of understanding unspoken assumptions about identity and experience. But our most important debt is to the historians, in particular ChaeRan Freeze, Olga Litvak, Iris Parush, and Shaul Stampfer, whose focus on everyday reality (marriage, divorce, education, literacy) and intellectual life (the Jewish Enlightenment) brings us closer to the world in which brivnshtelers were written and read.

Unlike memoirs or novels, written with an eye to immortality, brivnshtelers were not meant to last, and certainly not to be studied.[17] Looking at them now, we see in them the reflection of the needs and desires of ordinary people in an era of great change.

NOTES

1. Collection of Zimman Family, n.d. Letters 123/125.

2. Singer, *Collected Stories*, 274. The story does not appear to have ever been published in Yiddish.

3. *Eyn nayer brifenshteler in dray obtheylungen* (1900), 147; also in Alek, *Oytser mikhtovim* [*Otsar mikhtavim*] (1906), 79. We have preserved the original nonstandard spelling of the word brivnshteler.

4. Bernard Bray makes this point with respect to seventeenth-century France, calling letter manuals a "microcosm" of the society. He also notes a possible tension between the conventions taught by manuals and the feelings of the user: "In teaching the art of letter-writing, the manuals teach the art of the lie" (*L'art de la lettre*, 29–30).

5. For example, see Avraham Paperna, *Meyroyts igroys* [*Merots igrot*] (1874) and *Mikhtov meshulesh* [*Mikhtav meshulash*] (1878).

6. The playful manual is Arukh, *Arukhs brifenshteller* (1892); assimilation-oriented manuals are Hirsh Lion Dor, *Eyn nayer brifen shteler* (1887), Frishman, Paperna, and Mrs. Hess, *Igron shalem* (1911), and Harkavy, *Amerikanisher briefen-shteler* (1901); youth and modern life are prominently featured in *Bernshteyn's nayer yudisher folks-brifenshteler* (1912).

7. Poliak-Gilman, *Der nayer obraztsover brifenshteller* (1904), 20.

8. Ibid., 32.

9. *Eyn nayer brifenshteler in dray obtheylungen* (1900).

10. There are a few later publications of brivnshtelers, but these are outliers. Missing from the YIVO library in summer 2011 is a book noted in its catalog, *Khosn-kale brief* by Avrukh, published in Warsaw in 1931. Whether this is a reprint of a work published earlier is not known. There is also a late 1930 edition of *Dr. P. Berliner's moderner yidisher brivnshteler* noted in the catalog of the Medem Library in Paris. Sixty years later in 1992, A. Safra published *Idishe briv: briv-shteler tsu lernen zikh shraybn Idishe briv* in New York. Almost all Yiddish letter manuals in Europe were published in the Russian Empire. Only a few were published in the Austro-Hungarian Empire. Why this is so deserves further study.

11. *Eyn nayer brifenshteler in dray obtheylungen* (1900), 110–111.

12. See Max Weinreich, "Levin Lion Dor's brivenshtelers," for a discussion about one oft-reprinted series of brivnshtelers.

13. *Shteler* is the Yiddish version of the German word *steller,* as in *schriftsteller,* writer, or someone who puts something into writing.

14. Carlebach, "Letter into Text," 127.

15. There are other examples of plural forms in Yiddish that appear only in compound nouns, such as *ferds-ganef* (horse-thief) in some dialects of Polish Yiddish, and there may be other linguistic reasons for the use of the plural *brivn* in the word *brivn-shteler.* Our thanks to Paul Glasser for his observations on this topic.

16. Barton and Hall, *Letter Writing as a Social Practice,* 1.

17. While the study of English-language, Russian-language, and French-language letter manuals is an established field (see, for example, Eve Tavor Bannet. *Empire of Letters;* Lina Bernstein, "The First Published Russian Letter-Writing Manual"; Carol Poster and Linda C. Mitchell, *Letter-Writing Manuals and Instruction from Antiquity to the Present;* Cécile Dauphin, *Prête-moi ta plume*), there have been no full-length studies of brivn-shtelers. Judith Halevi Zwick surveyed Hebrew letter-writers in *Toldot sifrut ha-igronim* and the late Joseph Bar El examined a few individual brivnshtelers in his unpublished dissertation, "The Yiddish 'Briefenshteler'" (in Yiddish). *Mamme Dear* by Lewis Glinert presents translations of letters from a popular brivnshteler by Oyzer Bloshteyn.

ACKNOWLEDGMENTS

The fragile books we have explored here were not written with longevity in mind. That any of them survived is testimony to the dedicated work of libraries around the world, especially the YIVO Institute for Jewish Research, the Jewish Theological Seminary, the New York Public Library in New York, and the Russian National Library in St. Petersburg. At YIVO, Yeshaya Metal and Herbert Lazarus were always ready to answer questions and find sources. In St. Petersburg, the warm and erudite Vera Knorring of the library's Division of the Literatures of Asia and Africa presented us with books we never knew existed. Anatoly Nakhimovsky chased down references and masterminded digitization. Zachary Baker of Stanford University and Brad Sabin Hill of George Washington University supplied us with a constant stream of references and ideas. Brad's advice on bibliographic and transcription issues was indispensible. Ann Ackerson of Colgate University worked marvels with interlibrary loan.

We offer our special thanks to Janet Rabinowitch, director of Indiana University Press, for her early interest in our project, and to Vera Szabo for her expertise in Yiddish translation and numerous helpful corrections and suggestions. Jeffrey Edelstein was our eagle-eyed proofreader and indexer. Shoshana Olidort and Anat Guez assisted with Hebrew. The Eisenstadt and Zimman families, who had commissioned translations of private correspondence from Roberta, kindly allowed us to publish excerpts. To our colleagues and friends, unstinting sources of ideas, references, and encouragement, we express endless gratitude: thank you, Aleksandr Bratus', Jeffrey Edelstein, Gennady Estraikh, David Fishman, ChaeRan Freeze, Paul Glasser, Marion Kaplan, Ellen Kellman, Cecile Kuznitz, Mikhail Krutikov, Chava Lapin, Olga Litvak, Chana Mlotek,

Harriet Murav, Alexander Nakhimovsky, Avrom Nowersztern, Nancy Ries, Sarah Swartz, Robert M. Seltzer, and Daniel Soyer.

Colgate University has been unfailing in its support. Alice's colleagues in Jewish studies—above all Lesleigh Cushing—and in the new Program in Russian and Eurasian Studies have created a congenial place for writing and teaching. For making Colgate work so well, particular thanks go to Lynn Staley, head of Research Council, Helen Kebabian, director of Corporate, Foundation, and Government Relations, Constance Harsh, director of the Division of University Studies, and President Jeffrey Herbst.

The idea for this project was born at the YIVO Institute for Jewish Research, where Alice and Roberta served on the staff of *The YIVO Encyclopedia of Jews in Eastern Europe.* Not long after, Alice turned up as Roberta's student in a seminar in reading Yiddish handwriting at the YIVO Summer Program in Yiddish. While she never learned that tricky skill, the subject matter of the seminar—private correspondence—proved extremely interesting. From real letters, which could never be assembled as a representative sample, it was a short hop to brivnshtelers, and from there to a long-lasting collaboration.

Brivnshtelers, as the reader has seen, are obsessed with family. So it is fitting for the authors to conclude with gratitude toward their own families. From Alice, thanks to John Stone and Barbara Schaefer, for always being there, and to Sasha, Sharon, Isaac, Chitra, and little Maya, for all the joys. Roberta gives warm, loving thanks to her parents, Malcolm and Estelle Newman, for their unflagging support and encouragement.

TRANSLATION AND ROMANIZATION

Letters in brivnshtelers have their own peculiar challenges for the translator. These are texts written in a variety of styles, sometimes graceful and heartfelt and sometimes awkward and stilted, even by letter-manual standards. Written across a century, the letters reflect stylistic changes in written Yiddish: the Germanisms that mark the prose of the early nineteenth century are largely purged in books published later at the turn of the twentieth. Letters include Hebrew salutations, abbreviations, and sometimes quotes from the Tanakh and other holy books, along with Russian words transliterated into Yiddish.

In our translations, we have striven to portray the prose of Yiddish brivnshtelers in all its diversity. We have approached with a light hand the occasional artlessness of the prose, choosing to hew closely to literal translation as much as possible, and have not attempted to rationalize the prose of the different authors into one homogenized style. We have also preserved, as much as we could, the punctuation used in the letters (for instance, inserting ellipses if they appear in the originals), as well as variant spellings of names. Other translation choices are noted in the annotations to the translations.

For transliteration of Yiddish, we have followed the long-established YIVO romanization system. For Hebrew, we have followed the romanization system of the Library of Congress, though in a simplified form, without the special characters used to represent *khet, tet, kuf,* and *sin.* For Russian, we have followed the Library of Congress, with exceptions made for a few proper and place names (e.g., Trotsky, Moscow). All Russian Empire place names have been romanized according to Library of Congress rules for Russian. Our multilingual writers often had Yiddish,

Hebrew, and Russian variants of their personal names. When referring to them within the text, we have mostly adhered to the choices made by *The YIVO Encyclopedia of Jews in Eastern Europe*. When our bibliography cites works by the same author in different languages, we have transliterated the name used for that language. So, for example, S. An-ski is the author of Yiddish works, and S.A. An-skii of Russian ones.

To avoid anachronism, Hebrew titles of books published in Eastern Europe, as well as a few other phrases in Hebrew, are romanized according to YIVO rules of transliteration to reflect Ashkenazi pronunciation, with the more modern Hebrew transliteration following in brackets.

Finally, a number of inconsistencies in brivnshteler texts have affected the way this book looks and reads. Brivnshteler writers never agreed among themselves about how to present letters. Some letters start with dates and places, and the fictional correspondents have full names, and sometimes everything is generic. In all these cases, we have followed the styles of the individual brivnshtelers.

Dear Mendl, Dear Reyzl

ONE

The World of the Brivnshteler

ENCOUNTERING MODERNITY

The age of the brivnshteler was an age of modernization, which some Russian Jews pursued, some resisted, and most accommodated to one degree or another. The brivnshteler served as an agent of change, guiding Jewish readers in their adaption of new social, cultural, and economic realities. It was also a reflection of change, encompassing within its pages almost the full range of Jewish responses to modernization.

The earliest Russian brivnshtelers appeared against a backdrop of political and social fragmentation. In the early nineteenth century, the authority wielded by the rabbinate was under attack, as the spread of Hasidism gave rise to a competing religious establishment. The cohesion of Jewish communities was further broken by the military draft instituted by Nicholas I. With no good way out, community leaders used the children of the poor to fulfill conscription quotas dodged by the rich through influence and bribes. The *kahal*—the autonomous Jewish community council—continued to run local communities even after being formally outlawed in 1844,[1] but its authority over individuals was considerably weakened.

Another challenge to the religious elite served as a forceful instrument of modernity. The Haskalah—the Jewish Enlightenment—was a reformist rethinking of Jewish intellectual and community life that started in Berlin and reached Russia in the early nineteenth century. Proponents of the Haskalah, *maskilim*, drew from the ideas of the European Enlightenment, as well as from Hebrew translations of medieval and Renaissance works of philosophy, science, and history. The self-appointed teachers of their nation, they became, in the formulation of Olga Litvak, a Jewish intelligentsia—"the bearers of a modern Jewish metaphysics and the founders of a new Romantic religion."[2] As implacable opponents of Hasidism but critics of complete secularization, maskilim pursued a modernizing agenda that included spiritual and cultural renewal as well as the social and economic integration of Jews into the broader society. While most remained religiously observant, they espoused ideas that the Jewish establishment considered subversive.

The story of the maskilim intersects with that of the brivnshteler because of the Haskalah's emphasis on the acquisition of non-Jewish languages (initially German) and its interest in broadening the scope of Jewish education. The first authors of brivnshtelers were maskilim. But these early Jewish intellectuals were also fundamental in reforming the institutions and subject matter of Jewish schooling more broadly. In the 1840s, when the intentions of the imperial government could be interpreted generously, some maskilim bypassed Jewish channels of influence to cooperate directly with Russian authorities. They shared with Russian government officials the idea that Jews should be transformed into productive subjects of the modern state and saw education as the key to promoting acculturation. Traditionally minded Jews, seeing the same linkage, did what they could to resist.

A law of 1844 mandating the establishment of government schools for Jews was followed, over the next few years, by the opening of specialized primary and secondary schools under the control of the Ministry of Education. Fearing that this largely secular education would cause Jewish religious identity to fatally unravel, Jewish communities replicated their response to the military draft and filled the schools with orphans and the children of the poor.[3] But the unexpected success of the educational recruits led some prosperous parents to change their minds. The draft deferment that accompanied enrollment was a strong incentive, but so were practical benefits of secular study.[4]

To get a sense of what secular schools looked like from the point of view of a maskil, we can turn to an 1865 brivnshteler by Hirsh Lion Dor. Through the medium of a model letter, Lion Dor is ecstatic in his praise of the new curriculum, which he sees as the foundation for Jewish renewal, self-respect, and prosperity under an enlightened imperial government:

Day in and day out, in the schools which opened in Vilna a few years ago, young children blaze ahead in skill, in languages, in the sciences, which was unheard of until our age. Before, no one could write or do arithmetic or open their mouths in any language. They were the laughingstocks of other nations. Now, however, everyone possesses the greatest sophistication. There are finally very skilled men, in Russian, German, French, and other languages; in arithmetic . . . like the greatest mathematicians. It is lovely to behold and beautiful to hear. . . . Their livelihood is taken care of. They will never know need and won't have to go looking for a way to make a living as in the past, when some of ours, in impoverished circumstances, finally came home [from yeshiva] and had no way to make a living. And so, understandably, they barely managed to find jobs as a janitor [*strazhnik*] via a friend, family member, or acquaintance for a low salary, earning their bread with sweat to support a wife and children, all because they hadn't been educated and had no skills or profession. . . . But through the favor of the government and the help of our educated Jews, who with the schools have opened the eyes of our clever children . . . each and every one of them will study and dedicate themselves to good, which will be pleasing in the eyes of God and the other nations, and especially our government.[5]

The educational reforms involved girls too, though differently. Girls from well-off families had never been as sequestered from secular subjects as their brothers. Because women did not engage in the study of religious texts but did participate in economic life, girls from families who could afford it learned Russian and German, the two significant languages for entry into the outside worlds of culture and business. At the most basic level, girls of marriageable age were supposed to be capable of drafting a business letter—a specialty of the brivnshteler. Higher up the social scale, merchant families who moved or aspired to move in Russian circles expected their daughters to be conversant with Russian and German high culture.[6]

Wealthy girls could always be educated by private tutors. But in the 1840s, enlightenment-minded educators began to open schools for them as well, more than one hundred between 1844 and 1881.[7] Even some religious Jews sent their daughters to these schools, in the belief that education would make them more marriageable.[8] As modernization progressed, education became decoupled from marriage, and young women pursued it with intensity. By 1909, the law faculty at the Bestuzhev Higher Women's Courses in St. Petersburg—the most prestigious postsecondary institution for women in Russia—had a Jewish enrollment of 20 percent, despite the restrictions on Jewish residence in St. Petersburg that remained in effect until February 1917.[9]

The new educational opportunities open to girls and women are reflected in the pages of late-nineteenth-century brivnshtelers, where letters about girls seeking education are not uncommon. *Bernshteyn's nayer yudisher folks-brifenshteler* (Bernshteyn's new Yiddish folk brivnshteler) includes a letter from a young woman living in a city, begging her mother to send her niece to live with her so that the little girl can get a proper education. The young woman is making a living—no husband is mentioned—and she will either send her little niece to school or teach her herself. But little Rokhele must leave their "God-forsaken shtetl where there is no school and not even a proper teacher."[10]

The education law of 1844 also aimed at the reshaping of Jewish religious life. In addition to primary school, the law mandated the establishment of secularized rabbinical seminaries, which the Yiddish-speaking public called *rabiner shuln* to distinguish them from yeshivas. The two rabiner shuln, one in Vilna and the other in Zhitomir, had the goal of producing a new class of Russian-speaking rabbis whose limited immersion in Talmud would be preceded by four years of secular fortification in modern languages, Latin, mathematics, physics, and penmanship.[11] More impressive in theory than in reality—instruction had to take place in German because the students couldn't handle Russian—the curriculum did not bring any sweeping changes to Jewish religious life.[12] But the rabiner shuln did play an important role in the creation of secular Jewish culture. The writers Mendle Moykher Sforim (Sholem Yankev Abramovitsh) and Yitskhok Yoyel Linetski, as well as the pioneering playwright Avrom Goldfadn, all studied at the rabbinical seminary in Zhitomir. The maskil Avraham Paperna, author of a number of Russian, Hebrew, and Judeo-German letter manuals, studied at both Zhitomir and Vilna.

The students of the rabiner shuln—by 1855, a combined total of around five hundred—were drawn largely or perhaps exclusively by the secular subjects, which put them on the path to entrance exams for Russian secondary schools (gymnasia) and universities.[13] Bowing to the inevitable, authorities dropped the "rabbi" part of the curriculum in 1873, and turned the schools into pedagogical institutes. The future writer and editor Abraham Cahan studied at the one in Vilna. Despite his loathing for the imperial government and anything connected with it, Cahan saw the institute's mission in the same unclouded terms as had his predecessor Lion Dor, as a laudable way "to prepare teachers for a new kind of Russian preparatory school for Jewish children." Enrolling in the school was a way for Jewish adolescents to join the larger society, not just by studying the same subjects as Russians of their own age, but even—as Cahan remembers without irony half a lifetime later—wearing a uniform, just as they did.[14]

Cahan was hardly alone in his enthusiasm. By the late 1870s, before the government developed second thoughts about the desirability of educating Jews and established exclusionary quotas, Jews constituted more than 10 percent of secondary school students in the Russian Empire.[15] This move toward secular studies represents, of course, only one side of the picture: traditional religious education continued to be the route for most boys, and girls from poor families got very little schooling at all. But expectations had changed, as had desires.

The growing interest in secular education is part of the rise of a Jewish middle class, evident even as the great majority of Jews lived in poverty.[16] Brivnshtelers reflect the social aspirations of readers as well as their struggles not to descend down the class ladder. The threat of such descent is evident in letters that bring up the precariousness of business and employment. But potential rewards also beckon, seen in occasional flights of fancy projecting the possibility that readers could travel in the social circles of extremely wealthy Jews. The 1901 bilingual Yiddish-Russian *Der hoyz-korrespondent* (The household correspondent) includes a letter from a young man to a prospective father-in-law, whose daughter he met at a ball given by the fabulously wealthy Baron Gintsburg. Fantasy aside, anxieties brought about by ascending the class ladder could be allayed by brivnshteler letters that modeled proper etiquette. A reader who had to write to a prospective father-in-law of a higher class might consider himself lucky to have *Der hoyz-korrespondent* close at hand.

The brivnshteler came of age in the aftermath of a fateful event: the assassination of the liberal Tsar Alexander II in 1881. Jewish hopes for political and social progress were set back by the wave of pogroms that followed the assassination, as well as by a series of exclusionary laws issued over the next decade. These laws limited Jewish trade, restricted

Jewish entrance into professions, and cut off higher education for all but a tiny percentage. Jews previously permitted to live in Moscow, such as artisans, army veterans, and wealthy merchants, now had these privileges rescinded. The May Laws of 1882 made new Jewish settlement in rural areas illegal, even within the Pale.[17] Laws restricting where Jews could travel or live were part of a longstanding policy that accorded certain impediments (or, alternatively, privileges) to the various legally designated social groups in the Russian Empire. It can be argued that Russian peasants had it worse. But the peasant cause engaged the sympathy of the entire liberal intelligentsia. The ever-constricting Jewish future was, by and large, a problem just for Jews.

A search began for new ways to negotiate Jewish identity in the modern world, giving rise to new Jewish ideologies—Zionism, Jewish socialism, and Diaspora Nationalism. Some of these originated before the pogroms, but it was in the decades that followed that they captured the Jewish imagination.[18] There were demographic changes as well. After 1881, mass emigration from the Russian Empire increased dramatically. More than 2 million Jews emigrated from Eastern Europe to the United States between 1881 and 1914, an estimated 1.6 million of them from the Russian Empire.[19] Tens of thousands of others emigrated to Europe, Canada, Latin America, and South Africa.

Other countries were not the only attraction for Jewish migrants. Even before 1881, the prospect of making a living or even achieving prosperity had drawn thousands of Jews to Russian cities outside the Pale. By the end of the nineteenth century, more than 300,000 Jews had taken up legal residence elsewhere in the Russian Empire, including major cities such as St. Petersburg and Moscow.[20] The amount of illegal settlement is hard to calculate, but is well attested to in memoirs and literature. In one of his *Menakhem Mendl* stories, Sholem Aleichem's bumbling hero finds himself in what he fears is a police raid on his Jewish boarding house in Yekhupets, Sholem Aleichem's name for the city of Kiev. The financial markets of Kiev/Yekhupets were full of Jews, most of whom were not allowed to stay in the city overnight.

Brivnshtelers would address many of these changes, though often with a time delay. Manuals from the 1880s are similar to those published before the pogroms and the start of mass emigration. They project a sanguine view of economic and social progress: Jews do business, seek education, and engage in steadily modernizing modes of private life. Into the twentieth century, a longstanding wariness of politics made brivnshtelers vigilant in avoiding any reference to anti-tsarist sentiment and activities. There are no mentions of political parties such as the Bund, the Russian Social Democratic Labor Party, and other revolutionary organizations to which Jews belonged. The silence persists even after censorship was lifted in the wake of the Revolution of 1905. It was still, after all, illegal to engage in revolutionary activity, and espousing radical ideas in print would have taken considerable daring. Another likely factor is the inertia of genre: since brivnshtelers had never before dealt with politics, there was no particular imperative to break the mold. About the closest that some of the letter manuals come to politics is an affinity for Zionism. Mordkhe Betsalel Shnayder's 1901 bilingual Hebrew-Yiddish *Koyvets sipurim u-mikhtovim* [*Kovets sipurim u-mikhtavim*] (Collection of stories and letters) cautiously promotes the project of a Jewish home in Palestine.[21] Shnayder's book is also supportive of official policies aimed at Russification, a view not shared by all of his fellow authors, as we can see in a letter from one post-1905 manual complaining that life in the Russian Empire did not present a lot of opportunity for Jews.[22]

As we move closer to the twentieth century, an increasing number of model letters focus on emigration, primarily to North America, but also, in a handful of cases, to South America and Palestine. While Jewish socialism remains a forbidden topic, the style and substance of letters reflect a growing responsiveness to the problems and lives of working-class people. There is an occasional acknowledgment of serious Jewish poverty. Above all, by the early 1900s, letters show a robust turn to colloquial Yiddish, which had become the language of a vibrant new literature, an emerging system of secular education, and, in politics, the preferred medium of Diaspora Nationalism and the socialist Bund.

Politics, like modernity and change, draws attention more than stasis does. If only for that reason, we should keep in mind that throughout the nineteenth century, many Jewish institutions, customs, and lives continued without sharp breaks with the past. The brivnshtelers of the era reflect this duality, with some authors striving to present new content that would be relevant to new life situations encountered by readers and others representing continuity with the past by printing recycled letters from times gone by.

THE BRIVNSHTELER AND
TRADITIONAL EDUCATION

A distinctive facet of the brivnshteler is the niche it occupied in the traditional system of Jewish education. We are not talking here about state-sponsored Russian schools or Enlightenment-oriented private schools, and still less about the interwar period when, for the first time, a variety of Russian-, Polish-, Yiddish-, and Hebrew-language secular schools was available to Jewish children. Graduates of these schools would not have needed the kind of instruction offered in a brivnshteler. But before World War I, Jews with more restricted opportunities did rely on them. Teachers used the manuals as handwriting textbooks, in both private lessons in the home and formal lessons in religious schools. And people who could not afford teachers turned to them for the self-study of foreign languages, arithmetic, and sometimes basic Yiddish literacy.

In their capacity as informal writing and general educational primers, brivnshtelers were attempts to compensate for the inadequacy of traditional education. From the last decades of the nineteenth century roughly through the first decades of the twentieth, they tried to fill the gap between the religious texts that boys were taught and the secular knowledge that many desired, and between the Jewish reverence for education and the achievements—sometimes very limited—of the boys and girls, or men and women, whom the system failed.

The particular focus of most brivnshtelers was writing in Yiddish and foreign languages. Not coincidentally, modern languages and a subject called "penmanship" was central to the curriculum of Enlightenment-oriented schools founded by maskilim. A document in the YIVO Archives shows the course of study in a Vilna elementary school, established around 1855.[23] Secular subjects included Russian, German, and Hebrew (Hebrew grammar would not have been taught in a religious school); arithmetic, geography, history, and penmanship. While Judaism was not excluded from the curriculum, its changed role is signaled by the term used to refer to it: *religyon,* a Yiddish word never applied to study in traditional schools. The six hours a week devoted to religyon represents a third of the curriculum: a significant percentage that was nonetheless a massive reduction of the time spent on religious texts in traditional schools. And it is unlikely that students were seeing much of the Talmud, which had been replaced by textbooks written by the maskil Leon Mandel'shtam.[24]

Enlightenment schools specifically for girls were not enormously different. Eliyana Adler's book on Jewish schools for girls includes a photocopy of a printed advertisement for a girls' school that opened in Vilna, also in 1855.[25] The advertisement shows a largely secular curriculum that dovetails in significant ways with both the boys' curriculum and the emphasis on language, writing, and penmanship promoted in brivnshtelers. The school advertised three grades, for a fee of ten silver rubles a year. Grade one (following Russian practice, this would have been for ten-year-olds) is devoted to reading and penmanship in Russian, German, and Yiddish. The only other subject is arithmetic. Grade two adds geography, grammar in German and Russian, reading in French, and religyon, glossed in Russian as *zakon bozhii* (divine law), the phrase used for Christian instruction in Russian schools. "Writing exercises" are central.

The particular role of Yiddish in these schools deserves some comment. Its low status meant that it played no role in the boys' curriculum whatsoever, and even in the girl's school, the study of its grammar was omitted because it was commonly supposed that Yiddish, alone among languages, did not have one.[26] The teaching of Yiddish was actively discouraged in some Enlightenment schools. Shevel Perel, the head of the Vilna girls' school that did teach Yiddish composition, sought government support for a ban on exactly that, saying that the letters of the Yiddish alphabet are as "as ugly as Turkish and Arabic" and that if Jews went on reading, speaking, and writing Yiddish they would never be able to break their ties to the language.[27] Eventually, Yiddish disappeared from the course of study in most schools for girls.[28]

Writing exercises and penmanship were not a specifically Jewish obsession. When Jews started applying to gymnasia, the private Russian secondary schools that served as a gateway for the educated elite, they faced dictation in Russian as a crucial part of the entrance exam. Brivnshtelers fit right into this mindset. With their focus on spelling and their supply of grammatically correct prose in one or more languages, they replicated, in accessible form, the standard educational practices in the non-Jewish part of the Russian Empire. While no brivnshteler attempted instruction in history, geography, or religyon, an overview of arithmetic was occasionally provided in appendices.

None of these subjects was covered in the traditional curriculum for Jewish boys. Their education began with kheyder: a daylight-to-dusk religious primary school. Kheyder was universal: orphans and boys whose parents could not pay for it were educated through a community-supported version called a *Talmud Torah*. In the first level of kheyder, little boys learned basic alphabet and deciphering skills. They read the prayer book and the weekly Torah portion, translated word-for-word into standard Yiddish equivalents. The next step was to read the Torah with Rashi's commentary. Gifted boys proceeded to the study of Talmud, where memorization was replaced by argumentation and intellectual pyrotechnics. Not all boys were gifted, and very few continued their study beyond the age of thirteen, when they were sent to work.[29]

The word "kheyder" means room, and the room belonged to the *melamed*—the teacher—which meant that his wife and children, the cooking and the illnesses and all the activities of the household, hovered in the background. *Melamdim* ranked low in the shtetl hierarchy and were often as poor as their pupils. Those pupils included the occasional little girl: in an entry in his diary, made during his ethnographic expedition to Volhynia and Podolia in 1912–1915, the writer and folklorist S. An-ski (Shloyme Zaynvl Rapoport) reports visiting a kheyder with several girls among its students.[30] But most girls stayed only for basic literacy: the study of Talmud was exclusively male. Girls whose families could afford it hired tutors for them or sent them to schools from which they were likely to emerge not only familiar with secular subjects, but considerably more familiar with them than their traditionally educated future husbands.[31] On the other hand, many girls got no education at all.

Descriptions of the kheyder in memoirs range from nostalgic to bitter. Doba-Mera Medvedeva (Gurevich), the grandmother of the historian Michael Beizer, portrays the kheyder circa 1900 from the point of view of a melamed's daughter. She focuses on her father's unending workday, his concern for the poor, and—in a bitter aside—the prospects for girls like her in that setting:

> He taught poor children for free. Although the shtetl had a group of poor children whose tuition was covered by the Society for Helping the Poor, there were some parents who were ashamed to send their children there. So my father would teach them even though he was overwhelmed with work, and would get up early and go to bed late, and spend all his time with the

children. From 7 to 9 in the morning he would teach children who were not in his class, and also in the evening, from 8 to 10, he would work with his main class, consisting of 8 to 10 children, mostly boys. Girls weren't usually sent to school, first because it was a waste of money, and second because parents in that day thought it was superfluous for girls. Why take her away from housekeeping?[32]

Some boys did not thrive at kheyder. The best known example is fictional: Sholem Aleichem's beloved scamp Motl, from the novel *Motl, Peysi dem khazns* (Motl, Peysi the cantor's son). When we first meet Motl, he is a prime example of a Talmud Torah failure. Inventive and imaginative but not inclined to the academic, Motl spends his school days helping the teacher's wife sweep the floor and playing with the cat. Motl's boredom with years of enforced study of the alphabet is comic, but not the real reason his education grinds to a halt. That reason is poverty. With his father dying and no money in the family to feed him, Motl has to leave home to go to work.

Like most Jewish boys, Motl could read. While the 1897 census shows the rates of Jewish literacy to be alarmingly low (only 48% of males and 27% of females claimed to be literate in any language),[33] historian Shaul Stampfer makes the reasonable assumption that Jews being questioned by Russian census-takers might not have told the truth, or might have considered that from a Russian perspective, Hebrew and Yiddish didn't count.[34] Jewish investigators who carried out their own studies found higher rates. In Minsk, for example, in 1901, a study of craftsmen found that 87 percent of men and 82 percent of women who were master craftsmen were literate in Hebrew and Yiddish, with numbers slightly lower for apprentices (76% and 66%).[35] That still leaves a sizeable minority of both men and women who were worse off than Motl. And the number of genuine illiterates was growing at the turn of the century because of increasing poverty among Jews, especially in the slums of industrial cities.[36]

Knowing how to read did not mean knowing how to write. A study carried out in 1913, again among Jewish artisans, found many who could read Hebrew and Yiddish but did not know how to write either language: 15 percent of Vilna artisans fell into this group, along with 29 percent in Warsaw and a distressing 45 percent in both Berdichev and Bzheziny.[37] In Ayzik Meyer Dik's 1871 novel *Di yuden in lite* (The Jews in Lithuania) a twenty-two-year-old yeshiva-educated man becomes the rabbi of a small town, where he comes face to face with the reality of not being able to write:

> Aside from being learned, I was hardly a human being at all. First of all, it became apparent that not knowing how to write was a great disadvantage, and at that point I could not even form an alef. I undertook my first signature on a rabbinical court judgment with sweat and shame. They had to first trace my signature on the document with a pencil and then I went over it in ink.[38]

Sholem Aleichem's Motl feels exactly that kind of shame when he is handed a handwritten letter with the expectation that he can read it aloud. He cannot read handwriting because he has not been taught to write it, despite his desire to learn. Handwriting is the only piece of formal education that Motl wants, and it is explicitly the one he isn't offered. It was people like Motl and Dik's rabbi who were the brivnshteler's targeted purchasers. In the preface to his 1865 brivnshteler, Hirsh Lion Dor promises that readers will be equipped to spell correctly and write what they mean. And most important, they won't have to seek someone else to write their letters and thus parade personal business in front of a stranger.[39]

Many boys thrived at kheyder, becoming fluent in reading Hebrew and Aramaic, and, later on, adept at the intricacies of Talmudic argument. The traditional path for them was either to go on to yeshiva, usually far from home, or undertake a less formal course of advanced study in the local *besmedresh* (the study house, ubiquitous in Jewish communities as an adjunct to the synagogue). Yeshiva boys became part of an intellectual meritocracy, supported by the Jewish community's version of financial aid. What this meant was that students slept in the study house and got their meals through a system of "eating days." There was a certain reciprocity in this arrangement: householders who hosted students at their table accrued religious merit and also status. From the point of view of the householder, the more brilliant the student, the greater the reflected glory. From the point of view of the student, a reputation for intellectual prowess brought not only meals—for some, so many that invitations would be traded—but often the possibility of a good match. One plausible conclusion to advanced study was *smikhe*, rabbinical ordination. Another was marriage into a well-off family that would provide support (*kest*) while the young man studied for a certain number of years prior to starting a business.

As the twentieth century approached, the lure of secular studies presented a challenge to this way of life. But higher education in the Russian Empire was a possibility primarily for young men whose well-off families adhered to the ethos of the Haskalah or were oriented toward acculturation. Less privileged Jews who wanted a secular education faced the huge impediments of poverty, parental opposition, and, beginning in 1887, a new barrier: as the number of university-educated Jewish doctors and lawyers began to grow, Russian Christians competing in the same fields prevailed on the government to limit the number of Jews in higher education. The so-called *numerus clausus,* a policy reversal that affected precisely those Jews who wanted to acculturate, restricted the percentage of Jewish students to 10 percent in the Pale, 5 percent outside of it, and 3 percent in the capital cities of Moscow and St. Petersburg. In 1901 (this time, because of fear of Jews as revolutionary agitators), the numbers were set even lower.[40]

Another problem for Jews was lack of preparation. To be admitted to a Russian gymnasium (or to either of the Jewish pedagogical institutes that replaced the government rabbinical seminaries), one needed to do well on an entrance exam. This meant proficiency in arithmetic and the ability to do a clean Russian dictation. The historian Nikolai Poletika, who was not Jewish, describes in his memoirs how he and his brother took such a writing exam in Kiev in August 1905:

> In walked a hefty man in a blue uniform who began dictating about a peasant who ate first one cake and then another cake, but remained hungry. Then he ate bread and was full. For us, the dictation was easy. But the next day we found out that we both got Bs, not because of mistakes, but because of cross-outs and smudges. On reading selections from an anthology, however, we did fine.[41]

Jewish students did manage to pass through these gateways, some by excelling at the exams and others by bribery; Abraham Cahan had to bribe an official simply to get to take the exam.[42] As for the First Kiev Gymnasium, the school attended by Poletika, until the administration excluded Jews altogether in 1911, twenty Jewish students studied there. Out of a student body of seven hundred, this represented, as Poletika notes, almost precisely the 3 percent permitted after 1901.[43]

Poletika's Jewish classmates likely came from Russian-speaking homes: by 1905, this was easily possible. Jews who came from Yiddish-speaking homes, with an exclusively Jewish education, faced a barrier that was much greater. In their case, breaking through to get into a Russian school, or into one of the commercial schools established by Jews to bypass the numerus clausus, or even to university abroad required prodigious feats of self-instruction in arithmetic and foreign languages.

In his Russian-language novella *Pionery* (Pioneers), An-ski describes how ex-yeshiva students in the 1880s threw themselves into learning Russian. The method was to take a dictionary and use it to decipher the most complex contemporary texts:

> I asked a gymnasium student I knew to bring me the hardest book available in the Russian language. He brought me a whole volume of Belinsky. I made a vow to read this book to the last page, and read it so that not a single word would remain unknown. I got a Hebrew dictionary and started reading. I had to look up every word. But I told myself: let me die over the book, I'm going to succeed.[44]

An-ski's "pioneers" learned the Russian language and Russian progressive politics simultaneously, studying radical literary critics like Belinsky with the same intensity they once devoted to the Talmud. Focused as they were on high-culture, antiestablishment texts, they probably would not have touched a brivnshteler. Nonetheless, brivnshtelers had a role to play in the complicated system of formal education and self-study, beginning at the very lowest levels and continuing—at least in the ambitious intentions of some authors—to respond to the needs of men who were as educated as An-ski's heroes, but a little less adventurous.

Almost everybody who was taught to write was taught by a shrayber (literally a writer, but in this context, a teacher of handwriting and spelling). This was a man—or often, in the case of girls, an educated woman—who came to the kheyder or the home for an hour's lesson. Memoirists from Pauline Wengeroff to Puah Rakovska remember their shraybers; Abraham Cahan boasts about his, a tall blond man with a goose-feather pen.[45] The most comprehensive description comes from Fayge Shargorodska, who resurrected an already fading past for a YIVO journal in 1926:

> In would come a worn-out man, Shloyme the shrayber, sit himself down right away and call, "Feygele, come and write." So right away, I would go up to him with my sewed-together notebook. Silently and solemnly, he would rule two

pages and write on the first line of each page "I traveled to Odessa to buy merchandise," read it out to me, and tell me to copy it. When I finished my work—at first, with great effort, like childbirth—he picked himself up and was off to another, to a third, to thousands of Jewish children to teach them to write their own *shure grus* [sentence for copying].[46]

None of these children, she continues, had any idea what they were writing —neither the meaning of the word "merchandise," nor its connection to Odessa, nor the role that Odessa played in Jewish life. What they knew about Odessa (which had the reputation, in traditional circles, of an apostate city) was that "the fires of Gehenna burned for seven versts around it."[47]

Like certain business letters written for one brivnshteler that then re-appear over and over again in different books, the combination of Odessa and merchandise seems to have gotten around. A friend of Shargorodska's who had grown up in a maskilic environment very different from her Hasidic one used the very same shure grus.

The poet Leyb Kvitko, cornered in a café and asked how he learned to write, confirmed that it was by copying a shure grus. When asked which one, he thought for a moment and said, "Hmm, well, for example, 'Uncle went to Odessa to buy merchandise.'"[48]

Brivnshteler writers saw their work as a possible substitute for the shure grus. Writing in 1890, Tsvi Hirsh Goldshteyn-Gershonovitsh reminds his readers of the enormity of the shrayber's task: "For the small reward of 3 rubles he must be busy and running around the entire day in order to earn a piece of bread for himself and his family. But who would imagine that this harried man, who can't serve the interests of his students beyond the allotted hour because afterward he has to immediately run off to another student, can properly meet the needs of his clients?" Even worse, the author writes, the shrayber has had nothing to teach from. He, Goldshteyn-Gershonovitsh, aims to change that with publication of his modest book.[49] A couple of years later, another brivnshteler author, Arukh, went one step further and claimed that "with this *brifen-shteller*, no teacher is needed, that's my rationale."[50] Many Yiddish letter manuals, in fact, have sections printed in a cursive ("handwriting") font, the idea seeming to be to offer both a lesson in penmanship and practice reading handwriting (though the graceful "handwriting" presented would have borne little resemblance to the penmanship readers would have encountered in real letters).

Brivnshtelers can be considered the first Yiddish textbooks, published as they were in the vacuum of any sort of formal Yiddish educational framework.[51] While their primary focus is to teach the writing
of Yiddish, there were occasional forays into more ambitious territory.
For instance, the very early anonymously authored *Mesader igeres* [*Mesadar igeret*], a brivnshteler from 1825, has several letters that are there
mainly to deliver science lessons and other bits of secular knowledge:
one writer reports in detail on a trip to "Baghdad, in an American area,"
in which he witnessed various aspects of the whaling industry; another
describes a visit from a "German" who taught the writer's daughters
all about the process of harvesting pearls. Other letters deliver lessons
on human anatomy and trivia, such as the year Columbus discovered
America, 1491 [*sic*].[52]

But even *Mesader igeres* [*Mesadar igeret*] focused on providing basic
Yiddish prose to copy and emulate. Grammar and usage is another issue.
While brivnshtelers often introduced the alphabet and explained the difference between vowels and consonants, neither *Mesader igeres* nor the
many books that followed gave explicit instructions on what kind of language was acceptable and what was not. But if brivnshtelers uniformly
sidestepped the dos and don'ts of proscriptive grammar, that mainstay
of primary education outside the Jewish world, proscriptive grammar
was in fact their function. By copying prose, a user learned proper spelling and good style.

With the approach of the twentieth century, just about all manuals
have opening sections that present, in addition to the alphabet, properly
spelled lists of men's and women's names, days of the week, forms of address, and common Hebrew words that a less educated user would not
know how to spell because their spelling is not phonetic, as is the case
with Yiddish words of German or Slavic derivation. The opening section
of the anonymously authored *Eyn nayer brifenshteler in dray obtheylungen*
(A new brivnshteler in three parts), published in Vilna in 1900, is typical.
The title page advertises the book's contents:

1. Hebrew letters.
2. Handwriting with all the rules for learning writing and spelling of names
   of both genders (male and female), also Hebrew words and abbreviations
   needed for writing letters, in good order according to the alphabet.

3. Yiddish letters in printed font with vowel signs. Also numerous letters on various useful topics, written very well in an easy language. Also assorted anecdotes and good fables to read and copy.

The specific needs of girls are the focus of another manual, Alek's *Oytser mikhtovim* [*Otsar mikhtavim*], *oder brifenshteler fir yudishe kinder* (Treasury of letters, or a letter manual for Jewish children), published in 1906. Its foreword notes that "there are women, young ladies" who don't know how to spell Hebrew words and terms properly. The author will pay particular attention to teaching them how spell *loshn-koydishe* (Hebrew) words that appear in Yiddish, which he will list alphabetically because "no females are yet familiar with *shoreshim* [the three-letter roots of Hebrew words]." He believes, however, that what he provides will enable his students to write the words without mistakes so that "they won't be laughed at."[53]

The heyday of the brivnshteler was a time of contention about Yiddish orthography and usage. Debates raged over whether to purge the language of Germanicisms and Slavicisms in vocabulary, spelling, and syntax. Some participants in the debate wanted to bring written Yiddish more in line with actual spoken Yiddish, while others preferred the idea of elevating the masses and the language by developing a serious literature. Yet another approach called for stressing Yiddish's classical origins in Hebrew and Aramaic through the use of Hebraic spelling and diacriticals.[54] Those who were passionate about Yiddish saw the lack of standardization as "a weapon in the hands of the enemies of the Yiddish language." By enemies they meant champions of modern Hebrew as the national language of the Jewish people or proponents of weaning Jews away from Yiddish in favor of state languages like Russian, Polish, and (in America) English.[55]

Under the influence of the maskilim, *daytshmerish* (Germanic) spelling was common in printed Yiddish literature, and brivnshtelers were no exception in this regard: almost every single example of the genre employs daytshmerish orthography.[56] Aleksander Zederbaum, editor of *Kol mevaser,* defended himself against those who criticized *daytshmerism* by claiming that readers were "used to" the Germanic spellings from existing translations of the Bible and other religious literature. He expressed the hope that more and more Jews would become educated enough to read this sort of Yiddish, which would then serve as a special sort of literary language. Zederbaum's contemporary Shiye Mordkhe Lifshits attempted to rationalize and phoneticize Yiddish spelling and to purge it of daytsh-merism in a series of dictionaries, but was largely unsuccessful. Daytsh-merish spelling remained the norm—Sholem Aleichem used it, as did the early Yiddish newspapers *Der yud,* which began publishing in 1899, and *Der fraynd* (1903). The reality was that no uniformity of spelling or usage existed in the Yiddish literature and press of the late nineteenth and early twentieth centuries. While the standardization of Yiddish spelling was high on the agenda at the Czernowitz Yiddish conference in 1908, the subject was completely overshadowed by the fierce debate about Yiddish itself and whether it should be designated as the single national language of the Jewish people. It was not until after World War I that serious initiatives to standardize Yiddish spelling and usage took shape. [57]

Brivnshtelers reflect this orthographic anarchy. A good example is the 1912 *Bernshteyn's nayer yudisher folks-brifenshteler* (Bernshteyn's new Yiddish people's brivnshteler), which does not employ a single orthography—some words have daytshmerish spellings, while others don't. But in his preface, Bernshteyn rails against the use of foreign words. Yiddish correspondence, he complains, is often "written in a strange, daytshmerish language and must encompass within itself an entire ocean of outlandish, flowery phrases about 'sonne,' 'mond,' 'engels,' [sun, moon, angels], etc."[58] He notes the shift from German to Russian, but approves of neither:

> The bloated German verse which replaced the simple old-Yiddish letter style held sway over the Yiddish letter almost single-handedly for a long time. . . . In the last few decades . . . there has also been an influx of masses of Russian words and Russian verse (in Poland, naturally, Polish). . . . For the time being, the influence of our new literature has not yet had much of an impact on everyday Yiddish life. The Jewish middle-class householders, the semi-intelligentsia, the workers, etc., are still very far from having the respect for themselves and for their language that would keep them from mixing in dozens of unnecessary German and Slavic words every step of the way. This entirely spoils the rhythm, integrity, and character of the Yiddish language

FIGURE 1. (*facing*) *Yidish-taytsh* and Hebrew square font in Shalom ha-Kohen's *Ksav yoysher* [*Ketav yosher*], Vilna, 1864.

— 23 —

מיטהיג אויך מיך פֿערוואונדערט . — דאו גפֿאלד האבט מיך מיינעם
הערן מֶעקעל אויפֿלאובעטוווואהרטעו געגעבעו, דא מיך דעסטעו ניבט
בעטרארף, הינדעם מיך נאך פֿאן דעם רייזענעטועדע האבע, וועלכעם
מיר דיינע ניטע או רייבליך מיטנאחב ; אונד מים אויסגאחבעו או מיינעם
פֿערגענניגעו פֿערצוועהט מיך מיין גוטער מֶעקעל, נאטט זעגנע מיהו !

מיך ווערדע דיינעו ראטה בעהערצליגעו, אונד מיר מיינגע
טטוגערדעו לאו מיינער ערהאֿלונג בעטטיגוווען . ביזהער אבער וואר עם
נאטעווענדיג, מיינעו פֿליים לאו פֿערדראמפֿעטעו, אום דאו פֿערזיימטע
מין פֿריהערער ליים נאבלוהאלאן, דא מיינע מיטטגילאר מיר מין דעו
וויסטענטטאֿבטעו וויט פֿארגעטקלאמוועו וואהרעו . יעלט אבער דא מיך זיך
נאַטטאֿלאֿב בחאֿד טרריייבט האבע, ווערדע מיך עם מים מיינעם פֿליייס
ניבם מעהר אֿם זעהר מיבערטרייבעו . לעבע וואַהֿל ! גריסט מיר דים
ליעבע מוטער אונד מיינע געטטוויסטער .

דיין געהאֿרזאמער זאֿהו .

ח) מכתב הדוד לאחיו

נפלאת היא בעיניך , אחי מדוע החשיתי עד כה לבלי הודיעך
מאומה מבנך בבורך , והפצרת בי לגלות אזנך באמת ותמים , הנכוחים
מעלליו אם לא , ואני צר לי להדאיב נפשך בשמועה לא טובה , על
כן החרשתי . אמנם אף אם אמרתי אכחד תחת לשוני , כלכל לא
אוכל מהגיד האמת , כי לא עת לחשות הוא . מאז ששה חדשים נהפך
לב הנער והיה לאחר , נמוטו פעמיו ארחות עקלקלות , לא יאבה שמוע
קול תוכחתי יאטים אזנו למוסר מוריו ומנהליו , ויכל כהבל ימיו
וילך שובב כל היום , יסוב עיר , יתהלך בחוצות ויצמד לנערים
בני בליעל , המשחיתים דרכו לבשתי ולכלמתי , ומדי בואו לביתי
ושאלתיו איה אפוא היית ? כחש יכחש לי לאמר : הייתי שם ופה
לשמוע למד פלוני ולקח פלוני , וכאשר חקרתי ודרשתי אחריו , אשמע
כי לא כן , אך שקר ענה פיו , גם שלום אין לו עם בני ביתי , כי
ידבר עמם נאצות , יכעיסם גם כעם , יכביד עליהם טרחם ומשאם
לנקות ולתקן בגדיו הקרועים ונתעבים תמיד בפרוע פרעותיו ; ובזה
יחרחר ריב ויגרה מדון , ויהפך לב עבדי ואמהותי לשנוא לו . —
והנה אהבתי אליו תמנעני להכותו בשבט מוסר , ואדבר על לבו יום
יום , פעם בדברי חנינה ופעם במבטא קשה ותוכחת מרה , אך הכל
ללא יועיל , ושרתי דברי . על כן אמרתי אגלה את אזנך , ואנסהו

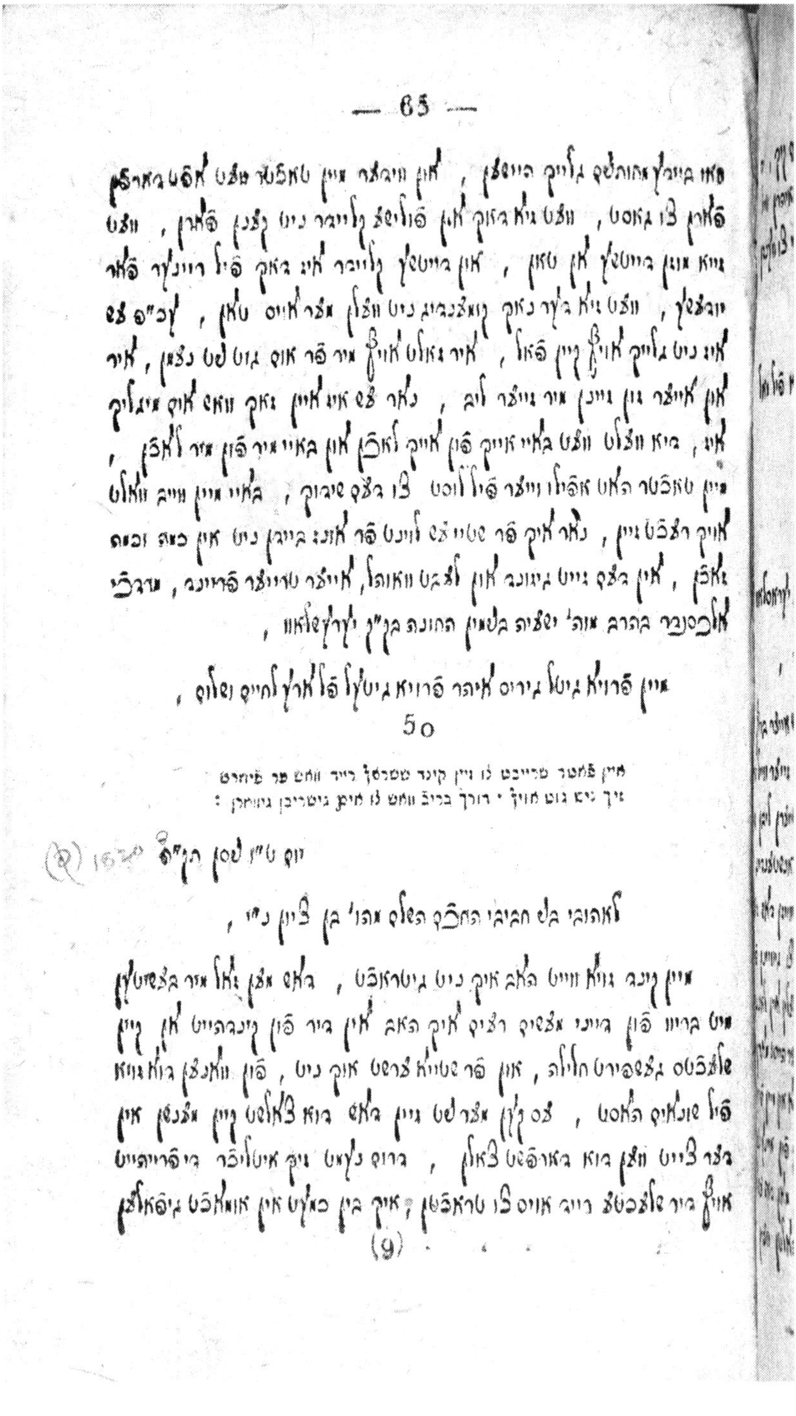

— 65 —

50

(9)

אוצר מכתבים

אדער

בריפענשטעלער

פיר יודישע קינדער

ווארשא

БРИФЕНШТЕЛЕРЪ

т. е. Письмовникъ.

Типо-Лит. Ф. Баумриттера, Красинск. пл. 6, Варшава 1906.

FIGURE 3. (*above*) Title page of Alek [A.L. Kartuczinski], *Oytser mikhtovim* [*Otsar mikhtavim*]. Warsaw: F. Baymritter, 1906. This illustration appears on the title pages of a number of different brivnshtelers.
Courtesy of the National Library of Russia, St. Petersburg.

FIGURE 2. (*facing*) Yiddish in cursive font with introductions in *yidish-taytsh* font in *Mesader igeres* [*Mesadar igeret*], Vilna, 1830.
Courtesy of the Library of the Jewish Theological Seminary.

FIGURE 4. Cover of *Bernshteyn's nayer yudisher folks-brifenshteler.*
Warsaw: Ya. Kelter, n.d.
Courtesy of the National Library of Russia, St. Petersburg.

FIGURE 5. Cover of Oyzer Bloshteyn, *Der nayer fielbeserer ales Bloshteyn's brifenshteler: mit dem zhargon-lehrer tsuzamen* [*Bloshteyn's briefenshteler*]. Warsaw: Y. Y. Raynerman, 1924–1925.
Courtesy of the Dorot Jewish Division, the New York Public Library, Astor, Lenox, and Tilden Foundations.

FIGURE 6. Title page of Yoysef Gorodinski, *Gorodinski's Korrespondent.*
Der nayer brifenshteller. Der postalion. Berdichev: Yoysef Berman, 1910.
Courtesy of the National Library of Russia, St. Petersburg.

and indeed turns it into something like a "half-German" and "half-Russian" cobbled-together *zhargon* [jargon].

. . . In letters to their friends, they write *ich komme, ich werde gehen, du hast mir versprochen* [German for "I come, I will go," and "you promised me," transliterated into Yiddish], and so forth. This is not even to speak of the dozens of other atrocious barbarisms which must arouse disgust in every person of superior cultivation and aesthetic sensibility![59]

Well into the last days of the genre, some brivnshtelers demonstrated little regard for either purity of language or consistency of spelling and style. The anonymously authored 1855 *Khalifas igroys* [*Halifat igrot*] (Exchange of letters) leaves out many vowels and renders the letter *yod* as a *vov* with a *shuruk* (dot midway up its stem). Goldshteyn-Gershonovitsh's late 1913 trilingual *Der praktisher zhargon-russish-daytsh Briefenlehrer* (Practical Zhargon-Russian-German letter teacher) incorporates many transliterated Russian words in its Yiddish texts. The 1906 *Oytser mikhtovim* [*Otsar mikhtavim*], *oder brifenshteler fir yudishe kinder,* which looks like its publisher assembled it from pirated material, refers to Yiddish as "our Jewish German language" and indiscriminately mixes letters written in daytshmerish Yiddish, less daytshmerish Yiddish, and Judeo-German. Would this sort of hodgepodge have disturbed the average Yiddish reader? Given the general lack of orthographic standardization in Yiddish literature and the affinity of German to Yiddish, quite possibly not. Judeo-German may have seemed like an extra-fancy sort of Yiddish, perhaps not entirely comprehensible, but to a large degree accessible to a Yiddish-speaker. Brivnshtelers themselves promoted this sensibility, often urging their readers *not* to write in the Yiddish they actually spoke in everyday life.[60]

Orthographic controversies were in any event the province of the well-educated. Many brivnshteler users were in the position of Dik's fictional rabbi or Sholem Aleichem's Motl: they could not write at all, because their families had been unable to sustain even the modest expense of hiring a shrayber. Jewish communities funded Talmud Torah schools for poor boys because religious life could not function if Jewish men could not read the prayer book and honor the Talmud. The ability to write may have been crucial for the economic well-being of individuals and even of the community as a whole, but it was not a religious imperative, and Jewish communities, often impoverished themselves, did not fund it.[61]

If the community was disengaged from a skill it failed to see as a public good, some individuals pursued it on their own. In autobiographical essays that YIVO solicited through contests right before and after World War II, learning the mechanics of writing is a recurrent and poignant theme. For many of the contestants who grew up in poverty, learning to write represented a conscious achievement, even a kind of personal liberation.

A good example is Ben Reisman, first-prize winner in YIVO's 1942 contest in the United States and Canada. Reisman was born in Kalush in Galicia in 1876. He studied Talmud—he could read, in other words, both Hebrew and Aramaic—but had never had a writing teacher. Orphaned and sent out to work, he was in despair over his inability to read Polish or write in any language whatsoever. He finally achieved that skill when he was away from home for a week, staying with a sympathetic uncle:

> I told him that I would like to learn how to write. So he took a shingle and a piece of chalk and wrote, "alef, beys," and so on, and I started to learn how to write Yiddish. The girls wrote the a-b-c on a piece of paper for me, and I would erase it and write. Within about four or five days, I was able to write the following words, "Dear uncle, I received your dear letter in good order." I could also write several Polish words.[62]

Reisman's practice Yiddish sentence recalls the shure grus. But another essayist, Rose Silverman, recalls teaching herself how to write with the aid of an actual brivnshteler:

> I couldn't read or write, but I knew that it was very bad if you couldn't. My will is apparently stronger than anything. I found a printed alphabet in a prayer book or a Haggadah—I don't remember. About each individual letter, I asked: What is this? After that, I started to put words together in my head. Then I asked about the punctuation. I kept my head in the prayer book all the time, until I learned to read a bit. But writing, how would I learn to write? Sometimes a coincidence is the best thing. By coincidence, I came upon a Yiddish letter-writing manual in which the Yiddish alphabet was written down, and I quickly comprehended it. I already knew the meaning of all the letters. Reading and writing soon became clear to me.[63]

As Ben Reisman's memoir attests, young Jews were eager not only to learn to write in Yiddish but also to learn and perfect their Hebrew and to acquire foreign languages like German, Russian, and Polish. In that regard, the brivnshteler also had an important role to play, particularly in its earlier incarnations.

Some early manuals promote language learning for a specific audience: men who had been through advanced study at a yeshiva. The most important author of such manuals was the maskil and pedagogue Avraham Paperna. Written in Judeo-German between 1874 and 1889, Paperna's books offer no lessons in how to write actual spoken Yiddish. What they advertise instead is the acquisition of proficiency in German written in Hebrew characters (the 1889 Paperna includes some letters in actual German as well), along with Russian and Hebrew. The multiple printings, including several without Paperna's name, are testimony to the popularity of the approach.[64]

Hebrew, Russian, and German were explicitly high-culture languages. The assumption was that Paperna's readers knew Hebrew, the accepted language of written communication between Jewish male elites, though they might have needed help in composing a good letter in it. For business, they needed either German or Russian. German was a language they most likely did not speak, though they might have been more or less able to decipher Judeo-German; Russian was needed to communicate with non-Jews, as well as with any government institution. By the turn of the twentieth century, Russian had supplanted German as the non-Jewish alternative to Yiddish. Hebrew, by contrast, was the hallmark of intelligentsia associated with the Haskalah. When Zionism came into the picture in the last decades of the nineteenth century, proficiency in Hebrew acquired a new dimension as a mark of secular Jewish self-awareness.

Foreign languages were also taught in dedicated textbooks, often advertised on brivnshteler back covers. Both Paperna and the equally prolific Khaim Poplavski wrote textbooks using the Ollendorff Method, which pioneered pattern sentences to showcase particular grammatical constructions.[65] Brivnshtelers weren't as modern. But for a kheyder graduate used to learning languages through text and translation—a sophisticated text read with a memorized oral translation—a brivnshteler made sense. In his memoirs, Abraham Cahan describes how this worked. For a while in his boyhood, he was obsessed with the idea of modernized Hebrew. His father, who had maskilic leanings, gave him the means to learn it: "At that time, a Hebrew brivnshteler by Naftali-Maskil Eitan had come out, with the title *Mikhtovim lelomed* [*Mikhtavim le-lamed*]. My father bought the book and had it bound for me. First he studied every letter with me, just as one would study a chapter of Tanakh [Bible] in kheyder. Then I copied out the letter a few times until I knew it by heart."[66]

People like Cahan were drawn to Hebrew because it evoked a proud national past. Russian, by contrast, was a necessity of the here and now, essential for business, study, high culture, and social interactions with gentiles and assimilated Jews. While Jews in the Russian Empire had always commanded a certain level of marketplace Ukrainian, Belorussian, or Polish, Russian, the language of the state, was in a different category. Despite the pogroms and exclusionary laws, Russian was the language of education and prosperity.

Historian Steven Zipperstein gives statistics from a study of a Jewish lending library in Poltava (Ukraine) from 1904 to 1905. Out of a total of 35,200 books borrowed in the course of the study, 80 percent were in Russian, 13 percent in Hebrew, and 7 percent in Yiddish.[67] And this was a Jewish library. Even Russian libraries had a Jewish clientele. "If it weren't for the girls and the young Jews, you might as well close the library," wrote Chekhov, describing a provincial town in a short story of 1898.[68]

Later bilingual brivnshtelers accommodated this interest in Russian by pairing Yiddish letters with Russian translations. This type of book could serve two categories of users. Those who wanted to learn how to write Yiddish letters could focus on Yiddish texts, while those bent on learning Russian could concentrate on that, with recourse to the Yiddish for translation of unfamiliar Russian words or phrases. Other languages also figure. It was not uncommon for brivnshtelers to include a few sample German letters in their business sections. One Zionist letter manual used Yiddish letters on facing pages to teach modern Hebrew.[69] In America, Alexander Harkavy would use the brivnshteler as a familiar vehicle for teaching English.[70]

In addition to providing opportunities for self-instruction, brivnshtelers were preoccupied with the subject of education itself. Letters referring to young men who have left the shtetl to study are ubiquitous. (There are some about women, though fewer.[71]) A frequently encountered series involves a boy sent to live with his wealthy uncle to pursue his education in a city. While the exact nature of this education (secular? religious?) is often not made clear, the desired outcome is obvious: the boy is supposed to study hard.

Brivnshtelers oriented toward the less educated often tout the practical value of learning. Young men who have not been good students have
to leave home, sometimes to far-off America, where they regret their ill-
spent youth and write to their parents, asking for money to purchase a
return ticket. Their studious counterparts who have learned languages
and arithmetic, or who can write in a good hand, get jobs as clerks and
don't have to emigrate. A particularly melodramatic variant on that theme
comes in a letter from a brivnshteler of 1904, in which the value of language proficiency is given dramatic embellishment:

> Ach, what a misfortune I've met with these past few days. It's painful for
> me to be silent and screaming won't help me either. . . . This week the last
> 300 rubles I had left from my wedding money after three years of board-
> ing with my father-in-law and mother-in-law was stolen out of my bag.
> Now I'll have to throw myself off a bridge. . . . The money was in five-
> ruble coins covered in fat and there was a gold watch made in a factory in
> London engraved with the number 300. . . . My good fortune is this: while
> I was boarding with my in-laws I learned to write Yiddish and Russian,
> and arithmetic.[72]

Writing correctly in Yiddish and Russian and knowing arithmetic—all
skills that could be picked up from a brivnshteler—are as valuable capital
as a gold watch and money. As a story in a brivnshteler, it constitutes a
perfect piece of self-advertisement.

THE BRIVNSHTELER AND THE HISTORY
OF MODEL LETTERS

The brivnshteler has a long history. Going back deep into the Western
past, we find ourselves in Sumer and Egypt, where the development
of writing meant the necessity of training scribes, and training scribes
meant exercises in copying texts.[73] Students in Sumer, where writing
emerged in the fourth millennium BCE, practiced cuneiform with model
sentences, fables, and contracts.[74] In Egypt, apprentice scribes copied out
hymns, literature, business documents, legal documents, and letters,
sometimes assembled in pedagogical collections.[75] The most famous collection was put together during the Middle Kingdom (the beginning
of the second millennium BCE). It enjoyed a long shelf life: the copy
that has come down to us, known as Papyrus Lansing, dates from the

Twentieth Dynasty, hundreds of years later. Papyrus Lansing appears to be a student's copybook. It is full of spelling errors and other mistakes.[76]

Papyrus Lansing consists of two letters. One is a letter from a master scribe to his own recalcitrant apprentice, exhorting him to study for the spiritual and practical purpose of a good life:

> By day write with your fingers; recite by night. Befriend the scroll, the palette. It pleases more than wine. Writing for him who knows it is better than other professions. It pleases more than bread and beer, more than clothing and ointment. It is worth more than an inheritance in Egypt, than a tomb in the west.[77]

The theme of forsaking the material pleasures of the world for the chaste rewards of education would persist as a theme in letter-manual prose across history and culture. Another theme that would remain potent is that of the wayward son. In Papyrus Lansing, as in Jewish manuals millennia into the future, the young man's flaw is that he will not study. Seeing his pupil's future at risk, the teacher is distraught:

> I spend the day instructing you. You do not listen! Your heart is like an (empty) room. My teachings are not in it. Take their (meaning) to yourself!
>   Do you not recall the (fate of) the unskilled man? His name is not known. He is ever burdened (like an ass carrying) in front of the scribe who knows what he is about.[78]

Like some letters in brivnshtelers (see, for example, "Courtship and Marriage" or "Modernity and Mobility"), Papyrus Lansing can be read as social criticism. The ancient writer has harsh things to say about the lot of peasants, soldiers, potters, merchants, sailors, and workers on obelisk-construction crews, among many other life paths. Literacy, however hard-won, is the key to avoiding all that: far better to be a scribe than a manual laborer.[79]

The European strain of model-letter books traces back to the Roman *ars rhetorica,* which migrated to every country touched by classical culture. Like Papyrus Lansing, the Latin and Greek Bologna Papyrus from the third or fourth century CE seems to be the work of a student, in this case someone "who painfully attempts to write in an educated manner."[80] Following the Renaissance and the rise of printing, painful attempts at writing engaged an ever-larger portion of the European population and began to take place in the vernacular. In England, letter manuals in English rather than Latin appeared in the second half of the sixteenth century, intended for users outside the educated elite.[81]

In the mid-seventeenth century, manuals that taught "good manners and the art of courtship" were imported from France into England,[82] though within decades, a competing approach that deemphasized aristocratic ideals was already catering to the needs of a less-educated class oriented to business.[83] French manuals were more conservative, retaining their loyalty to *savoir-vivre*[84] until the genre lost its audience in the late nineteenth century, a victim of better public education.[85] With the gap of about a hundred years and some local variations, the same tension between bourgeois models and aristocratic ones resurfaced in Russia. And among both Russians and Russian Jews, the availability of public education after the Revolution brought the genre to a close. American brivnshtelers enjoyed a slightly longer run, with reprints published into the late 1920s, probably catering to the dwindling number of Jewish immigrants or Americanized Jews who wished to communicate with family back home in Europe.

While the content of Jewish manuals is steeped in Jewish specificity, their early chronology makes them very much a part of the European history of the genre. Hebrew-language collections appear at the very outset of Jewish publishing in the sixteenth century, assembled from handwritten manuscripts that were already in circulation.[86] Judith Halevi Zwick, who has written a detailed account of these books, notes that one of the very first, the *Igroys shloymim* [*Igrot Shelomim*] (Letters of greeting) printed in Augsburg, Bavaria, in 1534, appears on the publisher's list of religious texts. At the very least this indicates the importance of the genre, which, as Zwick observes, must have been seen as crucial to the day-to-day functioning of a religious community.[87] But she also remarks that the books were widely derided, presumably because they were cheap and used for secular purposes rather than serving the goal of enabling fulfillment of ritual obligations or of furthering Torah scholarship.[88]

True to its title, the *Igroys shloymim* [*Igrot Shelomim*] provides the user with formulaic greetings to honor a recipient. A rabbi, for example, merits this: "He who sits on the chair of awe. From him shall come forth Torah through speaking and through explication. His appearance is like awesome ice. May God protect him from trouble and misfortune."[89] After greetings and blessings come texts whose everyday but dramatic nature is apparent from the subject headings. The first letter takes up the situation of a man "who is angry at his friend because he has slandered him." The second, escalating one step further, is for someone "who wants to let his friend know that he is capable of taking revenge but would rather not do so."[90] The *Igroys shloymim* continued to be reprinted through the seventeenth century.[91]

One of the first manuals to provide Yiddish (in its West European variant) alongside Hebrew was the *Igeres Shloyme* [*Igeret Shelomoh*] (Letter of Solomon) of Shelomoh ben Yehudah Leib Segal Medasa, printed in Wandsbeck, near Hamburg, in 1732.[92] The author explains the presence of Yiddish in the book as an instructional aid for children not yet comfortable with Hebrew.[93] The idea that some adults, too, might benefit from a Yiddish translation would probably have been understood as insulting. A *haskamah* (rabbinical endorsement) in the book reports that Segal had to undertake its publication because of extreme poverty and the need to raise money for his daughter's dowry. He was a melamed and these are the model letters he uses for teaching. Foreshadowing a later development of the Haskalah, Segal recommends that Jewish children also learn a foreign language, in this case Latin.[94]

Another foreign language appears in the early nineteenth century: German, in the form of Judeo-German. The combination of Hebrew and Judeo-German is prominent in two Enlightenment-era manuals that had long afterlives in the Russian Empire: Moshe Shmu'el Neumann's 1815 *Sefer Mikhtevey ivris* [*Mikhtave 'ivrit*] *oder ebraisher und daytsher briefshteller* (Letters in Hebrew, or Hebrew and German letter-writer) and Shalom ha-Kohen's 1820 *Ksav yoysher* [*Ketav yosher*] (Proper writing).[95] The books share the same goal: to instruct Yiddish-speakers in German and the equally high-prestige Hebrew through the useful medium of letters. Otherwise they are very different. Neumann is above all a pedagogue: unique among the genre's authors, he meticulously annotates his letters for the language learner. Shalom ha-Kohen, an Enlightenment poet and all-around intellectual, writes model letters that are as close as we come to epistolary novellas. His letters are arranged in lengthy sets, united by the same recurring characters and a genuine narrative line.

Like their earliest Yiddish counterparts, the early editions of the Shalom ha-Kohen and Neumann books are printed in the semi-cursive *yidish-taytsh,* typeface commonly found in Yiddish translations of the

Bible and other texts that targeted a female readership, with Hebrew printed in square letters. (See figure 1.) The connection with women is explicit in another name for this typeface, *vayber-taytsh* (women's Yiddish). Until about the middle of the nineteenth century, it was common for Yiddish to be printed in cursive fonts. For instance, in figure 2, letters are printed in this style of font, with introductions rendered in yidish-taytsh.[96]

From the very beginning, *igronim* oscillated between the sacred and the secular in accordance with the time and the community. Sixteenth-century igronim in Venice highlight worldly values and beautiful writing,[97] while East European collections over the next two centuries reflect the intense religiosity of Ashkenazi communities and showcase a Hebrew that is much less fluent.[98] Many nineteenth-century authors use the genre to promote maskilic ideas, and not without success: prefaces of later igronim sometimes credit the earlier books with leading the authors from darkness to light.[99] In a further conflation of sacred and secular, some igronim were published with the word *sefer* at the beginning of their titles, for example, the 1856 *Sefer Mikhtevey ivris* [*Mikhtave 'ivrit*], attributed to Neumann and Kohen. "Sefer" was generally reserved for religious books, while a *bukh* (book) was the usual designation for a book with secular content. Calling a letter-writing manual a sefer seems to have been an attempt to elevate its status and render its secular content more "kosher," even as it spread maskilic, and thus subversive, ideas.[100]

Zwick finds a number of nineteenth-century books, even some published in Warsaw, within the Russian Empire, that address contentious issues like the conflict between Hasidism and Zionism, and Jewish discomfort with the Russian draft.[101] Brivnshtelers are much more circumspect about anything controversial. Unlike igronim, they have little to say about religion and steer clear of politics both inside and outside the Jewish world. While they reflect the enormous political changes going on around them and even the ideologies of their authors, those reflections are filtered through a vision of private life.

YIDDISH LANGUAGE, YIDDISH PUBLISHING, AND THE BRIVNSHTELER

The first brivnshteler known to have been published in Russia was the anonymously authored *Mesader igeres* [*Mesadar igeret*], which appeared in Vilna in 1825.[102] The next few decades saw the publication of about half a dozen other Yiddish titles, including several by Avrom and Hirsh Lion Dor.[103] But the real rise of the brivnshteler came in the last quarter of the nineteenth century, in tandem with a new era for both Yiddish and Yiddish literature.

The everyday language of East European Jews began to be consistently referred to as "Yiddish" only in the 1890s. Until then, there was no single commonly accepted name for the language. Among the more popular were *taytsh* (German, or "translation") and *loshn Ashkenaz* (the Ashkenazi language, though this could also mean just German).[104] By the mid-nineteenth century most people called Yiddish *zhargon*, a pejorative French word introduced by German maskilim in the late eighteenth century to denote a language they viewed as a hodge-podge, highly inferior to "pure" competitors like Hebrew or German. As the term moved eastward, it lost much of its sting—though not all of it.[105] The YIVO Archives has a letter from Leon Trotsky mollifying a correspondent offended by Trotsky's references to "zhargon" in his autobiography. Writing from exile in Istanbul all the way to the Bronx, Trotsky apologizes for any misunderstanding: back in Odessa when he was growing up, "zhargon" was the word everyone used.[106] It was not until around the time of the Czernowitz Conference, the first international conference on Yiddish, in 1908, that "zhargon" was firmly replaced by the term "Yiddish" in public life.[107]

The lack of a standard word for Yiddish is evident in brivnshteler titles, where it can be the cause of bibliographic confusion. When the word "zhargon" appears on a title page, it is pretty clear that the contents will be in Yiddish; but when "loshn Ashkenaz" appears, it is anyone's guess whether the material within will be in Yiddish or in Judeo-German. Typography provides no clue: the special vayber-taytsh font and similar cursive fonts were used for both Yiddish and Judeo-German to mark them off from Hebrew text printed in a square font.

Compared to Hebrew and Aramaic, the languages of Jewish holy books, Yiddish was held in low esteem as the language of women and family life. Lack of prestige in no way implies lack of use: until the spread of Hebrew-language schools between the two world wars, very few women knew Hebrew, and, as we have seen, relatively few men had more than a basic Jewish education. These people, if they wanted to read,

read in Yiddish—including men who could and did read books of ethical literature that were published in Yiddish for women. The oral nature of a lot of religious discourse meant that even among male elites, most discussion about religious texts and questions was in Yiddish. Hasidism was spread largely in spoken Yiddish, without the help of written texts. Outside of the educated elite, women and men got their religious instruction from the sermons of preachers. These too were delivered in Yiddish, the only language most of their listeners would have understood.[108]

The rise of the Haskalah among Jews in Central and Eastern Europe beginning in the late eighteenth century brought a new and organized hostility toward Yiddish in Russia and Poland. The maskilim rejected traditional Hebrew-Yiddish bilingualism in favor of one that was Hebrew-German or Hebrew-Russian. The Hebrew-German combination had been promoted in Germany by Moses Mendlssohn and members of his circle. In the romantic conception of the maskilim, Hebrew was the noble language of a glorious Jewish past. Biblical Hebrew in particular was considered the language of the soul. Like Yiddish, rabbinical Hebrew, the Hebrew of the Diaspora, came in for condemnation because of its haphazard grammar and inclusion of Aramaic and other foreign words.[109]

The enthusiasm of the maskilim led to the creation of a new Hebrew literature in the usual Enlightenment genres: poetry, novels, and parodies. Maskilim produced Hebrew-language books on science and math, and translated novels from European languages. The other part of maskilic language reorientation—the replacement of Yiddish by German—was directed at Jews who hoped to assume a respected place in the world of Western culture and learning. To make good on the promise of the European Enlightenment, Jews needed to recast themselves as educated Europeans. Learning standard German was an important milestone toward achieving this goal.

Whether the linguistic goal was Hebrew or German or both, the hope for a modernized Jewry was predicated on the abandonment of Yiddish. Leading Berlin maskilim such as the historian Heinrich Graetz derided Yiddish as "a half-bestial language." Yiddish in this view was a degraded dialect, certainly not capable of serving as a vehicle for high culture or a means of conveying elevated secular ideas about philosophy or politics. The same attitudes prevailed farther east in Russia and Poland. The maskil Yitshak Ber Levinzon was among many who asserted that Yiddish had "no grammar and no rules or restrictions concerning parsing and spelling."[110]

One attempt to wean Jews away from Yiddish was the promotion of a kind of anti-Yiddish: German written in Hebrew characters, as utilized in 1783 by Moses Mendlssohn, the leading exemplar of the German Haskalah, in *Nesivoys ha-sholem* [*Netivot ha-shalom*] (The paths of peace), his German translation of the Hebrew Bible. Sometimes referred to as Judisch-Deutsch, or, as we have been calling it here, Judeo-German,[111] it appears to be based on the idea that a Yiddish-speaker would find learning German easier if he encountered the language in the Hebrew alphabet.[112]

Most of the Jewish letter manuals published in Eastern Europe before the 1890s are written in Judeo-German.[113] Many of these books have been cataloged over the years as Yiddish. But their language, which at first glance might appear to be Yiddish, is wholly German in syntax and vocabulary, entirely lacking words of Slavic or Hebraic origin.[114] Since the Judeo-German brivnshtelers were not intended by their authors as Yiddish, but rather as weapons in an ideological war against it, we have largely excluded them from the purview of this book.[115] We do not, however, exclude books written in daytshmerish, the most common style of language and spelling in later nineteenth-century brivnshtelers.

Other proposed substitutes for Yiddish had their own problems. Even those who championed Hebrew had to acknowledge that there was little in the way of a potential readership for works in that language.[116] And while Jews in German lands were quick to forsake Yiddish for German, the situation in Russia was different. While statistics on library use point to a rapidly growing interest in Russian reading, not all Jews could use libraries, still less borrow books in Russian: at the time of the 1897 census, only a third of all Jewish men and not quite 20 percent of Jewish women claimed Russian literacy.[117] And these statistics say nothing about what language they were using in everyday life. Even truly bilingual Jews needed Yiddish to communicate with non-Russian-speaking family members who belonged to the older generation.

One spur to the development of Yiddish prose occurred, oddly, among maskilim, who saw the language as a useful tool in their struggle to contain the spread of Hasidism, a movement they viewed as the very embodiment of everything standing in the way of the modernization of Jewish life. To combat the influence of Hasidism, the Galician maskil Menakhem Mendl Lefin promoted the creation of a maskilic literature in Yiddish. In 1814, he published a Yiddish translation of the Book of Proverbs, purposely shying away from Judeo-German and the archaic literary Yiddish of women's literature in favor of the more modern, Slavicized Yiddish actually spoken by his intended audience. His decision to write in Yiddish was nonetheless controversial among some of his compatriots, who saw it as a betrayal of the ideals of the Haskalah. And even he regarded writing in Yiddish as a temporary measure, a necessary evil on the road to reform.[118]

A few decades later, in the 1840s, Lefin's approach was taken up by the maskil Ayzik Meyer Dik, a teacher in a state-sponsored Jewish school in Vilna. Dik began publishing novels in Yiddish, through which he hoped to deliver moral lessons to Jews not educated enough to read Hebrew or Russian. While he was held in low regard by his fellow maskilim, he was the first modern Yiddish author to be published by a major publishing house, Romm, in Vilna, which signed a long-term contract with him in 1864. Dik became the first important writer of popular Yiddish fiction. But even he was self-deprecating about his work in Yiddish, confessing, in Hebrew, "I degraded my pen by writing numerous stories in the language which, to our great shame, is the spoken dialect of our people in this country."[119]

During the first half of the nineteenth century, the maskilim had, in any case, few outlets for literary expression, whether in Hebrew or Yiddish. In 1836, the tsarist government closed all Jewish presses in the Russian Empire except for Romm in Vilna and Shapira in Zhitomir. These two presses refused to publish maskilic literature out of fear of alienating their more traditional readers.[120] The writings of maskilim, for the most part, languished in desk drawers or were privately circulated in manuscript. It was not until the 1860s, under Alexander II, that the ban on Jewish publishing was relaxed. Freewheeling Odessa, already a bastion of the Haskalah, became a new center of Jewish publishing, and in 1862, the first Yiddish periodical, *Kol mevaser* (The herald), began publication there. It provided a venue for new Yiddish writers, such as Sholem Yankev Abramovitsh (Mendle Moykher Sforim), Yitskhok Yoyel Linetski, and Avrom Goldfadn, all of whom believed that writing in Yiddish would provide a much wider audience for their work.

The readership of *Kol mevaser* was more educated than the masses who were devoted readers of Dik.[121] While it has been commonly held that educated Jews were not much interested in Yiddish before the end of the nineteenth century, Alyssa Quint reports that in the 1860s, there were literary salons in Warsaw, Vilna, Odessa, Mogilev, Berdichev, and other places in which Yiddish, not Hebrew or Russian, was "the favored language of entertainment." She also notes a problem with the populist beliefs of early Yiddish writers: most of their readers were other maskilim. And even when less-educated Jews read, for example, Dik's novels, they were not consciously choosing innovative reading material. From a popular point of view, there was no reason to see Dik's novels as appreciatively different from the *mayse-bikhlekh* (storybooks, or chapbooks) with which ordinary people were familiar.[122]

An example of maskilic enthusiasm for Yiddish, as well as excitement about the existence of *Kol mevaser*, can be found in a letter in Lion Dor's 1865 brivnshteler. The letter is framed as a thank-you note from Yankev Leyb Blumentsvayg to his father, who has sent him a package of books in *idesh-daytsh* (Yiddish). Yankev Leyb reiterates all the doubts an intellectual can have about the language—it has no grammar; it's not backed up by a dictionary; it's not a tool for fine art—and counters that a writer who can overcome those impediments is truly great:

> I marveled at how clearly and pleasantly the language is presented and written, in idesh-daytsh, with beautiful examples, such as discussions and also ethical teachings, especially the stories in which one can find moral lessons. It so happens that at the time, some young people, my good friends, were visiting me and they asked, "What good and what use are they, these Idesh-daytsh books?" They said, "What is it? A sefer [a religious book]? A bukh [a secular book]? There's no language, no grammar." Then, I explained to them and gave them to understand: "Just listen, my friends! What you're saying is so unintelligent. Isn't it true that we call someone who creates a work, and has a good instrument at his disposal, good tools, and also good raw material, an artist? But when someone creates a beautiful work without tools and fashions it out of coarse stuff, is he not truly a master of his craft? Certainly, my friends: someone who uses language, who has learned from a grammar book and thoroughly studied a dictionary, and has had a lot of practice is a good writer, a poet with a good mind. But the idesh-daytsh language is mixed with many foreign words and doesn't have a grammar . . . nonetheless, see here, brothers, what beautiful compositions we have in the world today, published by authors. It is truly a pleasure to read these beautiful

writers: the fables of the sage, Herr Zweifel, or the [work of the] newspaper writers of the well-known sage Zederbaum's idesh-daytsh *Kol mevaser,* and also the works of other very learned men, who explain everything so that the masses can clearly understand. And even the knowledgeable say that their pure words and precious examples are a pleasure to read."[123]

The first edition of Lion Dor's brivnshteler was published in Vilna by the Hebrew printing press of Shmu'el Yosef Fuenn, a leading maskil. With its miscellany of subject matter—model letters, fables, ethics lessons, poems, ethical precepts, and even an arithmetic primer—the book serves almost as a transitional object. The fables and ethics lessons mark continuity with older forms of Yiddish literature, while the letters themselves (exhortations about the value of modern secular education and glowing reviews of the new government schools established for Jews) place the manual squarely in its time and place. But Lion Dor's enlightened attitude toward Yiddish points his book toward the future, as part of a growing trend.

Fuenn was also the publisher of the first Yiddish novel of Shomer (Nokhem Meyer Shaykevitsh). Shomer became famous for his prolific output of potboilers, both novels and plays, and was perhaps the most popular Jewish novelist of his time, the 1870s–1880s. His work was derided by critics in the burgeoning Yiddish literary establishment, most famously by Sholem Aleichem in his 1888 pamphlet, *Shomer's mishpet* (Shomer's trial), which cast Shomer as a purveyor of literary trash (*shund*) and hence an impediment to the development of serious Yiddish literature. The link between shund and brivnshtelers can be seen in the careers of both Shomer and his fellow popular novelist Oyzer Bloshteyn. Both men not only published brivnshtelers, but became something like brand names, with many editions of their manuals appearing from the 1890s to mid-1920s, under various titles like *Shomer's briefenshteler, Shaykevitsh'es nayer briefenshteler* (Shaykevitsh's new brivnshteler), *Nayer Bloshteyn's briefenshteler* (New Bloshteyn's brivnshteler), and *Der nayer fielbeserer ales Bloshteyn's brifenshteler* (The new, improved, complete Bloshteyn's brivnshteler).

Not all the books so branded were written by the putative authors. At least one brivnshteler attributed to Shomer, the 1908 *Der nayer Shomer's briefenshteler* (The new Shomer's brivnshteler) is actually plagiarized from a work by Dov Arye Fridman, published in 1889 and in several later editions under the title *Der nayer praktisher brifenshteller* (The new practical brivnshteler). The use of *Shomer's* as a brand-name can only be the Vilna publisher's marketing strategy, as by 1908 Shomer had already been dead for three years.[124]

Bloshteyn enjoyed a similar, partly posthumous career. Several or even most of the brivnshtelers branded with his name and published well after his 1898 demise were actually by anonymous authors and contain a mixture of letters written by him and new content. The title of the first one to survive the ravages of time, *Der nayer rikhtiger Bloshteyn's briefenshteler* (The new correct Bloshteyn's brivnshteler, Warsaw, 189-?), presupposes an edition that was earlier and popular enough for the publisher to turn into a brand. Another Bloshteyn manual, *Nayer Bloshteyn's briefenshteler* (New Bloshteyn's brivnshteler), was published in Vilna in 1903, five years after his death. In New York in 1900 and 1905, the Hebrew Publishing Company dispensed with the author's name altogether, and retitled the text *Briefenshteler in shraybshrift* (Brivnshteler in handwriting). For reappearances in 1917 (Warsaw) and 1922 (Lublin) Bloshteyn's letters got an extravagant new title and a pedagogical appendix: *Der nayer fielbeserer ales Bloshteyn's brifenshteler: mit dem zhargon-lehrer tsuzamen* (The new, improved, complete Bloshteyn's brivnshteler, together with a zhargon primer). As late as 1926, another New York publisher took the letters and, perhaps feeling the need for novelty, at least in advertising, rebranded them under the name of Steinberg.[125]

These were the most famous of brivnshteler authors. About some of the others, little is known. Many, like Yoysef Arukh and Yoysef Gorodinski, were teachers, the former in Kishinev and the latter in Berdichev. Avrom Lion Dor (1793–1845) and his son Hirsh (no known dates), Shomer (1849?–1905), and Bloshteyn (1840–1898) were born early enough to have participated in the Haskalah, but some of the authors were of a younger generation, born in the 1860s or even perhaps later, and came of age in a new, post-maskilic era. As historian Shmuel Feiner notes, there was a qualitative difference between the maskilim of the first generation and the "nationalists" of the succeeding one, who accepted the basic tenets of the Haskalah, particularly regarding education, but had no interest in pursuing its particular ideological battles.[126]

The proliferation of brivnshtelers in the late 1880s took place in the context of a general upsurge in Yiddish publishing. An informal count of letter manuals with Yiddish content published from 1885 to 1914 yields twenty-eight new titles (not counting reprints or manuals published in America), while the number of titles published from 1800 to 1884 hovers at only about eight.[127] Modest as it may have been, the genre assumes greater significance and value when one considers that other forms of Yiddish literature were repressed. As David Fishman notes, in 1897 there was not a single Yiddish literary journal or newspaper in existence in the Russian Empire.[128] Beginning in 1883, Russian authorities severely restricted Yiddish theater. There were no legal Yiddish schools until World War I. Brivnshtelers joined the popular novels of Dik, Shomer, and others as one of the limited possibilities available to a Yiddish reading public.

The liberalization of tsarist policy after the 1905 revolution opened new opportunities for Yiddish literature. Yiddish newspapers were now permitted, allowing new dailies like the Warsaw-based *Haynt* and *Moment* to achieve wide circulation. Many smaller periodicals appeared, some affiliated with political parties. Book publishing flourished. New attitudes about the role of Yiddish in Jewish public life spurred some activists and intellectuals to challenge the hegemony of the anti-Yiddish old guard. In stormy meetings in St. Petersburg in 1905–1906, Yiddishist factions within the Society for the Promotion of Culture among the Jews of Russia (OPE) demanded that Yiddish be included alongside Russian and Hebrew in the organization's school curricula and cultural programs. More and more intellectuals became critical of integrationism and assimilationism in favor of nationalist and populist ideologies.[129] For those who espoused Diaspora Nationalism, Yiddish was seen as a bulwark against the disappearance of Jewish life and tradition. Populists saw the cultivation of Yiddish as essential to the democratization of Jewish life.

One can catch a glimpse of the tenor of the time and the new status enjoyed by Yiddish in a letter in the 1910 or 1911 *Bernshteyn's yudisher brieflehrer* (Bernshteyn's Yiddish letter primer). A young man in a shtetl writes to his friend in the city:

> No one reads like they do in the provinces. Every new work is for us the making of a new epoch, every feuilleton is discussed. . . . Recently, people have begun to read Yiddish literature. Yiddish writers are now considered fashionable instead of Russian writers, and the names of the classic Yiddish writers are constantly coming up in conversation.[130]

It is not clear exactly which writers the young man had in mind—most likely the classic triumvirate of Mendle Moykher Sforim, Sholem Aleichem, and Yitskhok Leybush Peretz. But the fact that he could use "classic" and "Yiddish" in the same sentence shows the enormous distance that Yiddish and Yiddish literature had covered in a remarkably short time.

THE BRIVNSHTELER AND YIDDISH LITERATURE

Brivnshtelers were not literature, though they have their literary moments. The genre existed on literature's margins, a step below shund, with which it shared a combined impulse to entertain and instruct. A glimpse of how the intelligentsia regarded brivnshtelers can be seen in a little story from Avraham Paperna's memoir. At the time it took place, the future maskil, pedagogue, and letter-manual author was a young man with Enlightenment interests, entranced with new Hebrew writing. A girl named Hindele, whose family boarded in the same house as he did, seemed interested in literature even though she knew no Hebrew: she would listen intently as Paperna and his friend read Hebrew poems out loud. Paperna was startled when Hindele asked for explanations: "Her insistent requests for us to tell her what was going on in one poem or essay or another I found out of place and impossible to fulfill. Could such lofty thoughts be understood by a woman's mind?" Hindele does not appear to have been cowed:

> [She] often complained to me that girls didn't get taught Hebrew as boys did, and that aside from the brivnshteler that she had already read and copied out hundreds of times, she had no kind of reading matter. I happily promised her to find appropriate stories in zhargon, and as soon as the *moykher-sforim* [book-seller] came by I bought her two books by A. M. Dik: *Khazkele aleyn* and *Shmaye der gut-yontev biter*.[131]

One can fantasize that Hindele had at hand the very first Yiddish letter manual to be published in Eastern Europe. *Mesader igeres* [*Mesadar igeret*] (1825) was literary by design and also exceptionally entertaining.[132] But whatever brivnshteler she copied and recopied, that book constituted her single printed source for entertainment and, possibly, knowledge about the outside world. Paperna, aware of better Yiddish options for a female reader, bought her some shund. It was the next step up.

In her history of Hebrew-language manuals, Judith Halevi Zwick argues that they served as a training ground for future writers, giving them a place and a reason to write in Hebrew about everyday life.[133] It is hard to make the same argument for Yiddish. While we have a few examples of popular novelists who wrote brivnshtelers (Shomer, Bloshteyn), they did not use the letter manuals for practice, but rather as a source of income that dovetailed with their pedagogical interests. There is not a single known example of someone who started out writing manuals and went on to become even a minor writer of Yiddish fiction.[134]

A related case has been made for the brivnshteler as "a bridge between letters and epistolary novels."[135] That makes sense in an abstract way, but not in a historical or causative one. The earlier East European brivnshtelers did not precede, but rather appeared in print around the same time as, the earliest Yiddish novels, while brivnshtelers in a more vernacular, unstilted Yiddish started coming to the market in the 1890s, at around the same time that fiction employing a similar style of Yiddish came into its own. Of course, it is possible that the Hebrew and Judeo-German letter manuals, which have a slightly earlier lineage, had an influence on the earliest writers of Yiddish fiction, but brivnshtelers, that is, actual Yiddish letter manuals, are unlikely to have played that role.

Yiddish literature may be unusual because of its late start. It has, for example, been argued that letter manuals focused on love were the source for the development of romantic fiction in seventeenth-century France.[136] But even there, by the time of the great eighteenth-century epistolary novels by Rousseau and Laclos, any ties to letter-manual prose had long been forgotten. The polyglot writers who created a modern literature in Yiddish were not living in a vacuum, and they did not recreate literary history. They adapted the techniques of modern literature to a new linguistic medium, taking into account the particularities of the Jewish audience and Jewish everyday life.

This is not to say that Yiddish writers didn't use the epistolary form. Sholem Aleichem, for example, has an epistolary classic called *Di ibergekhapte briv af der post* (Letters intercepted from the mail), about a correspondence between two friends, one recently deceased and the other still in the thick of things on earth. While Leybele in "the other world" awaits judgment for his many sins, Velvele in this world sends him the latest news. The premise is that Sholem Aleichem and newspaper

editor Aleksander Zederbaum have intercepted and published their letters. These letters are far more satiric than anything that would pass in a
brivnshteler—to which, in their detail and originality, they bear no resemblance at all. A different Sholem Aleichem story, "Mayn ershter roman"
(My first novel/My first romance), is closer to the idea of a brivnshteler in
that two tutors ghostwrite love letters for their hapless pupils; the narrator,
writing for the boy, falls in love with the girl before realizing that he is a
victim of the same ruse he himself has perpetrated. Though there are no
brivnshtelers in the picture, the story models an emblematic brivnshteler
genre: the love letter to someone you are about to marry but have never
or just barely met. Also recognizable from brivnshtelers is the focus on
education, meaning in this case the parading of knowledge about modern
culture in answer to the question "what should I read?" The "groom" in
the story advises his beloved ("my life, my soul, my Garden of Eden!") to
read Gogol, Turgenev, Tolstoy, Dostoevsky, Pushkin, Lermontov, Shakespeare, and Goethe (the list goes on). His "bride" not only knows all these
works thoroughly, but, continuing in the mode of satiric exaggeration,
turns out to be a Jewish nationalist devoted to everything Hebrew from
the Bible and Yehudah ha-Levi (whose work she knows by heart) straight
through to contemporaries Mapu, Levinzon, Smolenskin, and Gordon.[137]

The one Sholem Aleichem work that unquestionably—though only
partially—parodies brivnshtelers is the Menakhem Mendl series. This
is a linked set of stories in which Menakhem Mendl, a would-be seller
of stocks, bonds, currency, real estate (and more), writes to his wife
Sheyne Sheyndl as he thinks big and, a couple of pages later, goes bust;
the pattern then repeats. Menakhem Mendl is a dreamer, while Sheyne
Sheyndl is literal-minded and inescapably provincial. In his introduction
to the second edition (1910), Sholem Aleichem jokes that he has collected
Menakhem Mendl's letters and made them into a book, "almost a brivnshteler." This is, of course, outrageous, so Sholem Aleichem elaborates:

> Yes, indeed, a *briefenshteler* organized in six different sections. . . . If someone's
> a merchant and he wants to write a letter to his wife, for example, from Odessa,
> he should look in the first book, "London." A speculator on the stock market
> in wine and candles for the Sabbath, in shares, and other such merchandise,
> will find a good example in the second book "Stock certificates" or in the third
> book, "Millions."

Continuing in the same vein, the introduction suggests that readers who are agents or *shadkhonim* (marriage brokers), like Menakhem Mendl, will also find their letters in the appropriate sections. And since Jewish businesses generally go the way of Menakhem Mendl's, with absurd hopes followed by the inevitable crash, "nobody needs to work hard to put together a letter: they can take them just as they are. And if, perhaps, he is the one in a thousand for whom business is going well in the meantime, he can rest assured this won't be for long. Everything that is built on air and wind must, in the end, fall down."[138]

The manic content of the Menakhem Mendl/Sheyne Sheyndl correspondence could not be more distant from the intentionally banal world of the letter manual. What does tie it to the brivnshteler, and to old-fashioned correspondence more superficially, is its use of opening and closing honorifics.[139] These fancy Hebrew salutations ("The glory of Israel and of his generation," "May his light shine," "Dear Aunt, splendid among women"), sometimes given only as acronyms, were considered good form in letter writing. Lists or even tables of honorifics are a frequent component of brivnshteler front matter, where the acronyms are deciphered, translated into Yiddish, and matched with the appropriate relative (father, nephew, aunt). Menakhem Mendl and Sheyne Sheyndl use honorifics consistently but incongruously: before, for example, berating him for his incompetence and all-around uselessness, Sheyne Sheyndl gives her formal greetings "to my dear honored husband, the exalted sage and community leader Menakhem Mendl, may his light shine." Sholem Aleichem plays the discrepancy for great comic effect. Brivnshtelers, not surprisingly, are blind to the comedy. But they pay close attention to getting the honorifics right.[140]

With the passage of time and the distancing of emigration or revolution, some writers looked at the world of brivnshtelers and shraybers with nostalgia. In his poem *Sonaten-ring* (Ring of sonatas), the poet and playwright H. Leivick fondly remembers his father, a shrayber,

> Who would go from one house to another
> Dictating from Bloshteyn's brivnshteler, "bridegroom and bride"
> For the girls in a Russian shtetl in the northwest.[141]

Farther on in the poem, Leivick parodies a letter from a girl to her fiancé:

Highly esteemed, deeply loved bridegroom, live well,
First of all, I am writing to inform you—I report that I am,
The Eternal be thanked, in the best of health, and hope
To hear the same from you from today forward and forever more.

Secondly, I am writing to my bridegroom: though
The moon and stars shine in the heavens until dawn
It is dark before my eyes and my eyes run with tears,
Because fate has sundered this love of ours with hill and dale.[142]

In the poem "Yontev un vokh" (Holiday and week), the poet Y. Y. Shvarts is both ironic and sad. For Shvarts, writing in the United States, the absurdity of a business letter copied by children is imbued with unexpected meaning:

Sometimes he would give us a letter to write:
A "Dear Friend" letter to an in-law,
that on the Sabbath during Hannukah, if G-d wills it,
We will come to celebrate with him in person
And we thank him very much for his gift
The pocket-watch and the chain of pure gold,
And we also beg him please, absolutely,
convey our peaceful regards to the prospective mother-in-law and the bride.
A commercial letter to a reputable merchant:
He should be so kind and upon his honor, send us right away,
So many sacks of rye flour and also sifted flour
So much and so much fine white flour,
And for G-d's sake, without any flaws and at the same price,
Because from the previous merchandise, that is,
We suffered a major loss, or, to put it simply,
We became paupers.[143]

A different kind of irony is employed by the Soviet novelist Moyshe Kulbak. His novel *Zelmenyaner* (The Zelmenyaners), written in 1931, has a sequence in which an old woman learns how to write from a young man dispatched by the Party youth movement. She leaves a letter for her husband that is full of errors. She has also made, in his eyes, the mistake of writing the way she speaks, rather than in the elevated style that correspondence deserves. He concludes that she would be much better off working from a brivnshteler and reading Shomer: "'Copy from a brivnshteler,' he said, 'because the methods they're using now just don't seem right.... And you also have to read books. Books make you smart. There used to be a writer Shomer, you could learn something from him. The new ones are useless.'"[144] From a Soviet perspective, the old man and his old man's nostalgia are comically irrelevant: the Party youth movement is the way of the future. But a reader disenchanted with the present could secretly agree with him.

WHAT MAKES THE BRIVNSHTELER JEWISH?

What, aside from Yiddish, makes the brivnshteler Jewish? How does it differ from other letter manuals produced in the cultures in which Jews lived?

The world of the brivnshteler is not monolithic. The fictional correspondents of Yoysef Gorodinski's 1901 bilingual *Der hoyz-korrespondent* (The household correspondent) speak Yiddish and Russian, and behave a lot like Russians; across the ocean, however, the writers of letters in Harkavy's 1902 *Amerikanisher briefen-shteler* speak Yiddish and English and behave a lot like Americans. Since many Jews at the turn of the century were engaged in an accelerated and very intentional acculturation, it can be argued that all these assimilating characters were simply acting like Jews. But those examples are the extremes. Most brivnshteler letters show behavioral patterns that are much more directly Jewish.

The Jewish specificity of the brivnshteler comes through most strongly in its preoccupation with family, a preoccupation that reflects well-known stereotypes (except that brivnshtelers generally give fathers, rather than mothers, the presiding role). Relations between Jewish parents and children, most often parents and their young adult children, are suffused with anxiety in a way no non-Jewish letter manual would countenance.[145] Jewish courtship letters are also emotional, but more tentatively so than their non-Jewish counterparts, and even in matters of courtship, Jewish parents loom large. Another arena of Jewish specificity is education, which brivnshtelers emphasize to a degree that leaves the other manuals far behind. And brivnshtelers are wordy. European and especially American manuals consistently promote brevity, as we can see in the preface to a 1901 American manual advising the neophyte writer to express his desires "in as few words as possible—to couch them in polite, grammatical language—to write them legibly with all due regard for courteousness without 'toadyism,' respect without effusiveness, whether he be in business or in social life—whether he be friend, relative or lover."[146] In his American brivnshteler, Alexander Harkavy follows suit.[147] But for most brivnshtelers, more is better. In parental letters in particular, repetition of high-intensity sentiment is a sign of love.

Our comparison here is primarily with Russian manuals (*pis'movniki*), because when brivnshteler authors sought models to copy, that is where they looked. We also examine American letter-writers in comparison to the brivnshtelers published in America. Another significant language was, of course, German, the language of the Haskalah and of European high culture. Nineteenth-century German *briefstellers* are similar and in some cases identical in content to their counterparts in France and Russia. They differ a bit in national focus: German manuals give examples of correspondence from Goethe or Schiller, and Russian ones (though less often) from the Russian literary past; aristocratic titles and forms of address are localized. But the European manual was, in general, a transnational and often multilingual phenomenon. When Russians began writing their own versions, they started by translating from manuals written in German and French.[148] The cultural distinction that will concern us is a three-way one, with Russian, French, and German manuals as distinct from American ones as both of these groups are from the Yiddish.

One of the longest-standing categories of letter manuals in general is correspondence between fathers and their wayward but repentant sons. In a Russian manual of 1900, a son caught sinning in some unspecified way uses a kind of religious language to appease parental wrath:

> *My dear father!*
> I am full of grief and suffering that my unworthy conduct called forth your anger. My heart is full of anguish, my soul has no peace, my conscience, aware of its crime, is not clean. I fall to your feet and with heartfelt repentance ask your parental pardon. You gave me the gift of life. I owe my existence to your parental solicitude and care. Do not render me unfortunate, do not abandon your son to the vagaries of fate, replace your anger with kindness and allow me, in my moral torment, to appear before you and ask your forgiveness in person.[149]

While the letter itself is likely from an older source, the fact that it has been reproduced in 1900 indicates that someone, at least, found it relevant. The letter sustains a high existential and emotional pitch: we have, in short order, references to an anguished soul; the vagaries of fate; crime;

birth; and spiritual uncleanliness. So great is the paternal anger that the son cannot count on a personal audience. A more modern-sounding letter from the same year provides a different model. Here, the father initiates the correspondence, keeping a tone of restrained solicitousness:

> *Dear, wonderful son Volodia,*
>
> A month has now passed since you left us, and aside from a postcard from Tiflis, we have no news from you.
>
> You promised to write at least once a week, but apparently you have abandoned this good intention. In the meantime, Mama and I are worried and lose ourselves in speculation. I'm not going to start reproaching you; you will be your own judge and in the future will be more punctual and respectful.
>
> Uncle Kostia writes that you visited him, but he complains that you should come more often.
>
> I understand perfectly well that your new circumstances have changed your usual habits, but it's time for you to look at life in a more serious and sober fashion. Many young people at your age are already standing on their own feet. Don't put off your answer, but as soon as you get my letter, get your pen and write about your life abroad.
>
> I am sure that you will not put off fulfilling my request. We, thank God, are healthy. Mama kisses and blesses you.
>
> May God watch over you!
>
> *Your loving father*
> N.A.[150]

Neither of these approaches has much resonance for the brivnshteler. While Jewish sons also fail to write home and fall into the commission of quite specific sins (instead of studying, they carouse or go to the theater; they violate the Sabbath), Jewish templates for parent-child correspondence employ a wholly different emotional vocabulary. The fathers in the two Russian letters are distant from their misbehaving progeny, the more old-fashioned one because of his frightening anger, the modern one because he respects his son's autonomy. Brivnshteler parents could not be more different.

For one thing, they are never remote. For another, the concept of autonomy doesn't come up. After hearing of a son's bad behavior from a friend or an uncle, they spring into high-decibel argument. Often, as in the following Yiddish letter from a bilingual Yiddish-Russian manual of 1904, they remind their child of their own suffering on his account:

My dear child! From the moment that your friend Shmuel Leker brought us regards from you and told us all about your behavior, that you are spending your time with wicked friends, eating and drinking and gallivanting and the like and frittering away the money I send you . . . it's been like Tishebov for your mother, she's cried so much. I can tell you what she said and I told her everything. My dear child, I shed so many tears and cried so much while raising you, and spent many sleepless nights, when you were sick with pox or measles or other illnesses, and each time I wouldn't rest until God helped. I enrolled you in a kheyder so that you would be of use to both God and the world, and then I sent you to Khar'kov to my uncle so he would see to it that you graduated from the gymnasium. In the end, you have strayed from the righteous path. Now I curse all the days and years I have lived since I was born. As soon as you went away to study, my dear neighbor Shprintse predicted that you would soon be smoking cigarettes on *shabes* and other such things. We ask two things of you: first, that you turn away from the path of wickedness, because dear God gave man two paths. This will be good for you and for us. And if, God forbid, you don't do this right away, then don't bother writing to us anymore; we don't want your mouth uttering our names.[151]

In addition to demonstrating the Jewish parent wielding every weapon in his emotional arsenal, the letter tells us something about how the translator viewed the Jewish-Yiddish and Jewish-Russian cultural worlds. The Russian version leaves out the reference to Tish'ah be-av, the ninth of Av, the day of mourning for the destruction of the Temple, and replaces it with something more general ("I have been in anguish and sorrow"). It also reverses what the mother knows—in the Russian, the father spares her the worst details. Otherwise, compared to other brivnshteler letters that deal with wayward sons, the only thing slightly unusual in this one is its last line. More commonly, brivnshteler parents offer money and a ticket home.

Prodigal sons aside, children in French, German, and Russian manuals are a scarce commodity. The younger generation surfaces for formal greetings at birthdays and at the New Year: "My Dearest Father," runs a typical example from Froment and Mueller's German manual, "This day when you were born for my happiness reminds me of all I owe to Heaven for such beneficence."[152] Formality is the preferred mode even for a more spontaneous situation. In a letter that appears in German, French, and Russian, a boy writing for permission to come home for a vacation ("to tell you in person how sincerely I am devoted to you") gets a friendly but hardly ecstatic response: father and mother have conferred, and will write to the teacher to confirm that he indeed approves the boy's plans.[153] This is not, of course, to suggest that people behaved this way in real life—simply that the mood of letter manuals reflects an aristocratic esthetic that purchasers were encouraged to emulate.

Along with formality comes an attention to hierarchy. Russian and European manuals, as well as some American and bilingual Yiddish-Russian ones, pay close attention to social hierarchies. This is most obvious in the space devoted to forms of address for aristocrats and royalty, should a reader have occasion to write to them. But it also manifests itself in thank-you notes intended for people in the service class, like teachers and doctors. Yiddish manuals pay almost no attention to hierarchy at all. The only time it comes up is in letters addressed by a widow in dire straits to her husband's employer or the family's longtime benefactor. There are no letters addressed to officials to be found in Yiddish manuals, for the obvious reason that no rational person would have committed the folly of writing to them in Yiddish.

Like brivnshtelers, American letter manuals tend to be much less formal and more affectionate. But the similarity ends here. The predominating mode of American templates is good cheer—tempered, in face of illness, death, or financial difficulty, with fortitude and duty. In an American manual of 1900, a mother regrets the absence of her sixteen-year-old daughter, away at school:

> If only you could have been at home with us, that we might have had one of those old-time festivals! But, dear daughter, the path of duty demands many sacrifices of us all. You are where it is best for you to be, fitting yourself for the serious but delightful duties that must sooner or later demand your attention.[154]

In the face of life's reversals—acknowledged more often in American manuals than European ones—duty once again predominates. In a loving letter from the same 1901 book a father thanks his son for leaving college to help him out when his business fails:

> The generous spirit of your letter brought the tears to my eyes. I know well how much it will cost you to give up, or even postpone your college course. It will be hard to break off class associations, and leave the work that you find so congenial. I wish I could thank you for your noble offer, and tell you that

we could worry through without your help, but I find, that my affairs are in a worse condition than intimated in my last letter. Have not given up hope yet, still cannot conscientiously refuse any means of relief that comes to me. Go, my dear son, to your Uncle Henry's, and God bless you.[155]

The one exception to the fortitude rule concerns little girls, who are often in danger of studying too hard. The example below from 1884 is typical of the genre. A mother sends a note to the teacher:

Will it interfere with the discipline of the school if Louise leaves every day at one o'clock instead of two? She has masters for German and music every other afternoon, and I think is applying herself too closely to her studies. She informs me that the last hour in school time does not include any recitations, and thinks it will not hinder her progress in her studies to lose it.[156]

One area that Russian and American manuals have in common is the pursuit of pleasure. "Young people have a natural inclination toward pleasure," writes a 1915 Russian guide, which proceeds to explain how to dress and act in society so as to achieve it.[157] A letter from father to son in a different Russian manual also acknowledges that "youth inevitably inclines to pleasure," though the writer is a little more concerned about the moral implications: "Pleasures are necessary, but only for enhancing one's strength, so that after a summer of leisure one can turn with new energy to study and work." He contrasts pleasure with education, though not in a way that a brivnshteler would find familiar: "Education is our most important adornment."[158] Adults in Russian and European manuals pursue a more restrained kind of pleasure, with wording provided for invitations to dinners, musical evenings, and similar events in the home.

The American world is social in a more expansive way. The fictional correspondents in William B. Dick's 1888 guide issue invitations "to a Drive Out, to Make a Country Visit, to a Friend in the Country to Visit the City, to a Lawn Tennis Party" among many other activities;[159] they are also busy with charities. In Sheldon's 1901 guide, a young man in college tells his sister that college is "lots of hard work and lots of fun."[160] Fun seldom figures in the world of the brivnshteler. Pleasure is acknowledged, but related almost exclusively to births, marriages, and educational achievements. "There isn't much to say about how I have been amusing myself: I'm busy only with my studies," a young man tells his uncle in Judeo-German in a letter series that is very old, but reproduced many times through 1911, and whose sentiments are echoed in countless letters in Yiddish manuals.[161] Assimilation-minded Yiddish-Russian brivnshtelers refer to outings in the country (though more often to discussions about literature). Frivolous undertakings like dances come up in American brivnshtelers, but mostly because parents in the old country have heard about them and become very anxious about what their daughters are up to.

If the emotional center of the brivnshteler is the relationship between parents and children, in the French, German, and American manuals it is romantic love. Declarations of love are followed by proposals and responses to proposals, or as the situation warrants, with reproaches for coldness. Here is a typical love letter from a Russian manual of 1900:

> *Dear Zina, close to my heart!*
> The coldness of your recent letters turns my heart to ice and casts into my soul the terribly unbearable feeling of doubt and fateful premonitions. If this isn't the delirium of my sick imagination, then this is terrible. I said "sick imagination." Yes, my soul is sick, because, I repeat, the most dreadful premonitions have tormented me. Warm my soul with a kind word that will restore it, like noble balm to the wounded heart of a suffering man. Do this if only because it is your simple Christian duty.[162]

While the linkage of soul-sickness and Christian charity is not adaptable for a Yiddish courtship letter, the idea of love does transfer. But the combination of Jewish ways of thinking with European romanticism is not always elegant. In the example below, from 1891, Dov Arye Fridman attempts a merger of these two modes. His character Avrom starts out in the forest, a classic European romantic venue for thinking about love. It is not hard to imagine what the writer of "Dear Zina" would have done with a nature scene. Avrom makes a half-hearted attempt—he loves how the birds sing—but he is more comfortable in the world of intellectual argument. This world is not attuned to beauty, or to a hierarchy of concepts that do or do not belong in a love letter. It is natural for Avrom to start talking about meat, but the moment he does so, European decorum is out the window:

> Yesterday I went walking in the forest . . . and I went around deep in thought. I mused about whether love is really a child of God, a daughter of heaven, like the poets call her, or if love is only desire, an affliction, an evil thought. There is no such thing as sacred love. Today we love

this, tomorrow that. I can't say what the truth is, but God put the correct thought into my head. It seemed to me that love must surely be something different, must surely have another name. For example, I love meat, I love hearing how the birds sing, I love the pure, lovely air. But can I indeed say that I love them? I love meat, but do I kiss meat? I love birds, but do I know them? I love meat because I love myself, I love my body. But if I am granted my Rokhele, will I not kiss all her limbs? Will I not press her to my heart and say to her, you are my Rokhele, you are mine forever? Then can it be said that love is only desire? An affliction? No, dear Rokhele! Nothing will convince me of this. Love is divine, and therefore it is no disgrace to love a girl like you. Especially because you are my fiancée and one day you will also be my wife. It is no sin to love an angel like you.[163]

A sequence like this, linking the new interest in romantic love with the awkwardness of a young man brought up on religious texts, is conceivable in fiction—but as a model letter to copy, it makes sense only in a brivnshteler.

Another way to acquire romantic prose, particularly attractive to compliers of bilingual manuals, is by copying texts from previously published books and translating them. (Whether or not brivnshteler authors paid for the privilege is impossible to know.) Consider the following declaration from the Russian half of a bilingual Jewish manual: "Only you, dear Maria, represent all that I seek: intelligence without pretense, beauty without coquettishness and in general charm and modesty that delight all who know you." In the Judeo-German translation, "dear Maria" is excised, but the "pretense" and "coquettishness" remain.[164] In Alexander Harkavy's *Amerikanisher briefen-shteler*, a man named Joseph Marks writes to Miss Abrahams, regretting that her "maidenly dignity" precludes her from revealing what is in her heart. After being "received" at Miss Abrahams's house for over a year, Mr. Marks "cannot endure suspense any longer."[165] If Mr. Marks and Miss Abrahams sound like well-heeled American Protestants, the reason may be their origins in an American letter-writer, where an identical set of letters is exchanged between Miss Rebecca Kingston and Mr. Fred Hill.[166] While Harkavy's point might only have been to provide Yiddish-speaking readers with genuine American prose, the result is a kind of alternative world in which people with Jewish names behave like WASPs.

Another question that might be asked about brivnshtelers is how closely real Yiddish letters from before World War I resemble the model letters in the letter manuals. The answer is that they don't. People do not seem to have slavishly copied model letters, perhaps (hearkening back to the joke presented at the beginning of this book) all too aware that their correspondents might have the very same brivnshteler sitting on their own bookshelves. Interestingly, the all but ubiquitous opener in real correspondence, "I am in good health and hope to hear the same from you," almost never appears in model letters.[167] Where the brivnshteler and real Yiddish correspondence converge is in the realm of emotional expression. To say that real Yiddish letters are as emotional as those found in brivnshtelers is an understatement. Ordinary Jewish men and women did not hold back when it came to expressing their frustrations with their correspondents, or with the "paper life."

NOTES

1. Stanislawski, "Kahal."

2. Litvak, *Haskalah,* 32. In "Towards a Historical Definition of the Haskalah," 216, Shmuel Feiner notes that the "relationship between Haskalah and modernization was not clear-cut but ambivalent; support and enthusiasm on the one hand, constraint and control on the other."

3. Stanislawski, *Tsar Nicholas I and the Jews,* 105; also "Kazennye evreiskie uchilishcha."

4. Stanislawski, *Tsar Nicholas I and the Jews,* 105–107.

5. Hirsh Lion Dor, *Eyn nayer brifen shteller* (1865), 27–29. This book was reprinted in several editions, with the latest known edition appearing in 1887. Hirsh Lion Dor (birth and death dates unknown) was the son of Avrom Lion Dor (1793–1846), one of the first maskilim in Vilna, and a student in what was perhaps the first Jewish secular school in the Russian Empire: an elementary school at Vilna University that opened in 1808. Lion Dor senior was a teacher of Hebrew, Polish, German, and French and the author of the first Polish-Yiddish dictionary. Both father and son wrote brivnshtelers, and Hirsh also authored French- and German-language textbooks for Yiddish speakers.

6. Iris Parush, *Reading Jewish Women,* 40, 57, 72. Many memoirs of elite women testify to the importance of fluency in German and Russian, e.g., Wengeroff, *Memoiren,* or Zinaida Poliakova, "Dnevniki."

7. Adler, *In Her Hands,* 2. The Haskalah was deeply ambivalent about women. See, for example, Litvak, *Haskalah,* 43–44.

8. Adler, "Women's Education in the Pages of the Russian Jewish Press," 123, 131.

9. "Statisticheskii portret studentki iuridicheskogo fakul'teta VZhK," Iuridicheskikh fakul'tet Vysshikh Zhenskikh (Bestuzhevskikh) kursov, http://law.spbu.ru/ru/library /ExhibitionLib/ExhibitionLibTema/BectyKursi/WmanBectyKursi.aspx. According to the 1897 census, Jews were 4.04 percent of the population (Troinitskii, *Obshchii svod po imperii,* 4).

10. Bernshteyn, *Bernshteyn's nayer yudisher folks-brifenshteler* (1912), 46–48. Several library catalogs have attributed both this and another brivnshteler to the noted German

Jewish author and scientist Aaron David Bernstein (1812–1884). The actual author appears to be another Bernstein, first name unknown. Both brivnshtelers were published well after the death of Aaron David Bernstein; both are set in the Russian Empire, not in German lands; and both are strikingly modern in subject matter and language. The author's first name is not provided on the title pages of either manual.

11. Stanislawski, *Tsar Nicholas I and the Jews*, 84.

12. Dohrn, "Seminary."

13. "Ravvinskie seminarii."

14. Cahan, *Bleter fun mayn leben*, 1:192–193.

15. Nathans, *Beyond the Pale*, 208; Gitelman, *A Century of Ambivalence*, 31, 208.

16. Stanislawski, "Russia: Russian Empire."

17. Rogger, *Jewish Policies and Right-Wing Politics in Imperial Russia*, 68–69.

18. While Jewish life in the Russian Empire has been traditionally examined through the prism of crisis and revolution, some historians now question whether the events of 1881 mark as decisive a turning point in Russian Jewish history as was previously assumed. They suggest that the political, social, and cultural changes pointed to as characteristic of the late nineteenth century were actually underway much earlier, and were more a result of forces and processes within the Jewish community than the dramatic outcome of external events. See Nathans, *Beyond the Pale* (8–10) for a discussion of qualifications and amendments to the idea of 1881 as a turning point in Russian Jewish history.

19. Lederhendler, "America," 34.

20. Bartal, *The Jews of Eastern Europe*, 41; Nathans, *Beyond the Pale*, 83. This statistic does not include the unknown number of Jews living illegally outside the Pale.

21. See David Fishman, *The Rise of Modern Yiddish Culture*, 23–24. Hebrew, and perhaps by extension Zionism, was not subject to the same kind of stringent censorship as Yiddish because it was read by a very small readership and was thus seen as less threatening to the regime's agenda of Russification. Mordkhe Betsalel Shnayder (1865–1941) was a Lithuanian-born Hebrew scholar and writer of Hebrew textbooks.

22. Bernshteyn, *Bernshteyn's yudisher brief-lehrer: mit a kurtser yudisher gramatik* (1910 or 1911), 65–67.

23. As described in Stanislawski, *Tsar Nicholas I and the Jews*, 100–101.

24. Ibid.; Adler, *In Her Hands*, 88.

25. Adler, *In Her Hands*, 31.

26. Yiddish speakers who believed that the language they spoke had no grammar likely meant proscriptive grammar: rules that are taught in schools. Like German or English, Yiddish had numerous regional variants, but there was no educational authority or literary tradition to declare one variant standard and the others substandard. Spelling rules, as we discuss later, were inconsistent until the twentieth century. There may also have been some spillover from attitudes toward Hebrew. The study of Hebrew grammar was associated with the Haskalah and was emphatically not taught in traditional religious schools. Brivnshtelers, which provided examples of fluent Yiddish style, took the place of a proscriptive grammar in some ways.

27. Kazdan, *Fun kheyder un "shkoles" biz tsisho*, 93.

28. Adler, *In Her Hands*, 91.

29. Stampfer, *Families, Rabbis and Education*, 145–166.

30. Yiddish Literature and Language Collection, RG 3, 3260.1 YIVO Institute for Jewish Research, New York. In his autobiography *Moia Zhizn'* (54–55), Leon Trotsky

reports going to a coed school for a short while in a Jewish agricultural settlement in the Kherson province in the 1880s. In addition to learning arithmetic and how to read and write Russian, children in that school also studied the Torah. Trotsky himself doesn't refer to the school as a *kheyder*, using instead the neutral, rather modern Russian term, "school in an agricultural colony"—the colony itself was Jewish. In *Families, Rabbis and Education*, Shaul Stampfer notes, "Today it would be unthinkable for boys and girls to study together in ultra-Orthodox societies. However, in the early nineteenth century and even later it was quite common, though certainly not the standard, for little girls to go to heder with little boys, and the mixing of the sexes apparently was not regarded as worthy of note or reaction" (32).

31. Stampfer, *Families, Rabbis and Education*, 170. Girls learned how to run a Jewish household from their mothers. The secular nature of girls' education and its conse-quences is the subject of Iris Parush's *Reading Jewish Women*. Parush notes that very ob-servant families in late-nineteenth-century Russia had no problem sending their daugh-ters to Christian schools (87); such parents would never have countenanced having their daughters study Talmud, but valued training in languages and arts.

32. Medvedeva (Gurevich), "Dnevnik moikh prozhitykh dnei," 100.

33. Troinitskii, *Obshchii svod po imperii*, 3.

34. Stampfer, *Families, Rabbis and Education*, 197–198. Parush suggests that all data about literacy are unreliable. She notes that the ability to sign one's name was often taken as evidence of literacy but that there were people who could sign their names but not read and vice versa (*Reading Jewish Women*, 8–9).

35. Stampfer, *Families, Rabbis and Education*, 200.

36. Gennady Estraikh makes the same point about the "widespread myth" of Jewish male literacy in "Changing Ideologies of Artisanal 'Productivisation,'" 10.

37. Stampfer, *Families, Rabbis and Education*, 202. In "Multilingualism among the Jews of Hohenems," 33–47, Eva Grabherr notes that before the nineteenth century, knowing how to write was not all that common or even part of being considered edu-cated in Europe.

38. Dik, *Di yuden in lite*, 19.

39. Hirsh Lion Dor, *Eyn nayer brifen shteller* (1865).

40. "Protsentnaia norma."

41. Poletika, *Vidennoe i perezhitoe*, 7.

42. Cahan's matriculation at the Vilna Pedagogical Institute was preceded by a period of manic study with various tutors. But he was not permitted to take the exams because of lack of official information about his date of birth, common among Jews; when that was resolved through multiple bribes, he was already a few months too old. As he writes, "in such a situation Jews have a rule: find the nobleman's tailor." The tailor presented him to the director as his nephew: problem solved (*Bleter fun mayn leben* 1:257–262). In Isaak Babel's well-known "Istoriia moei golubiatny" (Story of my dove-cote) the hero, like Cahan, endures a period of manic study before taking the entrance exam for a gymnasium. He receives the highest grades, but one is lowered after another Jewish family presents a bribe, and their son gets accepted instead. Yet another descrip-tion of Jews taking a gymnasium entrance exam, this one from Vilna in the early 1890s, appears in Aleksandra Brushtein's autobiographical novel *Doroga ukhodit v dal'* . . . (The road leads into the distance, 343–346). For the oral part of the exam (reading and gram-mar), the Russian girls are examined first—publicly, as was the custom. Then they leave

the room and the seven remaining Jewish girls are given much harder questions. Of that group, two pass. Brushtein's book, published in 1957, only rarely touches on Jewish issues, which makes this particular incident, which ends the first volume, stand out. The Jewish girls are asked difficult grammatical questions about Russian. Brivnshtelers did not provide instruction in foreign-language grammar; that information would have to be acquired from a tutor, like the tutors engaged by Cahan and the parents in Babel's story and Brushtein's fictionalized memoir.

43. Poletika, *Vidennoe i perezhitoe*, 9–10.

44. An-skii, *Sobranie sochinenii* 3:63.

45. Wengeroff, *Memoiren einer Grossmutter*, 1:7; Rakovska, *My Life as a Radical Jewish Woman*, 23; Cahan, *Bleter fun mayn leben* 1:41–43.

46. Shargorodska, "Der shure grus," 67–68.

47. Ibid., 68.

48. Ibid., 69. As Parush notes, shraybers, like melamdim, were not held in particularly high regard, though they are sometimes credited by memoirists with exposing children in small towns to the ideas of the Haskalah (*Reading Jewish Women*, 69). Kazdan notes that the institution of the shrayber was a very old one, citing a statute in the 1623–1764 *pinkas* from the Vaad of Lithuania specifying that a shrayber be hired to teach the sons of poor parents (*Fun kheyder un "shkoles" biz tsisho*, 77).

49. Goldshteyn-Gershonovitsh, *Yudish-daytsher morall brifenshteller* (1890), unpaginated introduction. Goldshteyn-Gershonovitsh (birth and death dates unknown) was a private teacher of Yiddish, German, and Russian in Berdichev. In addition to several brivnshtelers, he also wrote a Hebrew letter manual, *Mikhtave neurim* (1891).

50. Yoysef Arukh, *Arukhs brifenshteller* (1892), 5. Birnboym reports that brivnshtelers were indeed sometimes used in kheyders ("Brivenshtelers," 468). The poet Avrom Reyzen, writing in 1933, reports that in the 1880s, brivnshtelers were used as instructional aides by shraybers, and that girls were sometimes instructed by a *rebetsn* (rabbi's wife) in writing Yiddish by copying text from a *taytsh-khumesh* (Bible in Yiddish translation) or a book of *tkhines* (book of psalms) (Avrom Reyzen, *Undzer shul*, April 1933, as quoted in Kazdan, *Fun kheyder un "shkoles" biz tsisho*, 101–102).

51. Kazdan, *Fun kheyder un "shkoles" biz tsisho*, 89. Kazdan cites the 1886 *Zhargon lehrer* by Yoyne Trubnik as the first real Yiddish textbook.

52. *Mesader igeres* [*Mesadar igeret*] (1825), 33–37, 52–56.

53. Alek, *Oytser mikhtovim* [*Otsar mikhtavim*], *oder brifenshteler fir yudishe kinder* (1906), 11–12. *Oytser mikhtovim* is one of those books whose content would seem to date it much earlier.

54. See Joshua A. Fishman, "Language: Planning and Standardization of Yiddish," for a summary of the different tendencies in proposals to standardize Yiddish.

55. Joel Entin and Leon Elba, *Fun idishe kval: A idish lehrbukh un khrestomatye*, 3, as cited in Mordkhe Schaechter, *The Standardized Yiddish Orthography*, 10.

56. The one exception to the rule: Arukh, *Arukhs brifenshteller* (1892).

57. Schaechter, *The Standardized Yiddish Orthography*, 2–10.

58. The correct plural of *engel* in German is *engel*. Bernshteyn may have been mocking his readers' incorrect usage.

59. Bernshteyn, *Bernshteyn's nayer yudisher folks-brifenshteler* (1912), 4–5. In his poem "Sonaten-ring," which recalls the poet's father, a shrayber, H. Leivick spoofs a letter from a brivnshteler that uses very daytshmerish language.

60. Birnboym, "Brivnshtelers," 468. This holds true throughout the history of the genre. *Bernshteyn's nayer yudisher folks-brifenshteler* (1912) criticizes "a well-known proverb" that urges one to "write the way you speak." No, he admonishes, one must write "better" than the way one speaks (3).

61. Shaul Stampfer makes this important point in *Families, Rabbis and Education*, 152 and 193; See 162–163 on the role of kheyder study in inculcating respect for Jewish texts even among those whose abilities did not permit advanced study. In *Reading Jewish Women*, Iris Parush argues to the contrary, that the reason writing was not taught was a rabbinical desire to restrict male literacy (68). In any event, it is clear that while the ability of men to read was understood to be a public good, their ability to write was not considered essential.

62. Cohen and Soyer, *My Future Is in America*, 43–44.

63. Ibid., 192.

64. The history of the Paperna books is typical of the plagiarism and recycling of the genre: Paperna's *Meyroyts igroys [Merots igrot]* of 1874 (Warsaw) was republished in 1889, also in Warsaw, as *Mikhtov meshulesh [Mikhtav meshulash]*, not to be confused with his *Mikhtov meshulesh*, published in Warsaw in 1878 but with a largely different content. The 1878 book also got republished in 1889 in Vilna, under the name of Shalom ha-Kohen, whose materials from earlier in the century Paperna had reused (with attribution). Yet another *Mikhtov meshulesh*, published under Shalom ha-Kohen's name in Vilna in 1884, has a different selection of letters, some of them copied from Russian letter manuals.

65. See, for example, Khayim Poplavski's *Der neyer vegvayzer* (1892) and *Nayer Shprakhfihrer* (1895). No stranger to self-advertisement, and obviously aware of the Jewish market for language study, Poplavski claimed to have a method for learning Russian, English, French, and German in 150 pages or less; this seems to involve vocabulary lists transcribed into Yiddish.

66. Cahan, *Bleter fun mayn leben* 1:114; the correct author and title of the igron is Naftali Maskil Leitan (Maskileison), *Mikhtovim le-lamed [Mikhtavim le-lamed]*, Vilna: 1870. For a description, see Zwick, *Toldot sifrut ha-igronim*, 160.

67. Zipperstein, *Imagining Russian Jewry*, 59.

68. Chekhov, "Ionych," *Polnoe sobranie sochinenii*, 10:30.

69. Inditski, *Ha-metargem* (1899). Yisroel Yekhiel Inditski (b. 1866) was born in Swislocz, but later settled in Bialystok, where he was a Hebrew teacher. He began publishing Hebrew textbooks in 1894, including a Hebrew bible with translations into Yiddish (1909), and also wrote a Yiddish textbook, *Idishe geshikhte*. He was a correspondent from Bialystok for Hebrew and Yiddish newspapers under the pen name Y. Fogelzohn.

70. Alexander Harkavy, *Harkavi's amerikanisher briefen-shteler un speller*, (1901; 1902) and *Harkavi's amerikanisher briefen-shteler: english un yudish* (1902; 1928). Alexander Harkavy (1863–1939) was a noted linguist and lexicographer from Nowogrudek, who settled in New York in 1903. He was the author of *Yidish-english-hebreysher verterbukh* (Yiddish-English-Hebrew dictionary; 1925), still in use today by scholars and students of Yiddish.

71. In P. Berliner, *Dr. Berliners moderner yidisher brivenshteler*, 27–29, Khanale brags to her father that now that she is not at home she is no longer the sleepy and lazy daughter they once knew. Her teachers praise her. Her father warns her not to work too hard but also to go out for strolls in the fresh air. He wants not only a learned daughter but a

healthy one. This book, published in the United States, appears to be a reprint of a European title.

72. Poliak-Gilman, *Der nayer obraztsover brifenshteller,* 34–35. The phrase "covered in fat" may be literal (coins hidden in a jar of shmaltz) or it may be an idiom. The Russian translation says "in fat," and is not an idiom.

73. Lichtheim, *Ancient Egyptian literature* 2:168; Kramer, *The Sumerians,* 235.

74. Kramer, *The Sumerians,* 235.

75. Lichtheim, *Ancient Egyptian literature,* 2:167.

76. Ibid., 2:168

77. Ibid.

78. Ibid., 2:168, 171

79. Ibid., 2:168–171.

80. Malherbe, *Ancient Epistolary Theorists,* 5.

81. Newbold, "Letter Writing and Vernacular Literacy in Sixteenth-Century England," 127.

82. Robertson, *The Art of Letter Writing,* 39.

83. Ibid., 65.

84. Dauphin, "Letter-writing manuals," 140.

85. Ibid., 117.

86. Carlebach, "Letter into Text: Epistolarity, History, and Literature," 127; Zwick, *Toldot sifrut ha-igronim,* 21.

87. Zwick, *Toldot sifrut ha-igronim,* 21.

88. Ibid., 25.

89. Ibid., 23.

90. Ibid., 25.

91. Ibid., 59.

92. Other Yiddish letter manuals published in the eighteenth century include *Loshn zohov* [*Lashon zahav*] (Amsterdam, 1743), first published in 1661 in Krakow, and *Loshn noki* [*Lashon naki*] (Amsterdam, 1769).

93. Zwick, *Toldot sifrut ha-igronim,* 76–77.

94. Bar El, The Yiddish "Briefenshteler," 65–68.

95. Parts of Moshe Shmu'el Neumann, *Sefer Mikhtevey ivris* [*Mikhtave 'ivrit*] are reprinted with small changes in the Hebrew in Paperna, *Mikhtov meshulesh* [*Mikhtav meshulash*], Vilna, 1876, 6–7; Paperna, *Mikhtov meshulesh* [*Mikhtav meshulash*], Warsaw 1878, 6–7; and Shalom ha-Kohen, *Sefer mikhtov meshulesh* [*Mikhtav meshulash*], Vilna, 1889, 6–7. The page numbers are the same because the sections were reprinted from edition to edition; probably, the plates were reused.

96. Harshav, *The Meaning of Yiddish,* 81. In "Language: Yiddish," 982–983, Dovid Katz reports that the printing of Yiddish in yidish-taytsh-style fonts held sway until the 1830s.

97. Zwick, *Toldot sifrut ha-igronim,* 37–38.

98. Ibid., 59–61.

99. Ibid., 157.

100. As David Roskies notes in *A Bridge of Longing,* 6, "The first generation of east European Jewish innovators became wolves in shepherd's clothing. Theirs was a treasonous art if there ever was one. They learned to imitate the sacred tale, the sermon, the spoken anecdote, so as to laugh them off the stage of history, once and for all."

101. Zwick, *Toldot sifrut ha-igronim*, 167, 221, 201.

102. In "Letter-Writing and Letter Writers," Richard Gottheil and Isaac Broydé mention an 1820 brivnshteler by Avrom Lion Dor, *Briefshteller,* but it is not known if this book is actually in Yiddish. Its title suggests that it may be in Judeo-Deutsch.

103. Brivnshtelers published before 1875 include *Khalifas igroys [Halifat igrot]* (1850); another book entitled *Mesader igeres [Mesadar igeret]* (1858) with completely different content from the 1825 book of the same name; *Shrayb lerer oder brifen formal for yudishe kinder beyde geshlekhter* (1867); and two frequently reprinted titles by the Lion Dors, *Eyn nayer kinstlikher brifen shteller* and *Mikhtovim [Mikhtavim], oder eyn nayer brifshteller.*

104. In *History of the Yiddish Language,* Max Weinreich notes that the lack of an official name until fairly late was not unique to Yiddish. Ukrainian had a similar trajectory (1:320–321, 317–318).

105. David Fishman, *The Rise of Modern Yiddish Culture,* 11; Miron, *A Traveler Disguised,* 47; Weinreich, *History of the Yiddish Language,* 321–322.

106. Letters Collection, RG 107 Box 6, YIVO Institute for Jewish Research, New York.

107. In *A Traveler Disguised,* 280, Dan Miron reports that the lexicographer Shiye Mordkhe Lifshits, an early champion of Yiddish, began referring to the language as "Yiddish" as early as 1862–1863, in the ninth issue of the early Yiddish newspaper *Kol mevaser,* but that even he wasn't completely consistent in his usage. The earliest Yiddish letter manual published in Russia, *Mesader igeres [Mesadar igeret]* (1825) refers to *taytsh* on its title page but also uses the term *yidishi shrift* (Yiddish writing) within.

108. Stampfer, "What Did 'Knowing Hebrew' Mean in Eastern Europe?" 129–140. In "The Phonology of Ashkenazic," Dovid Katz asserts that Yiddish should not be characterized as "low-status" prior to the Haskalah; that none of the three languages of Ashkenaz was "low-prestige" or "stigmatized" in any modern sense of these terms; and that all had their accepted and unquestioned place in the eyes of Jewish society, 47. In *The Rise of Modern Yiddish Culture,* David Fishman notes that among Hasidism Yiddish had a slightly higher status, in that some Hasidic holy books were in Yiddish, 4–5.

109. Kalman Weiser, "Nationalism," 36.

110. Miron, *A Traveler Disguised,* 36, 64.

111. Lowenstein, "The Yiddish Written Word in Nineteenth-Century Germany," 188. Lowenstein notes that Judeo-German served as a transitional language for many German Jews in the early nineteenth century, 179–180. According to Max Weinreich, the term "Judisch-Deutsch" can denote either Yiddish or German written in Hebrew characters (*The History of the Yiddish Language,* 1:268).

112. In "De Mortuis Nil Nisi Hebraice?" Michael Brocke and Christiane E. Mueller write about Jewish tombstones inscribed in Judeo-German, "With the onset of the nineteenth century Hebrew letters became only the outer garb of the inscription, implying nothing about the language, style and content of its text" (71).

113. A late example of a newly published brivnshteler with Judeo-German is the anonymously authored *Kaufmännischer Briefsteller und Haus-sekretar* from 1908, a quadrilingual book with Hebrew, German, and Polish as the other languages.

114. Daniel Lovins, "AJL 2004 Proposal to Rewrite Reference Structure for 'Judeo-German,'" presents a detailed discussion of this issue. While there is, of course, no clear line between the many different dialects of Yiddish and German, Lovins offers some helpful criteria for determining what is Yiddish and what isn't, as well as several

examples of Judeo-German works misclassified as Yiddish in library catalogs, including Mendelssohn's Bible translation. Our thanks to Zachary Baker for directing us to this unpublished paper. For more on Judeo-German and the continuum of German with Yiddish, see Steven Lowenstein, "The Complicated Language Situation of German Jewry, 1760–1914."

115. Some Yiddish scholars have accepted works in Judeo-German as daytshmerish Yiddish. For instance, in his entry on "Brivnshtelers," in the 1957 *Dertsiungs-enstiklopedye, Y.* Birnboym characterizes manuals by Shalom ha-Kohen and Moshe Shmu'el Neumann as daytshmerish Yiddish, while we label them as Judeo-German (1:473–474, 476). A chapter in *Gorodinski's korrespondent: Der nayer brifenshteller. Der postalion,* of 1910 advertises "Commercial letters (*reyn yudish*) [pure Yiddish], also a few in German," with the "German" consisting of letters in Judeo-German.

116. In *A Traveler Disguised,* 3, Dan Miron notes that Abraham Mapu's *Ahaves tsiyen* [*Ahavat tsiyon*] (Love of Zion), published in 1853 and "the most celebrated Hebrew novel of the century," had only sold 1,200 copies by 1857.

117. Troinitskii, *Obshchii svod po imperii,* 2:3. According to the census, 31.20% of men and 16.52% of women reported themselves as literate in Russian.

118. Miron, *A Traveler Disguised,* 39–41.

119. Ibid., 13.

120. A letter in the 1830 brivnshteler *Mesader igeres* [*Mesadar igeret*], published by the presumably small press of Menakhem Man and son Borekh, and Simkhe Zimel and son Menakhem Nokhem, provides a glimpse into the sort of alternatives to maskilic literature that were popular with consumers: a woman writes to her fiancé asking him to buy her a new prayer book with taytsh because she's heard they're about to publish a new one in Vilna with "improved" taytsh (18–19).

121. According to Boris Kotlerman ("Kol Mevaser"), in the ten years that it published, the publication apparently had only about 250 subscribers (though it most likely had many more readers). In *Ayzik-Meyer Dik and the Rise of Yiddish Popular Literature,* David Roskies notes that after the ban on Jewish publishing was relaxed, "a wave of popular chapbooks invigorated the market accompanied by a trickle of works that heralded the coming of the modern critical era. The reading public let itself be carried by the wave and all but ignored the trickle." (38)

122. Quint, "Yiddish Literature for the Masses?" 64.

123. Hirsh Lion Dor, *Eyn nayer brifen shteller.* 1865, 89–90. Eliezer Zweifel (1815–1888) was a maskil, a Talmud teacher at the Zhitomir Rabbinical Seminary, and a Hebrew and Yiddish writer. Aleksander Zederbaum (1816–1893) was an editor and journalist, and publisher of *Kol mevaser,* Russia's first Yiddish newspaper. This passage strengthens Quint's argument in "Yiddish Literature for the Masses?" 67–71, that contrary to commonly held beliefs that maskilim wrote Hebrew for each other and Yiddish strictly for the masses, some writers intended their Yiddish works for a more sophisticated readership.

124. Shaykevitsh, *Der nayer Shomer's briefenshteler,* 1908.

125. Steinberg, *Shteynberg's brifenshteler.*

126. Feiner, "Towards a Historical Definition of the Haskalah," 215.

127. This estimate is based largely on bibliographies found in Zwick, *Toldot sifrut ha-igronim;* Gottheil and Broydé, "Letter-Writing and Letter Writers"; "Pis'movniki"; and Zeitlin, "Bibliographie der hebräischen Briefsteller" (1919); as well as the catalogs of the

following libraries: YIVO, Jewish Theological Seminary, New York Public Library, National Library of Russia (St. Petersburg), and Hebrew University.

128. David Fishman, *The Rise of Modern Yiddish Culture*, 18, 23, 25. While Yiddish periodicals were banned in order to promote the Russification of Jews and to halt the spread of revolutionary propaganda, there was no such ban on Yiddish book publishing, which was overseen by a different department of the Ministry of the Interior. According to Fishman, no one in the department of press affairs read Yiddish, and it was therefore not possible to find reliable Jewish censors for Yiddish periodicals. But that begs the question of why it was possible to find reliable censors for Yiddish books.

129. Ibid., 33–47. OPE: the acronym for the Russian Obshchestvo dlia rasprostraneniia prosveshcheniia mezhdu evreiami v Rossii.

130. Bernshteyn, *Bernshteyn's yudisher brief-lehrer* (1910 or 1911), 59.

131. Paperna, "Iz Nikolaevskoi epokhi," 145. In *Reading Jewish Women*, Parush discusses Paperna's attitudes toward women's education in the context of the Haskalah (83–84).

132. As Yehuda Elzet notes, the anonymous author of *Mesader igeres* [*Mesadar igeret*] displays an awareness of its literary value in his foreword, when he maintains that the letters to follow are not only useful but a "pleasure" to copy. He also notes that there are striking similarities between some of the descriptive prose in this book and the novels of Ayzik Meyer Dik. While he doesn't go so far as to actually suggest that Dik is the author of *Mesader igeres* [*Mesadar igeret*], he suggests that Dik might have "come across" the brivnshteler (61–62).

133. Zwick, *Toldot sifrut ha-igronim*, 99, 105, 256.

134. Another lesser-known example of a brivnshteler author who was also a novelist was Eliezer Miller (b. 1849), whose novels, all published before his brivnshtelers, include *Af gots velt* (In God's world; Zhitomir, 1887) and *Di tsvy shoytfim* (The two partners, 1889).

135. Carlebach, "Letter into Text," 126; Kazdan says that brivnshtelers paved the way for Yiddish literature, and that the shraybers and melamdim were pioneers of Yiddish education who helped spread knowledge of Yiddish (*Fun kheyder un "shkoles" biz tsisho*, 84).

136. Bray, *L'art de la lettre*, 23–29.

137. Sholem Aleichem, "Mayn ershter roman," in *Ale verk*, 17:135–136.

138. Sholem Aleichem, *Menakhem Mendl*, in *Ale verk*, 10:i–ii. Shmuel Niger says that in 1902, Sholem Aleichem signed an agreement with a publisher in Bobruisk to produce an actual brivnshteler, but nothing seems to have come of this project (Shmuel Niger, *Sholem Aleichem* (New York, 1928), 217–227, as cited in Bar El, "The Yiddish 'Briefenshteler,'" 162–163.

139. Roskies, *A Bridge of Longing*, 154.

140. Not all brivnshtelers emphasize the use of honorifics. Many give the option of more simple salutations (e.g., "Dear mother") in at least some model letters, and the American *brivnshtelers* by Shomer and Eisenstadt largely do away with them. Real Yiddish letters from the turn of the century do not employ them consistently. The latter observation and all other comments on real Yiddish letters are based largely on Roberta Newman's familiarity with three large family letter collections and do not take into account class or regional differences, degrees of acculturation, or political orientation, all of which might affect usage.

141. Leivick, "Sonaten ring," 256.

142. Ibid., 257.

143. Shvarts, *Yunge Yorn*, 122. In "Brivenshtelers," Y. Birnboym affectionately refers to them *as di gantse toyre af eyn fus* (the entire Torah on one foot).

144. Kulbak, *Zelmenyaner*, 17–18.

145. The parent-child relations in the new Jewish upper class were modeled on Russian aristocratic norms (as reflected in Russian pis'movniki). It is in this area that we see the most striking difference between the behavior reported by upper-class Jews and the behavior reflected in brivnshtelers. The memoirs of the Poliakov family are a case in point. In his autobiographical essay ("Serebrianyi samovar," 5) Aleksandr Poliakov includes a striking couple of lines about not seeing his parents very often; though his mother read to him twice a week, she chose books that were beyond his comprehension, because she didn't see him enough to guess what his level of comprehension might be.

146. Sheldon, *Sheldon's Twentieth Century Letter Writer* (1901), 7. In *The Complete Letter Writer and Book of Social Forms* (1902), 3, editor Charles Walter Brown labels the "chief requisites of a letter" as "clearness, explicitness, and conciseness."

147. The advice from Alexander Harkavy's *Amerikanisher briefen-shteler* (1902), 1, is no different from that of Sheldon or Brown: "In writing a letter, one should have a clear idea of the points one wishes to make, and these points must have a proper order. The more important should come earlier, and the less important things must come later."

148. The German half of Froment and Mueller's *Deutsch-französischer Briefsteller* (Stuttgart, 1867) gets translated into Russian in 1872 and reprinted at least four times thereafter by two different editors. The title page of the 1907 edition gives its pedigree: "*Pis'movnik: obraztsy pisem vsyakago roda . . .* with the German text, according to the eleventh edition of the French pis'movnik of Froment and Mueller, put together by P. Fuchs, second edition, edited and corrected by Dr. S. Mandel'kern." It is worth noting that Solomon Mandel'kern was probably Jewish. The history of Russian manuals begins in translation. In her article "The First Published Russian Letter-Writing Manual," Lina Bernstein makes that point that this first Russian pis'movnik was a selective translation from two German books (99, 104); it was intended as a model for the new Europeanized behaviors sought by Peter the Great (100–102).

149. *Novyi russkii pis'movnik v 5 otdelakh*, 56. This manual, meant for immigrants to the United States, devotes its opening section to letters that an immigrant could use when writing home. The rest of the book, including not only the prodigal-son letter reproduced here but also an invitation to a duel, has nothing to do with immigration and is likely pirated from an older Russian or possibly European publication.

150. Zlatogor, *Russkii semeinyi pis'movnik*, 21–22.

151. Poliak-Gilman, *Der nayer obraztsover brifenshteller*, 26–27.

152. Froment and Mueller, *Deutsch-französischer Briefsteller* (1867), 46–47.

153. Fuks and Mandel'kern, *Obraztsy pisem vsiakago roda*, 40; Froment and Mueller, 38.

154. Chambers, *The New Century Standard Letter-Writer*, 122.

155. Ibid., 118.

156. Dick, *Dick's Society Letter-Writer for Ladies*, 219.

157. Nikolini, *Polnyi pis'movnik dlia vliublennykh* (1915), 12.

158. Sazonov and Bel'skii, *Polnyi russkii pis'movnik* (1887), 147.

159. Dick, *Dick's Society Letter-Writer for Ladies*, 6.

160. Sheldon, *Sheldon's Twentieth Century Letter-Writer*, 30.

161. Shalom ha-Kohen, *Sefer mikhtov meshulesh* [*Mikhtav meshulash*] (1889), 14. The letter is part of a series attributed to Shalom ha-Kohen (1722–1845) and was reprinted as late as 1920 in Frishman and Paperna, *Igron shalem* (20).

162. *Novyi russki pis'movnik*, 102–103.

163. Fridman, *Der nayer praktisher brifenshteller* (1891), 50–51.

164. David Frishman, Avraham Paperna, and Mrs. Hess, *Igron shalem*, 86.

165. Harkavy, *Harkavi's amerikanisher briefen-shteler* (1902), 138–139.

166. The letters appear verbatim in *Brown's Complete Letter-Writer*, 142. Since Harkavy and Brown both appeared in 1902, both authors probably lifted the exchange from another, earlier American letter-writer.

167. A rare exception can be found in *Gorodinski's korrespondent: Der nayer brifenshteller. Der postalion*, 20–22, where a letter begins, "I am well and hope to hear the same from you."

From the Pages of Brivnshtelers

MODERNITY AND MOBILITY

Introduction

The twin themes of mobility and modernity are ubiquitous in brivnshtelers published at the turn of the twentieth century. Young men and some young women travel to the big city for education or work, encounter its temptations, and suffer from loneliness and homesickness for their friends and family. While the city is presented in both negative and positive terms—it is a threat to the maintenance of Jewish tradition, but also the locus of economic and educational opportunity—the shtetl is not a preferred alternative. Those who have moved away from small towns may have a nostalgic memory or two, but they are quick to point out the lack of vitality and opportunity that drove them to leave home.

An early manifestation of modern thinking appears in a satirical letter from the earliest brivnshteler published in the Russian Empire. Letters 1–2 ("A German Jew Writes to a Polish Jew Asking for the Hand of His Daughter for His Son") mock Polish Jews for being backward. The Polish father rejects a good match for his daughter with a German Jew because of superstition (the in-laws have the same first names) and his fear about his daughter having to dress in more modern clothing.

Another sign of modernity appears in the many letters about education. As purveyors of education for an audience that was pursuing it at various levels, brivnshtelers were obsessed with the subject. The father seeking broader educational opportunities for his son is a model of enlightened behavior and close to a stock figure in brivnshtelers. Equally typical is his acknowledgment that if his son is to acquire a secular education, he is going to have to leave home. In Letter 3 ("I've Heard That There Are Schools for Boys in Berdichev"), from 1910, a boy's mother is blamed for keeping him from educational opportunities outside the shtetl. But now that she is dead, the father will send him to Berdichev, where there is a real school.

The sense of being trapped in the shtetl and the longing for secular knowledge are other common themes. Paperna's 1889 Russian-Hebrew manual *Mikhtov meshulesh* [*Mikhtav meshulash*] includes a letter from a young man to his close friend, who has gone off to "the capital city of P." After some time complaining that his friend hasn't written, and in general following the conventions of sentimental friendship that are a feature of the Haskalah as well as Russian Enlightenment culture, he gets to his point.[1] The friend knows what their small town is like, and he knows that there are no teachers, which make it impossible to learn anything serious: "So I ask you to be my advisor and help me make up for lost time; tell me what books would, if I apply myself assiduously, take the place of a teacher. If you can do this I will be forever grateful."[2]

Changes in thinking can be incremental within a family—the case with the enlightened father seeking opportunities for his son—or they can be radical, encompassing a group of friends of the same age. For Jewish men, the transition to modern thinking could be very complicated. One of the most vivid accounts of this transition—radical in its visible, physical manifestations, conservative in its retention of deeply rooted religious behaviors—is from a Russian-language story by S. An-ski, in which one young man urges another to cut off his *peyes* (sidelocks) as a grand gesture of secularization:

> "Listen!" Eyzerman turned to Tsiporin. "You've got scissors. Do a mitzvah, cut off my *peyes.*"
> "What's the hurry? You'll have time," Mirkin cut in with some annoyance, remembering the conversation with Hillel.
> "I'm ashamed to appear in front of people this way."
> "Go on, go on! Let's cut off his *peyes,*" said Uler. "He begged me to do it before. Go on, sit down. We'll take you to the bosom of the Haskalah."
> "A true maskil would let people tear out each individual hair," said Hillel modestly and very seriously. "By that feat, they would earn a place in freethinkers' heaven."
> Everybody laughed, but Eyzerman looked at Hillel in disbelief. He thought at first Hillel was serious.

Uler armed himself with scissors.

"How do you want it? Right to the skin? So that not a trace remains?"

"To the very skin. So that not even a memory remains."

"We have to say a blessing. We can't without a blessing," said Uler.

"Get it done already. . . . Don't hold him back," whispered Mirkin.

"All right. We'll manage without a blessing!" Uler agreed and completely
    shaved off both sides.[3]

While no brivnshteler goes as far as An-ski's fiction, brivnshteler writers were aware of these sorts of dilemmas and their relevance to their
audience, whose life experiences may have mirrored some of their own
struggles to break away from tradition. In Letter 4 ("A Young Man Hides a
Secular Book from His Father-in-Law"), from 1904, a young man has just
received a coveted but seditious gift: an anthology of Russian and German literature. He will hide it from his father-in-law, in whose presence
he is still playing the role of an observant Jew, a Hasid. In another letter
from the same brivnshteler, a different young man writes a very emotional
letter to his brother-in-law who has concluded his year of support (*kest*)
with his in-laws and is about to return to his own parents. The modern
element here is the expression of intense male friendship: the writer had
been hoping the two young men would have time to continue sharing
their life stories, but the period of kest concluded, and with it, their inti-
macy. The letter continues in a gloomy but much more traditional fashion
about problems investing money.

Whatever the author's personal beliefs, no brivnshteler is about to
reject religion either openly or radically, or advocate for an ideological
substitute such as Marxism or Zionism. (Marxism, a threat to the imperial government, is altogether absent.) But the winds of modern ideologies do ruffle brivnshteler pages. Letter 5 ("A Teenager Discovers Jewish History") is from a young man with a gymnasium education, which
assumes a privileged and at least partly secularized background. He is
astonished that the Jews have a glorious past replete with revolution and
heroism and eagerly shares his budding nationalist feelings with a friend.
Other oblique Zionist references come from bilingual Hebrew-Yiddish
manuals that promote Jewish national pride in the context of mastering
modern Hebrew. One book of this type, published in Vilna in 1899, includes a letter from a young man who lauds his friend's attempt at writing
in Hebrew but suggests that he really needs to learn some grammar and

Jewish history. The friend replies, assuring him that he is studying history by reading Graetz's *History of the Jews* translated into Hebrew (Letters 6–7: "Study Hebrew Grammar and Jewish History"). Disapproval for improper mastery of Hebrew is also stressed in another letter from this collection, in which the writer finds fault with his correspondent for not writing in Hebrew, though he understands that the young man learned the language only "theoretically" and not "practically." The recipient need not altogether despair—while he has a way to go linguistically, he has adopted the norms of sentimental friendship and is warmly thanked for expressing all his deepest thoughts and feelings.[4]

Another modern, not quite political path was secular Yiddishism. Two friendship letters from *Bernshteyn's yudisher brief-lehrer* (1910 or 1911), talk about the excitement generated by Yiddish literature and give advice on what to read. One of them is addressed to a young man who has up to now ignored anything Jewish. Coming fresh from European literature, he is advised to avoid Mendele and Peretz for the time being. They will be too Jewish for him, and he won't appreciate them. No, he should start with Shalom Asch's stories and Avrom Reyzen's poetry, followed by Yehoash, Morris Rosenfeld, and Shimen Frug.[5] The other letter talks about how young people are starting to speak Yiddish "more naturally"—a dig, presumably, at daytshmerish—and remarks that everyone has given up Russian literature to read in Yiddish. This letter sets up reading as just about the only good thing about life in the provinces. Apart from reading and admiring nature (itself a modern pastime), life is completely aimless. There is nothing to do except "make *motsi* [say the blessing over bread] ten times, bathe in tea, and read a couple of newspapers from the first line to the last: one gulps down the meat, the bones and skin all at the same time."[6]

When they get to the big city, Bernshteyn's characters are a little shocked, but resolute. Letter 8 ("My First Impression of the Big City") acknowledges the disorientation of urban life—literal disorientation, as the writer still can't find his way around. But it also conveys the excitement of being in the city, much of it centered in opportunities for education. A young women in the same manual weighs in with her own impressions in a letter to a girlfriend. Contemplating her loneliness, she admits to longing for the shtetl "where you are something, where you occupy a respectable place, where you have so many warm and loving friends around you."

But she will not "withdraw from the seething ocean that carries on its waves" the dreams of her future. Gradually, she has acclimated herself to "civilized life." She has no regrets.[7]

Bernshteyn's brivnshteler is one of the few written in the Russian Empire to reflect new possibilities for young women outside courtship and marriage. Bernshteyn's women are modern and mobile. Writing to her friend Esther, who has moved to Warsaw, a young woman refers to the scandal surrounding her departure. But the young people in the town consider her a heroine, and the writer also is full of envy for her personal freedom. She realizes that it is insufficient to sit in the shtetl reading books and waiting for her aunts to make a match for her. Every day, she dreams of joining Esther in the city to begin "systematically educating" herself (Letter 9: "Rebellious Girls").

Other letters present young women from explicitly poorer circumstances seizing control of their own futures, and trying to secure the future of a little girl in their family. In both cases, the little girls are orphans (they have lost one parent), a situation that was fraught with dangers of poverty and also neglect, if the surviving parent, particularly the father, remarried. (Letter 10: "A Woman Writes to Her Sister and Asks Her to Join Her in Minsk"; Letter 11: "Send Little Rokhl to Me in the City.")

An even more poignant story about an orphan comes from the Poliak-Gilman brivnshteler of 1904. Here, a little boy pleads for help from his sister and brother-in-law. He says he is entirely alone. He doesn't have clothes or enough food, and he has no possibility of getting an education. As he pleads his case, Poliak-Gilman gives him words from a well-known hymn in the liturgy for Yom Kippur (*ki hiney ka-khoymer*), which compares human beings to clay in the hands of a potter:

> Aunt doesn't want to give me food or decent clothes to wear. She doesn't let uncle pay for teachers and chases me out of the house every day. . . . For me, every day is like a year. Three years ago, when my parents were still alive, who would have treated me like this? Uncle was a bookkeeper in my parents' business until the wheel gave a turn. What have I come to? Yes, this is the truth. As the world says, a person is like a watch, who is at every moment in the hands of the Eternal, or like a piece of clay in the hands of a potter. But what has happened has happened. Now, give me some advice. You were there when my uncle was made trustee. Somewhere it must be recorded in the books at the notary about who has the will that our father left before he took leave of the world. So if you don't answer me with some

advice and a couple of rubles to get through these bad times—if you don't, I will have to come to you. But this I will say to you, if you help me out, I won't forget it as long as I live and God will repay you with seeing to it that your children will be protected and their parents won't, God forbid, be torn from the world at a young age. Since I have had a good cry in my letter, God will help me rejoice. From me, your brother and brother-in-law, who wishes you all the best, and awaits your reply,

Shmuel Teperovski.[8]

Most brivnshtelers walk a tightrope between their readers' desire for middle-class respectability and the specter of poverty, which was never too far off. In the case of this boy, knowing how to write a letter—the brivnshteler's most elementary function—gives him a way to seek justice and a better life. The willingness of some brivnshtelers to take up issues of social justice and poverty, along with an implied criticism of Jewish family life, is one sign of modernity.

Letters

1: A German Jew Writes to a Polish Jew Asking for the Hand of His Daughter for His Son[i]

Monday, the 6th day of Tammuz, 1821, Hamburg

To the well-known rabbi, the enlightened one, my teacher and rabbi, Mordkhe Aleksander, may he flourish,

As you know, here among us, no shadkhonim [matchmakers] are needed, and so I am writing you myself because I have heard that you have a clever daughter, attractive in appearance. Well, we too have been blessed by God, blessed be His Name, with a good, respectable son. I had him study for eight years in the Prague yeshiva at my own expense. He knows five hundred pages of Gemara and also happens to be exceptionally smart. He has been learning foreign languages for three years and he has mastered the Hebrew language; that is, the holy tongue with grammar, with all the rules that other languages have, because I also sent him to Berlin for three years to the Society for the Education of Young Men, where he became adept in the study of the Tanakh, to the extent that he knows as many of the psikhes [open portions] and stumes [closed portions][ii] as there are in the Tanakh altogether. German, French, and English are like mother tongues to him and when it comes to math, he could be a professor to the level of algebra. He is 17 years of age, attractive in stature, dresses in the German fashion, and his beard is beginning to grow and be visible. He is God-fearing, and you should know that if you're looking for a pious man among us, that's him; there is no chicanery involved, because he is very enlightened, and behaves as a servant of God ought to. If he behaved any differently, you can be sure that I wouldn't be considering a Polish Jew's daughter as a match for him. But because you are a great family and not bad in standing and the girl, your daughter, is clever and skilled, it seems to me that they would make a fine couple. As far as money goes, I will give him five thousand thalers, though among us it is not the custom to give a son any furniture or household goods, but because he is my son, who is the dearest in the world to me, I will give him, in addition to the money, pearls and diamonds worth 1000 thalers. He will receive two kanapey [divans]; a sofa; a deep chair; two desks; a big table with 30 drawer liners; three room tables, all inlaid with mahogany and ebony; 2 dozen hand towels; tablecloths enough for 34 people; 6 window curtains; as well as bronze dishes for the kitchen, and three mirrors. And so, if you agree, write to me about what you would give with your daughter in marriage, and then we will know how to proceed. May you live well, your friend and servant for eternity,

Markus Menhaym Kassel
My wife Gitl Flore sends many regards to you and your wife
Markus Menhaym, as aforementioned

i *Mesader igeres* [*Mesadar igeret*]*oder eyn nayer shrayb lehrer un brifshteller fir yidishi kinder beyde geshlekhter*, 62–65.

ii *Psikhes* are portions of the Tanakh that begin on a new line; *stumes* are portions that begin in the middle of a line after a blank space.

2: A German Jew Writes to a Polish Jew Asking for the Hand of His Daughter for His Son, reply

Sunday, the 11th of Elul, 1821, Jaroslaw
Herr Mordkhe Markus Menhaym Kassel, may he flourish,
My dear sir, you have bestowed upon me a great honor with your letter. I would also have written to you in taytsh,[i] *but I don't know it so well because I never learned it. I have heard quite a bit about your dear,*

precious son, the accomplished scholar, that he is a learned child. This is very acceptable to us and my daughter might indeed be happy about it. But I must point out to you that the match is not destined to be, the way we see it. First of all, it is very difficult to break a child of his habits. No doubt he will wear a long beard because he is God-fearing. My real objection is that you are called Markus (that is, Mordkhe), and I'm also called Mordkhe, and your wife and my wife are named Gitel,[ii] and among Polish Jews, great care is taken to avoid marriage if the names are the same. A certain commandment was laid down by a great man that this is very dangerous. And therefore no match can be agreed to because both in-laws have the same name. Furthermore, my daughter would often need to visit there and naturally won't be able to go there in Polish clothing. She would have to wear German clothing, and since German clothing is much finer than Jewish clothing, when coming back here she won't want to wear Jewish clothes anymore. So, the match can't take place under any circumstances and from all perspectives. Please don't take me the wrong way. You and your son are very beloved to us, but it's impossible. You would be a laughingstock in your world and I in mine. In fact, my daughter is really in favor of the match, and so is my wife, but my understanding is that this would not be worthwhile for either one of us in several respects. So be well and live well.

Your loyal friend,
Mordkhe Aleksander, son of Rabbi Yeshiye Binyomin
of the settlement and holy community of Jaroslaw
My wife Gitl sends many regards to your wife
Gitel Flore, may she live long and in peace.

[i] The word *taytsh* is used here to denote daytshmerish Yiddish
[ii] Variant spelling in original.

3: I've Heard That There Are Schools for Boys in Berdichev

Korostyshev, September 17, 1894

To my dear, praiseworthy sister Mrs. Feygah, may she live, in Berdichev,

The bearer of this letter is my oldest son. As you see, he is 11 years old. As is usually the case, I sent him to the best melamdim and teachers here, as far as my resources would permit. But unfortunately, in our small shtetl, there are never any good teachers or melamdim, because the ex-

*perts, the good lerers [teachers][ii] or melamdim who are good pedagogues
are not willing under any circumstances to give away their labor for free.
In our small shtetl, with its unsophisticated ideas about this important
subject, people still have very little grasp of how important the foundation, the first educational experience of a child is, and they do not
understand at all that the absolutely best teacher is necessary especially
at the start, at the level of the alef-beys [alphabet]. And how harmful
an effect a bad teacher or melamed has on an innocent child's education. In a word, my dear sister, when my wife, may she rest in peace,
was alive, she absolutely refused to entertain the thought that she could
live without her child and did whatever she could to thwart my goal: to
send him to you, in Berdichev of good fame, to study, because as is well-
known, in Berdichev and other big cities there is quite a different sort
of lerer and melamed. In particular, I've heard that Berdichev finally
also has schools for boys, as has been the case for a long time in many
other cities, where a specific curriculum is studied in an organized way,
and where, by law, the teachers and melamdim must be orderly people
and experts who understand their business and the importance of a
child's education. And so, my dear sister, all my hopes rest first of all on
G-d,[iii] and next on you, that you will have compassion on my dear son,
especially since he is, after all, an orphan. You will be doing a very good
deed to take him in and enroll him in that sort of school, where he can
learn everything altogether. First of all, it's very economical, just about
the best plan for the middle classes, for people like myself, that for 3 or 4
rubles a month, the child studies Hebrew, Russian, arithmetic, penmanship, and altogether everything that the Jewish child needs. Secondly, I
have heard from several people from Berdichev how orderly and organized the instruction is in these schools, that instruction is conducted in
the spirit of the Torah and with respect and that a fine child with some
aptitude is in the position, in the course of a few semesters, to become
a well-rounded person. I would be greatly honored, if G-d wills it, to
pay tuition and other expenses. Dear Sister, I only ask if you would be
so kind as to care for him and provide him with everything that a child
needs. Of course, if it is not too much of a burden for you to keep him, I
would be very happy, and ask you, as much as possible, to be a mother
to him, for which, aside from my brotherly gratitude, G-d will keep you
and your dear husband from trouble and grant you good fortune and*

*the greatest pleasure from your children. Regards to your dear husband
and your dear children and wishing you all the best.*

Your loving brother who awaits your reply,
Dovid Broyn

i Gorodinski, *Gorodinski's Korrespondent. Der nayer brifenshteller. Der
   postalion,* 32–34.
ii The author makes a distinction between a lerer (a secular teacher)
   and a melamed, usually a teacher of traditional subjects.
iii We have translated abbreviations and euphemisms for God, such
   as "Hashem" and "H'" as "G-d" throughout the text, but have used
   "God" to translate the Yiddish word *gott.*

4: A Young Man Hides a Secular Book from His Father-in-Law[i]

He who protects all of creation is with you.

*Thank you, my dear friend, for the present. The person who brought me
the book and letter—out of great joy, I didn't know what to do. I praised
him as if he had been sent by a count in a certain country.[ii] When I began
to read the book, I can't describe for you how much I enjoyed it, more
than if it was the best theater, because in it is everything that one could
ever come across. I especially enjoyed reading the jokes and fables. When
I am feeling gloomy, I forget about everything and start laughing. I even
know many of the authors from which the compiler took a little: Krylov,
Turgenev, and Schiller,[iii] and a few other such writers.*

*Today, I began to read about all the deserts, about all the desolate
places, about all the savage people who are so many and in so many
places. Until now I thought that our city was the world and that beyond
must lie nothing but the heavens with the earth.[iv] And so, the book has
opened my eyes. But I have to read it out of sight of my friends, because
if they find out, they will tell my father-in-law and mother-in-law. You
should know that my father-in-law is a Bratslaver Hasid[v] and I have
to play the role of modern-day Hasid, even though secretly, I am not
fooled. I adhere to the Torah of Moses and the Oral Law, and observe
the Shulkhan Arukh[vi] from morning to night. No one can know that
I'm reading a secular book because I will immediately be branded as an
apikoyres[vii] and get thrown out of kest.[viii] Today, I will write something
else. Don't think that I am such a good friend of yours only because you*

*have sent me this book. I have always held you in high esteem. So write
me letters more often, about your parents, don't forget our love and
friendship and I won't forget you either.*

Your brother-in-law and friend,
Yl'sh.[ix]

  [i] Poliak-Gilman, *Der nayer obraztsover brifenshteller*, 32.

  [ii] A possible reference to a popular song set to a poem by the German-
Jewish poet Moritz Hartmann. The poem was published in 1874
and translated into many languages, including Russian, Polish, and
Yiddish. The subject is a young man, a Hungarian count, about to be
executed for sedition. See Rothstein, "Vegn daytshn original fun 'A
graf fun Ungarn.'"

  [iii] This trio of famous, often-anthologized writers includes Ivan Krylov
(1769–1844), beloved Russian fabulist; Ivan Turgenev (1818–1883),
Russian realist novelist; and Friedrich Schiller (1759–1805), German
poet and dramatist associated first with the "Storm and Stress"
movement and later with Weimar classicism. Knowledge of all three
was standard for an educated Russian.

  [iv] The Russian version of the sentence in this bilingual book is slightly
different from the Yiddish, and makes a little more sense: "Up till
now I thought that beyond the city the heavens combine with the
earth and that's where the world ends."

  [v] Bratslaver, or Breslov, Hasidim were and are adherents of a group
tracing back to Rebbe Nakhman of Breslov (1772–1810).

  [vi] The standard compilation of Jewish law, based on Talmud and other
authorities, assembled by Yosef Karo in 1563.

  [vii] Yiddish *apikoyres*, Hebrew *apikoros*, from Greek *epicuros:* a heretic
or nonbeliever; someone who rejects rabbinic tradition. In some
nineteenth-century circles, a synonym for *maskil.*

  [viii] Room and board provided for a new couple for a specified period
of time by one or the other set of parents.

  [ix] Possibly an abbreviation of the name of the writer of the letter.

5: A Teenager Discovers Jewish History

Dear B. Rozenboym!

*May I only know from angry pox if I know what to write to you about!
But nothing: the paper lies spread out and inkwell and pen sit on the
table and I also have the time—so I will chat with you a little.*

So listen: you no doubt still remember the old times, my weakness for food and reading. You no doubt remember the bourgeois novels I was always so taken with. Today, imagine, there is news. I am intensely preoccupied with reading—guess what?—Jewish history! No doubt you are asking: what has brought me to such serious matters? I will explain to you what motivated me to suddenly start learning about our bygone history. In the course at the gymnasium, a significant amount of Roman history was covered, and when we came to the place where the Jewish "revolt" against the Romans and the bloody wars waged between these two peoples was mentioned, I found myself in for a weird surprise. Jews made a "revolution," Jews waged wars, Jews played such a significant role in the history of the ancient people—when was this? Who were the heroic leaders? And were these really the Jews from whom we, modern-day Jews are descended? These questions wouldn't let me rest and I decided to acquaint myself with all of Jewish history in general and with that epoch in particular. I assembled for myself a complete selection of Jewish history and sat myself down to study or read. And I tell you, in all seriousness, the more I read, the more the conviction grows that our history is one of the richest and most interesting, not even taking into account its relationship to the "histories" of the newly baked peoples who only yesterday emerged onto the historical scene, but also in comparison to the history of the other peoples of ancient culture!

Now I have arrived at the epoch of the Jewish "revolt" against the Romans and I am simply enchanted with every line that I read. How much unbelievable heroism they displayed! I don't know if you are acquainted with that epoch, but I tell you, that all the heroism of the Greeks and Romans which was described with such fanfare in our schoolbooks is puny in comparison to the heroism that our grandfathers displayed in the time of Vespasian[ii] and Titus. I want to talk much more with you about this matter, but it is already late at night and I have already also gone on too much about it. For the time being—enough!

In the meantime, be well and strong and don't forget to reply to your devoted historian . . .

D.

---

[i] Bernshteyn, *Bernshteyn's nayer yudisher folks-brifenshteler*, 49–55.
[ii] *Aspsinus* in the original.

6: Study Hebrew Grammar and Jewish History[i]

My beloved friend!

I got your letter written in Hebrew and I will give you my verdict (opinion)[ii] *on your letter: you have really accomplished a lot and according to my opinion (the way I see it) you have made great strides in your studies and have spared no effort to reach your personal goals. But there is one thing to which I find it necessary to draw your attention, a defect that you can improve on; that is (in other words), you should study the grammar of the Hebrew language, and not let the Tanakh*[iii] *out of your hands. Also, you should study Jewish history in order to know everything well (properly), the era in which the history (matters) that are told about happened (occurred) because it will be of great use. Just try and you will see I have given you good advice. Write letters to me frequently and I will reply and with this practice, you will learn a lot because there is no one smarter than the one who practices.*

Your friend _____

[i] Inditski, *Ha-metargem*, 39–42.

[ii] Synonyms and alternatives for some words and phrases in parentheses are in the original text, provided by the author as an on-the-spot thesaurus. Most parenthetical terms are in Yiddish, but some are in Hebrew.

[iii] Acronym for Torah, Prophets, and Writings: the Hebrew Bible.

7: Study Hebrew Grammar and Jewish History, reply

My dear pal!

I received your letter and read it with great pleasure and boundless joy because it convinced me that I haven't blundered and my self-love (egotism) hasn't blinded me to the truth. And how I inwardly rejoiced, seeing that you have rendered your verdict in my favor and that you haven't found it necessary to call my attention to more than two things in my letter, which I myself was already thinking about. I am reporting to you now that I am working hard at studying the grammar of the Hebrew language, and also that from today on, I will no longer be unfamiliar with Jewish history either, because I am also working hard at studying that. I am studying Graetz's Jewish History[i] *in a Hebrew translation by Rabbinowitz.*[ii] *Right now I'm reading the chapters*

that cover the heroism displayed by the Hasmoneans when, like lions,
they fought for the freedom of their people, fearlessly, even in the face
of death. In short, I will write you another letter and you will be con-
vinced that I am no longer unfamiliar with Jewish history.

Be well, and best wishes from your friend _____.

[i] A major figure of the German-Jewish Enlightenment, Heinrich Graetz
(1817–1891) is best known for his multivolume *History of the Jews*.

[ii] Heinrich Graetz, *Divre yeme Yisra'el (me-yom heyot Yisra'el le-'am 'ad*
yeme ha-dor ha-aharon), trans. Saul Phinehas Rabbinowitz (Warsaw,
1893–1911).

8: My First Impression of the Big City[i]

Dearest David!

Finally, today, I have a few free hours and I hasten to take advantage
of the opportunity to write this letter which I have owed you for so long.
So, listen:

The first impression that the city made on me with its immense
size and beauty was an unusual one. Imagine: I spent my entire life
in a small, poor, and dirty shtetl, and here I suddenly see before me
a metropolis, a huge, bustling city with towers, palaces, and parks. I
did, in fact, get flustered from the sight and for a long time couldn't
orient myself in the map of the streets, roads, etc. And I tell you the
truth, that even now, after I have finally gotten used to the bustle
of the city and finally know my way around a little—after all this, I
still haven't ceased to be amazed by everything and to marvel at its
beauties.

Aside from its surface beauty, the big city has yet other things of no
small significance: schools, high schools, and universities; libraries,
museums, theaters, circuses, and other places of recreation; and many
literary and scholarly societies.

About my personal life, I don't have anything to tell you. I sit all
day in my room and don't even have the time to get to know anyone.

Nu, it's getting late and I must end my letter. Now, dear, it's your
turn to write, and I don't believe that you will keep me waiting long for
your letter.

Yours . . .

[i] Bernshteyn, *Bernshteyn's nayer yudisher folks-brifenshteler,* 40–43.

9: Rebellious Girls[i]

Dear Friend!

I have no words, my dear, to describe the uproar, the talk, and the gossip that your sudden departure have caused in the shtetl. The adults whisper about you, about how you dared to do such a thing, and about your parents, who allowed it. It's the opposite, however, among the young people, who regard you as a heroine. All of them are secretly jealous of you: you won't have to suffer away in a small shtetl, where everything you do is seen by everybody and is on everyone's lips, and where one never sees the bright world. You are now in a more advanced society with loftier, more spiritual interests. You are studying and have a goal in life and will finally achieve what the best women of our generation dream of: to be independent. Not long ago, I read in a book that every human being's life should be like an opera: if the ending isn't to be tragic but instead, happy, then one's performance must be beautiful . . .

I tell you, Esther, you are the lucky one. It would have been worth it even if the only thing was your victory in the battle with your parents and the fact that you are the first among your girlfriends to go out into the greater world, where new people, new spiritual horizons await you, and most importantly: complete personal freedom!

Your departure made an unusual impression on me and I have experienced a revelation: I have begun to grasp that it requires no great talent to sit in a small shtetl and read books about life and spend one's time alone doing nothing until my devoted aunts start whispering that it is already high time . . .

But, dear, in the meantime, I can't compare myself to you: my parents are not your parents. In her own youth, your mother also dreamt of going to the big city to study . . . at least she quietly sympathized with you and didn't too vigorously oppose you when you came out with your decision. My mother, however (no use even talking about my father) is a fanatical yudene.[ii] All she does is beg God that her children won't behave any worse than she does, and if I did what you did, it would be worse for her than if I converted. Be that as it may, I will have to do what I have to do, even if my acts are not viewed favorably but with contempt.

Already, I dream of the day when I will take up bundle and sack, say goodbye to our Dvoryansker street, where we used to stroll all the time, as well as to the forests and the rivers, and leave to join you in the big city to begin systematically educating myself. Because, alas, what does our education consist of? Do I know much more than how to speak Russian without mistakes and read a novel? I have never felt as strong and young as I do right now. I feel that I am capable of working day and night, knowing that this will ultimately make it possible for me to be free, independent, and, as a matter of course, also happy! I am writing you all this so that you can appreciate your situation and won't become disheartened. I encourage you and this will give me courage, too. Brayndl and Khanele send you their warm regards. Right now, there is a guest here in town: Khaym Shats. He has come for a visit from Baku. He has a good job there and has become quite a different person. He asked about you and sends his regards. Be well and cheerful, my dear.

Yours, _____

ⁱ Bernshteyn, *Bernshteyn's yudisher brief-lehrer,* 57–58.
ⁱⁱ Used here as a derogatory term: a nosy, talkative, petty Jewish woman.

10: A Woman Writes to Her Sister and Asks Her to Join Her in Minskⁱ

Dear, devoted sister Gitele!

For a long time, I haven't written you any letters. How are you, dear little sister? As I recall that you are all alone, and how sad you must be there all alone at Grandfather's—it doesn't give me a moment's peace. It isn't going well for me, either. Since the death of our good mother, we have become wanderers, drifting around in the world. But you, Gitele, are, after all, the youngest, and my heart aches more for you. Little sister, if you knew how much Mother, may she rest in peace, loved you— she watched over you like you were the apple of her eye!

Write, little sister, about how you are and what you are up to at Grandfather's. I would like it if you would learn how to sew, and then I would bring you to Minsk so that we could be together. I am earning enough for everything that I need. I work in a box factory. The work is easy but one has to get up very early in the morning. We must be at our

*places by six. Nonetheless, it is much better than working as a servant
in a well-to-do home. Working as a servant was terribly difficult for me.
First of all, one isn't considered a human being by anyone, and secondly,
I couldn't stand the vulgar attitude of the rich "Madame." But thank
God that I had the opportunity to obtain a factory job.*

*The work—small cartons for cigarettes—is so easy that it doesn't
need to be learned and I made money already in the first week. If you,
Gitele, like this sort of work, I can bring you here right now. But I would
rather make you a seamstress. Tailoring is a more conventional job. So
consider it and write me an answer about it right away. In any case,
write to me often. But I hope to God, that we will soon be together. I
await your reply and remain, your devoted sister,*

Sheyndl Golkin[ii]

[i] Bernshteyn, *Bernshteyn's nayer yudisher folks-brifenshteler*, 60–61.

[ii] Gitl's reply mentions a father who has remarried, moved elsewhere,
and now has a new child whom he wants Gitl to come and care for.
But she doesn't want to be a nanny to her stepsibling and expresses
enthusiasm for going to join Sheyndl in Minsk. Still, she notes, "It
doesn't matter to me if I am a seamstress or a factory girl. In any case,
I will go to America when I get older. You will also go. [Our brother]
Shmuel will send us steamship tickets."

11: Send Little Rokhl to Me in the City[i]

Dearest Mother!

*I am writing to you with a suggestion that for sure you haven't been
expecting and which will arouse stormy emotions in you. I want you to
send little Rokhl here to me. I will keep her close by and enroll her in a
school somewhere or teach her myself. I am not making a fortune here,
but I live a respectable life and Rokhl will not want for anything here.
I realize full well that it will be very hard for you to part with this child
who is so dear to all of us and engraved so deeply on our hearts. But you
must consider that in the big city of V. it is possible for a child to make
something substantial of herself more quickly than in our little shtetl in
the boondocks where there is no school and not even a proper teacher.
And furthermore, as far as supervision is concerned, I assure you that
she will be very happy here with me. I will watch over her like the apple*

of my eye and will not let even one raindrop fall on her. You should know that I can't get this child out of my mind even for one minute and my whole goal in life is to see the child of our unforgettable Rivke who died so young be happy.

Think it over well, dear, and fulfill the request of your daughter, who awaits your answer impatiently.

Khane

ⁱ Bernshteyn, *Bernshteyn's nayer yudisher folks-brifenshteler*, 46–48.

PARENTS AND CHILDREN: RUSSIA

Introduction

Parental anxiety is part of the human condition. How one deals with it —what can be displayed and what must be repressed—is mediated through culture. If we look at brivnshtelers published around the turn of the twentieth century, we find a world that lives and breathes anxiety, anxiety verbalized as a kind of domestic art. There is no reason, in a brivnshteler, to hide what you feel. It is appropriate and desirable to make your child feel your pain. But guilt is not an end in itself. It is a potent means of changing behavior, of turning *tsures* (troubles) into *nakhes* (pleasure)—or if nakhes is too far a reach, then at least reassurance that nothing is terribly wrong.

Jews were not the only people grappling with the separations caused by mass migration. But the particular tone of brivnshteler letters and their sheer number point to a distinctive cultural response to the splitting apart of families and the loss of parental control. The compilers of these manuals saw their audience as needing guidance—or at least reassurance and empathy—as they converted face-to-face relationships with their children into "paper lives." Their model letters reflect the enormous tension that changing conditions provoked among parents, and by extension, in Jewish society as a whole.

Because brivnshtelers have an interest in demonstrating the effectiveness of their arguments, or perhaps because the genre valued an occasional happy ending, high-anxiety letters from parents are often followed by children's reassuring replies. We see this in Letters 1–2 ("Matisyahu and

His Son"). In the first letter, the father complains that the son hasn't written. He and his wife are beside themselves with worry. (Anxiety letters are
generally from the father but often refer to the sufferings of the mother,
which are always depicted as more dramatic and intense). Matisyahu tells
his son Gamaliel that he's doing a terrible thing to his parents, and that
even if some misfortune has struck, he must let them know. Eventually,
Gamaliel responds. All is well now, though the parental intuition was correct. His excuse for not writing is unassailable: he was lying unconscious.[9]

In a manual that specializes in anxiety, like E. *Miller's nayer brifenshteller in tsvey theyl* (E. Miller's new brivnshteler in two parts), even New
Year's greetings reflect the unease. Miller's first Rosh Hashanah greeting
has a son hoping that the new year will bring his parents freedom from the
misfortunes they suffered during the preceding year.[10] In another letter,
Shaul thanks his son for his Rosh Hashanah card and reminds him of the
terrible things the family miraculously survived. He also notes that they
are still giving the son financial help.[11]

Among the many troubles that brivnshtelers give voice to is parental
illness. It is worth noting how different Yiddish manuals are from Russian
or American ones in their approach to this universal problem. In non-
Jewish manuals, siblings who are away are gravely informed of a parent's
poor health; if the writer knows that they are not far, they are asked to pay
a visit. Brivnshtelers sometimes do this. But they also provide words for
siblings to use if they would prefer instead to vent their anger.

In Letters 3–5 ("Mother's Condition Is Hopeless"), we see that Miller,
once again, has focused on the fraught side of family dynamics. The
catalyst is a letter from Shimen to his sister saying that a friend passing
through told him that their mother was in very poor health. He's worried
and wants her to take Mother to doctors and even abroad if it will help.
He'll cover all expenses. The first reply has Shimen's sister informing
him that Mother's condition is desperate. Going abroad will make no
difference. Based on what local doctors say, "one can expect a catastrophe
any day now." An alternative reply runs through a different but equally
familiar familial script: though the mother has been sick for two years,
Shimen, "the boy, the future heir and *kaddish*, the wealthy success of the
family, the eldest son for whom Mother sacrificed her whole life" hasn't
made the time to come and see her even though he's managed vacations
at "various dachas." Miller supplies yet another possible reply, focusing on

the emotional effects of Mother's illness, which Shimen, as the successful son, has been spared. Her sickness has wrecked everyone's life and livelihood and made the house "a hill of ash." Right now, Mother is refusing to leave the country for treatment, but maybe if Shimen comes to visit he can convince her to go.[12]

A repeated subject of parent-child correspondence is the son who studies or apprentices at a business far from home. The stakes are high, with multiple possibilities for nakhes or, more commonly, tsures. The classic rendition of the son's tale as monitored by the father is the work of Shalom ha-Kohen, a member of the Berlin Enlightenment and author of a well-known manual in Hebrew and Judeo-German. While the anxiety dimension of his fictional letters is narrower than the no-holds-barred approach of Yiddish manuals seventy-five years later, his work remained in the public eye for a long time. With Russian translations added to the mix, his model letters were republished in full or in part well into the twentieth century.

Frishman and Paperna's 1889 *Igron shalem* (Complete letter-writer) gives the complete version of two sets of Shalom ha-Kohen letters in Hebrew, Russian, and Judeo-German. The letters, first published in Hebrew and Judeo-German in 1819,[13] might qualify as epistolary novellas except for their pedagogical function. In the second set in particular, each letter exemplifies a specific type of brivnshteler prose (the anxiety letter, the condolence letter, the congratulatory letter, the business circular) while at the same time advancing the plot. The two plots set out so many typical elements of the son-leaves-home story that a brief summary is worth our while.

The first letter of the first set is from a poor brother to a wealthy one, showcasing the proper use of wealth within the extended family. The poor man's son seeks knowledge of arts and sciences (*Kunst und Wissenschaft*—Shalom ha-Kohen was a maskil) and no one in the shtetl can provide it.[14] The brother, resident of a larger town or city, replies that he has long nursed this idea himself. All is well in the next few letters, as the son reports his safe arrival and warm reception, and the uncle reports only one problem: the boy studies too hard.

Such a surfeit of nakhes can only be followed by its antipode, and in Letter 8, tsures breaks loose. For the past six months, reports the uncle, the boy has abandoned his studies and hangs out with people who have

had a terrible influence on his morals. He quarrels with his uncle's family
and has brought shame and sorrow into the house.

The informant-uncle is a character who comes up repeatedly in stories
of this type. In the Shalom ha-Kohen series, as later, the father responds
to the bad news with an anguished letter. The son replies in elevated language, describing the tears that flow from his eyes and hoping for mercy.
But his penitent words mask an exonerating twist of plot. The son may be
apologizing, but he is actually not at fault. The fault lies with the servants,
who drew him into small transgressions and then exaggerated them to
lower the boy in his uncle's eyes. But the boy has faith in God and hopes
that God will restore the rights of the innocent and let the guilty fall into
their own trap.

Cognoscenti will see that Shalom ha-Kohen, in need of an exit strategy, has found one in the Purim story. There, a king who has been duped
by evil plotters learns the truth and condemns the plotters to the punishment they have been conniving for the honorable hero. In the brivnshteler
version, the uncle learns the truth and gives the servants the punishment
he had been planning for his nephew. The nephew is restored to his place
in the family, while the servants are banished. Also embedded in the
brivnshteler's happy conclusion is an ethical lesson. Before chasing the
servants away, the righteous and merciful uncle does not forget to give
them their wages.

The second set of letters moves the same three characters—father,
son, uncle—through a different plot, with each new set of circumstances
represented by the appropriate kind of model letter.[15] In the first one,
a classic anxiety letter, the father and mother are disturbed by dark
thoughts because the son has not written. The premonitions turn out
to be justified. Over the next few letters, we learn of the uncle's illness
(letter type: how to report an illness of someone you love) and then his
death. Fortunately, the uncle is righteous and farsighted—another little
ethical lesson that brings happiness to the hero, even in the sadness of an
untimely death. In his will, the uncle establishes the nephew as head
of his firm until his own sons come of age, and in his last moments further
sets the course of his nephew's future with the fateful words, "You know
that I have a seventeen-year-old daughter." The next letters are business
letters. In one, the nephew writes to someone who does business with
the firm, informing them of the uncle's death and of his own new posi-

tion; in another, citing orphans in the home, he gets his uncle's debtor to pay up. Returning to private correspondence, we get invitations to and announcements of a wedding, a birth, and a *bris*. In the final letter, the father whose anxious inquiry started the whole chain invites everyone to his seventieth birthday, which happens to be the same day as his fiftieth wedding anniversary. Life is good.

Throughout the history of the genre, letters about sons studying far from home follow many of the conventions established in the manuals of Shalom ha-Kohen and Avraham Paperna. Worried fathers correspond with gracious uncles who take their nephews into their homes and report on their behavior. Secular learning remains a focus, and fathers send money, books, and clothes.

While Letters 6 and 7 don't feature an intermediary uncle, they do show the development of the father-son genre later in the nineteenth century. Both letters come from an 1891 brivnshteler by Dov Arye Fridman, published again in 1908 with the famous (and by then deceased) novelist Shomer listed as the author. Each of them uses religious language to frame a maskilic attitude toward education, and each combines this advocacy with mundane, realistic references to clothes and books.

In Letter 6 ("Send Me Money for Decent Clothing"), a son named Sholem Birenboym asks his father Moyshe for money to buy religious books and also secular ones. The interesting thing here is the absence of emotion: the need for both kinds of books is given equal emphasis; no explanation is needed. Much more emotion goes into Sholem's request for proper clothes: "I am embarrassed to go among people in ripped clothing."[16]

Letter 7 ("Buy Books, Get Clothes, Pursue Wisdom"), from Borekh bar Shimen Zak to his son Sholem, dated 1889, presents a maskilic argument for secular learning. The secular knowledge Borekh has in mind for his son is not much more than a working knowledge of Russian, though the language is not actually specified by name. Author Dov Arye Fridman makes a general case for learning foreign languages by taking a long-term view—the entire Jewish experience in the Diaspora, which proves how important it is to know the language of the people in charge. Fridman's caution may be tied to his understanding of his specific audience, brivnshteler readers for whom any diversion from religious learning is contentious. So Borekh begins his argument by saying, mildly, that nonreligious learning is valuable in itself. Then, in very strong words, he describes what happens when rabbis are "without the language of the land." When speaking to government officials, they behave like "mutes," and Torah is dishonored.[17] His argument concluded, Borekh gets back to the practical business of letter writing. He tells his son that he is sending money for clothes and books.

The main points of these letters (learn languages; here's some money for clothes) are maintained even in brivnshtelers whose orientation is wholly secular. A good example is Letter 8 ("Beloved Child, Study Yiddish and Russian") from Poliak-Gilman's 1904 manual. Along with his pedagogical advice, the father has sent a silk hat and a few rubles. The suggestion to study languages—note that Yiddish, absent earlier, is now on an equal footing with Russian—is offered without any religious justification. Though in this case the father has received only good news, parental anxiety is not entirely absent: this short letter includes two references to the son's health.

Study and work don't always go well; sons misbehave. But sometimes, as in the Sholem ha-Kohen story, a father who hears that his son has gone down the wrong path has been misinformed. Letter 9 ("Truth Rises to the Top Like Oil on Water") is from a son who claims that he is the victim of slander. Like the son in Shalom ha-Kohen, he starts by following the prodigal-son script, which calls for an abject apology. Quoting King Solomon, the young man praises his father for teaching him righteousness and expresses concern that anger will be damaging to his father's health. With that out of the way, he asks why the father is listening to gossip. The letter has touched all bases: genuine prodigal sons can copy everything up to the specific excuse; sons who have been framed can learn at what point, diplomatically, to reveal it; and parents can hope that their anxiety will turn out to have been unfounded.

Faced with a misbehaving son, the first step is an angry letter. The usual form is open exasperation, mixed with reminders of everything Father and Mother have done for the young man by taking care of him when he was sick and providing him with an education, and sometimes even employment. "You are making us angry and crazy with your fantasies and demands," writes one infuriated father. "If you are really thinking about a job, you must guard your job like the eyes in your head. You must realize that these days jobs are scarce, as well as how much effort and health it cost me before I got this job for you."[18] In another letter, from a 1904 manual, the wayward son is reminded that his mother "ran to the doctor so that he would write a prescription even though we didn't have a cent." A few sentences later, "then there were the problems with your kheyder, the teachers' assistants, and your melamdim. In the summer, your mother would immediately run to look for you by the river. She was afraid to let you swim, in case, God forbid, you would drown."[19] In an extreme situation, "tough love" can be used to bring a wayward son in line: "Don't think you're coming home. No! I'll chase you away because I don't have the means to support you."[20] But usually, as in Letter 10 ("Your Letter Did Not Bring Us Any Pleasure"), the parental rant concludes with an offer of money or a train ticket home.

In the world of the brivnshteler, daughters are much less frequently the recipient of parental anxiety and anger. The young woman who has gone away, usually to marry but occasionally to work, does not slack off like her brothers and is almost never accused of immoral behavior. There are some rare exceptions. In Letter 11 ("A Young Girl Must Be Careful"), a mother writing from Lutsk tries to warn her unmarried American daughter about dishonorable suitors (her daughter replies that she's learned by watching what has happened to other girls and that God will protect her). Other letters target married daughters who are accused of succumbing to the lure of secular entertainments and neglecting their families. Letter 12 ("Please Come Visit") reverses the usual parent-child role by having a daughter hector a mother who is not living up to societal expectations. Rivke's mother hasn't provided any material support, and she has embarrassed her daughter in front of the in-laws by never visiting.

Acculturation also has its effect on parent-child relations. Perhaps the most dramatic example is an exchange of letters between parents and a son who is serving in the Russian Army at the start of the Russo-Japanese War (Letters 13–14, "We Live in Great Anxiety"). The guilt-inducing worry in the letter from the parents is already familiar to us. It is the son's reply that illustrates the particularly modern dimension of this correspondence. Yoyl Moyshe reports himself to be just fine. In fact he's excited, and very patriotic. His letter beautifully portrays a young man caught between Jewish behavioral patterns (he knows how to dig at his parents, even as he reassures them) and Russian ideas of manliness and heroism in battle.

Letters

1: Matisyahu and His Son[i]

Dear Son!

In the last month, we have already written you three letters and have not had the good fortune to have received a reply to any of them. We are sick with worry. I and your mother—may she live—cannot rest for a moment because of our great sorrow and grief. We cannot believe that such a long silence on your part is without a good reason, so this makes us very uneasy and our imaginations have given rise to various scenarios that we can't bring ourselves to put down on paper. In any case, your torturing us with your silence is a great injustice. If—God forbid—you've met with misfortune, you should have notified us right away. Maybe we can be of assistance to you. In the meantime, your not writing is the biggest misfortune for us because we imagine that the worst has happened. Therefore, we sincerely beg of you, that if our health and life is precious to you—and this we don't doubt for a second—you must write us the truth about what is going on with you and not hide anything from us.

Your father,
Matisyahu

[i] Miller, E. *Miller's nayer brifenshteller in tsvey theyl*, 9–11.

2: Matisyahu and His Son, reply

Dear Parents!

In reply to your last letter, I can tell you that in reality, your fear was not without foundation. My not replying to your recent letters was not some sort of caprice on my part or sheer fancy, but was due to a certain important reason, which I expect, you yourself should understand. No doubt you recall that when I was visiting you last time, I told you that I didn't feel well and also that I had been consulting with different doctors and that I was even thinking of going abroad for the summer. And exactly a month ago, my illness suddenly got worse and took a very intense and dangerous form, and my wife and the whole family were confused and didn't know what to do, whether to write you the truth or not. I myself lost consciousness and didn't know what was happening to me.

The situation was so bad that at the end of last week, my wife was about to telegraph you that you should come because the illness had taken a dangerous turn. But thank God, there was a turning point that very evening and the situation improved. And today, I got out of bed and my very first task was to write you this letter to let you know that your son is alive and, with God's help, will live.

Your son,
Gamliel

3: Mother's Condition Is Hopeless[i]

Dear Sister!

In the last few days an acquaintance passing through told me very sad details about the state of our dear mother's health: that her stay in V___ hasn't brought her much in the way of improvement in health, and that she is feeling very weak, and looks really terrible, as well. This news made me sick with worry, and my heart is broken that I can't see, with my very own eyes, how mother is. Therefore, I am turning to you with the suggestion that you should take all measures that are possible for you to improve the state of our dear mother's health. You should consult with the best doctors in the city. Maybe it would be a good idea to travel abroad with her. On my part, I am prepared to take on all the expenses. I deeply regret that it isn't possible for me to be at her side. But I am ready to provide as much money as needed as long as it can help her. In the meantime, I am asking you to send me honest reports about the health of our dear mother, for which I will be very grateful to you.

Your brother,
Shimen

[i] Miller, E. *Miller's nayer brifenshteller in tsvey theyl*, 13–17.

4: Mother's Condition Is Hopeless, reply

Dear Brother!

In your last letter, you demanded, my dear brother, that I write you the truth about the state of health of our dear mother. And to my deep regret, I will tell you that the sad news you received from your acquaintance about the situation of Mother's illness is true. We have done everything in our power to help her but there is nothing that can be done. And her condition grows worse from day to day. Also, about your suggestion that we should travel with her abroad, we've already given this a lot of thought, but the local doctors have told us that it would be pointless, and from what they say, we can expect a catastrophe any day now. This is the sad truth about our dear mother's condition that I have up until now kept hidden from you. But now I find it necessary to reveal everything to you so that you should know how things are. Maybe you can figure out a way to come and see her, because God knows, if you do not come as soon as possible, it might be too late . . .

Your sister, who writes to you with a broken heart
and eyes filled with tears,
Leah

5: Mother's Condition Is Hopeless, another reply

Esteemed Brother!

I will tell you the truth: I didn't want to write this letter to you, and shouldn't have, because you don't deserve to be written to. But because my head is spinning right now on account of the bad condition of our mother, I won't be diplomatic. Aside from that, in this letter I will express my great anger and resentment about your cold attitude toward the illness of our dear mother, because truly, this is a big disgrace on your part, and a terrible insult toward our mother. For more than two years she's been deathly ill and you haven't found it necessary to come to visit her, to see how she is and what is happening with her, while at the same time, every year you have found it possible to travel to various dachas[i] and baths. Aside from this, during the entire time that Mother has been ill, you haven't given a thought to whether she needed material support, and the whole time we haven't seen a tsebrokhenem groshen [broken cent] from you. You have dumped everything on me. I'm the one who has to sit day and night at the side of the invalid, the one who has to summon doctors, make frequent appointments, take her to V_____, and fill the most expensive prescriptions in existence. Everything falls on me, a sick, ordinary woman, and you, the boy, the future heir and kaddish,[ii] the wealthy success of the family, the eldest son for whom Mother sacrificed herself her entire life, you—you're exempt from everything, you're free of all the trouble and financial obligation. But now, when you've heard by accident that we don't have long to suffer from Mother anymore; now that her hours are numbered, you have shown up with your goodness and open hand. But you're too late ... it's now too late.... The patient is quiet and at rest and no longer needs any help....

Your sister,
Devoyre

ⁱ Country vacation houses.
ⁱⁱ The reference is to the Mourners' Kaddish, traditionally said by male mourners for eleven months after the death of a close relative. The birth of a son was an assurance that this prayer would be said for the parents, hence the name, which in this case doesn't refer to the prayer but to the person who will eventually say it.

6: Send Me Money for Decent Clothingⁱ

Warsaw, B' Bekhukosay [be-khukotay]ⁱⁱ 1888

Shalom to my beloved father, my great teacher, the noble, shining star of our generation, Moyshe Birenboym.ⁱⁱⁱ

I am writing to inform you, dear father, that yesterday, I arrived safely at my destination, and my dear uncle welcomed me with all-embracing love and honor, and also gave me my own room in which to sit and study. I am very happy that I came here because I will be able to achieve the goal that I have striven for all my life. Also, all the children of the house love me a lot. They go around with me in a very brotherly way. They can hardly be without me for a minute, and keep asking me what I want, what I have asked for and requested. I hope that in the course of time I will achieve great results and that you will be happy with your son and will have pleasure from him, amen.

Now, I am asking you, dear Father, to demonstrate your good heart and send me money so that I can buy decent clothing in order that I can be among people and be the equal of respectable people. That is also very educational, but I am embarrassed to go among people in ripped clothing. I also need a few rubles for different bikher and sforim^{iv} because without tools there is no master craftsman, and without sforim, one can't study. I expect that you will grant my request quickly and *will immediately send me everything I need. Your son who respectfully awaits your reply,*

Sholem Birenboym

ⁱ Fridman, *Der nayer praktisher brifenshteller*, 31. Dov Arye Fridman (1845–1920) was also the author of books on arithmetic and bookkeeping, as well as a Hebrew primer.

ⁱⁱ Reference to the Torah portion and Haftarah for the 27th of Iyar, Lev. 25:1–27:34 and Jer. 16:19–17:14.

ⁱⁱⁱ An example of a formal, flowery Hebrew salutation. This letter is full of Hebrew words, as befits a young, educated man. Some Hebrew words are glossed in Yiddish in the original.

^{iv} Secular books and books with religious content.

7: Buy Books, Get Clothes, Pursue Wisdomⁱ

Lublin, the 2nd of Av, 1889

Peace be unto to my dear and esteemed son, Sholem, may his light shine.

Your letter gladdened my heart because it has convinced me that you are traveling on the path of good and righteousness that is pleasing to both God and man and that you are diligent in your studies. May G-d grant that your heart will always be devoted to God and that you will hasten to the gates of the Torah with all your heart and soul, because these days, the Torah is the best merchandise and a corpse is better than a person with no faith, as our sages say, blessed be their memory. You should also make an effort to learn something practical, that is, you should not take the path of many young men who study only so that they can show off their own virtues and accomplishments. The Torah is not precious to them at all; they just want to make a name for themselves. Therefore, [when you study Torah] you should study in order to know the law, that is, the six orders of the Talmud, and the commentaries. You can also study other disciplines,ⁱⁱ but don't be distracted from your lessons. The other disciplines are also essential, and without them, nowadays, a rabbi can't succeed. If only all the rabbis had learned the language of the land, they would be able to speak with the important officials rather than stand there as if mute and the honor of the Torah would not be dragged down to the bottom of hell. And now, my dear son, I am sending you a couple of outfits, an under-kapoteⁱⁱⁱ and a great-

coat so that you can be among people. As you wrote in your letter, you
will also receive a few rubles to buy bikher and sforim that you need for
your studies. In any case, just make sure that you don't waste time on
foolishness, and don't forget to write me frequent letters, because it is my
greatest desire and joy to read your letters. Your father, who loves you
with all his heart and awaits your letters.

Borekh Bar Shimen Zak

ⁱ Fridman, *Der nayer praktisher brifenshteller*, 32–33.
ⁱⁱ Secular subjects.
ⁱⁱⁱ A *kapote* was an ankle-length coat, fitted to the waist. A long shirt
   was worn underneath.

8: Beloved Child, Study Yiddish and Russianⁱ

Dear and beloved son,

*Yesterday I received a letter from dear uncle. He wrote me that you are,
thank God, in good health, and that you are treading the proper and
preordained path, that you are not spending your time frivolously, but
only in study and writing. Oh! How lucky I am to have such a son. I
haven't stopped rejoicing about this happy news. May the Eternal One
see to it that I will always have such joy and that you will thoroughly
fulfill God's wishes and do good, and that the Eternal One will always
be with you. Doing good is the foundation of being a human being
because without this, man is just like a senseless animal. There is only
one thing that I ask of you: put aside 1 or 2 hours a day to learn how
to write Yiddish and Russian, because this is essential in commercial
business. Those who can't write are not suited to any business. And so,
please, dear child, see to it that you learn those languages and how to
do arithmetic. Also, please, devoted son, write letters to me often about
how your health is, about your writing and studying, and write about
everything. Write proper letters and you will gladden the hearts of your
loving parents. I have sent you via the bearer of this letter a silk hat and
a few rubles for small expenses. Even though it is only a small present,
you should value it as if it were the biggest present, because it was sent to
you by your parents who wish you well and hope to eventually send big-
ger presents and to hear from you and be gladdened by your letters . . .*

ⁱ H. Poliak-Gilman, *Der nayer obraztsover brifenshteller*, 3–4.

9: Truth Rises To the Top Like Oil on Water[i]

With great joy to my beloved father!

Dearest Father and devoted teacher and close friend,

With your letter of last week you made me very sad. It doesn't bother me that you accuse and shame me in the letter. Even if you had accused and shamed me even more and preached morality to me even more, every word would have been as sweet as honey to me, because every father has the obligation to instruct his child in the path of righteousness. As King Solomon said, when a child cries in his youth, he will walk on the righteous path in adulthood.[ii] But one thing does bother me, Father, and that is that I think that when you wrote me that letter, you were angry, and that this caused harm to your health. Why do you need to believe the slander and gossip that this person told you? What happened is that before he left, he came to me and asked me to loan him two rubles, with the plan that when he got home, he would send the money back to me by mail. But I know him: when he takes, you never get it back. I didn't want to give it to him, and so when he got home, he immediately went to you and slandered me. Everything he says is untrue. You can write to Uncle and ask about me, because truth rises to the top like olive oil on water. As I write these words to you, I am imagining you just as if you were standing in front of me, and I ask you if you really believe such things about me? You taught me that Jerusalem and all its inhabitants were destroyed on account of slander and gossip. I am asking you, please from now on, don't write such things, only happy things, and I too will be happy. Please fulfill the request of your obedient son,

Isak Shenker

[i] Poliak-Gilman, *Der nayer obraztsover brifenshteller,* 27.

[ii] Possibly a reference to Proverbs 22:6: Train a lad in the way he ought to go/ He will not swerve from it even in old age (*The Writings: Kethubim,* 237).

10: Your Letter Did Not Bring Us Any Pleasure[i]

Volkovishki, May 6, 1903.

Beloved son, Shloyme!

Your letter did not bring us any pleasure. Don't think that we expected anything else from you—we always said that this would be how your

quest would end. You have frittered away your time and our health!
What are you running after? Do you lack for anything in your parents'
home or have we ever asked you to earn money? We always told you:
stay at home, educate yourself, look after the business, and get out
of your head this fantasy about earning money, independence, and a
free life. But you were stubborn and went off. Nu, what do you have
to say now? It looks like in the future you'll be careful. We wonder
only why you are so foolish and are even now still asking, "Where
should I go and what should I do?" Come home, to your parents.
Turn to them and do what they tell you to do. We are sending you
fifteen rubles in this letter for travel expenses and to put an end to all
this foolishness.

Your parents,
Ezriel and Toybe Pozen

ⁱ Bloshteyn, *Nayer Bloshteyn's briefenshteler*, 31.

11: Beware of Men in Americaⁱ

Lutsk, June 28, 1898

Khanele, my child!

I have received your letter of June 15. I kissed the paper on which I rec-
ognized my daughter's handwriting, I even kissed the envelope with its
American stamp.

The American stamp! It made me realize that my daughter, my
sweet Khanele, is in America, on the other side of the ocean, at the end
of the world. When did I ever imagine that my beloved child would end
up so far away from me that I would lose the hope of seeing her?

But no! I won't think of such things. I will hope that I will yet live
to see my daughter at least one more time, to hug her and kiss her pretty
cheeks one more time . . .

You have delighted me, my child, with the news that you are, thank
God, in good health, and that you hope to find your good fortune in
the new world, because you are being courted by many gallant young
gentlemen.

To tell the truth, the expression "many gallant young gentlemen"
leaves a bad taste in my mouth. I would have been more pleased if you
had written me that one gallant young man was seeking to win your

love, because from many young gentlemen a young girl's head can spin, so that she doesn't know what to do, whom to choose from among them. My child! Do you understand that a young girl must be careful these days when she is surrounded by so many suitors? Are you familiar with the sort of people that most of these suitors tend to be?

I must admit that I have just asked you a stupid question. How would you know about such things? You are still a young child, you were brought up in a small shtetl, and you are still unskilled in the ways of the wider world, so I consider it my responsibility, my child, to make you aware of a few important matters that can help you protect yourself against great misfortune. You should know, my daughter, that big-city young gentlemen are not stingy with their compliments to a pretty girl. Most of them do not really mean the words that come out of their mouths, so you shouldn't believe every one of them. Even if one of them kneels before you and swears that his love for you is great and eternal, you should thoroughly, very thoroughly investigate whether his vow is true, because there are many scoundrels in the world who, in order to attain their own dark ends will not hesitate to swear to anything.

And when you are finally convinced that a young man sincerely loves you and truly intends to marry you, you must first of all know how to deal with him. Don't give yourself over completely into his hands. You must use all your resources to make sure that he won't lose respect for you, because love without respect will very quickly come to an end. He must respect you and this you can only pull off if you hold him at a certain distance from yourself.

These sorts of things can't be written about in detail. But I believe that a smart child like you will understand the sense of my words.

I wait with the greatest impatience to hear news of your engagement to a fiancé who is worthy of possessing you. Write to me often, my daughter, very often, so that with your letters you will delight your mother, who thinks always only of you.

Devoyre

---

[i] Shaykevitsh, *Shomer's briefenshteler*, 31–33.

12: Please Come Visit[i]

Warsaw, August 12, 1894

Honor to my dear parents![ii]

First, I can tell you, my dear parents, that this month, praised be G-d, I have been fortunate to finish kest.[iii] When you, my dear parents, see what my father-in-law, may he live, has already, blessed be G-d, set us up with, you would certainly take great pleasure that you won't have to pay for any of it. Dear Father-in-law and Mother-in-law have rented an apartment for us and bought furniture as a gift to remember them by. (There is nothing more I could ask of them, God forbid. I have no complaints.) They have more than done their duty. But now may G-d make them happy and also bless us with a good livelihood so that we won't need theirs. My dear husband and my two children, may they live, Moyshele and Khanele, send you their very loving regards and wish you health, happiness, and a long life.

Dear Mother! I must mention to you that it would be right and proper if you would come for at least a couple of weeks, to convince people, especially my father- and mother-in-law, that you take an interest in me and also in our children, to the extent permitted by your circumstances. Aside from this, I would really like to see you.

Your daughter, who loves you with all her heart,
Rivke Ehrlikh

[i] Gorodinski, *Gorodinski's korrespondent: Der nayer brifenshteller. Der postalion*, 1.

[ii] This letter has many Hebrew words and a couple of Russian ones.

[iii] Room and board provided to a newly married couple by one or the other set of parents for a specific number of years determined as part of the marriage agreement. During the period of kest, the young man would study or prepare to set himself up in business.

13: We Live in Great Anxiety[i]

14 July 1904

Dear beloved son Yoyl Moyshe Kostetski!

Ever since we accompanied you to the Zdolbonov railway station, the tears have not dried from our eyes. We live in great anxiety, nothing in the world can make us forget you. If you saw your mother, you already wouldn't recognize her. Imagine, beloved son, compared to her, I'm a hero, my heart is full to overflowing, and yet I still have to give her strength.[ii] *Sometimes she looks so terrible that I am simply afraid to leave her alone. So, dear child, we ask you, please, write to us about your health and courage and you will bring back our courage until God has mercy on us and brings you back to us.*

From us,
Your father Yerakhmiel and your mother Khane

[i] Poliak-Gilman, *Der nayer obraztsover brifenshteller*, 44–46.

[ii] As in Letters 1–2, the mother is depicted as falling apart, as opposed to the (relatively) strong father, a situation that can be presumed to reflect both new and old conventions about gender.

14: We Live in Great Anxiety, reply

8 August 1904, Tshifu[i]

Dear and highly esteemed parents!

What did you want from me with your letter? Until now, I have been cheerful and happy, and your letter caused me so much pain that it is impossible for me to bear. Why are you carrying on this way? Why do you allow yourselves these fantasies? I am, thank God, not doing badly. In fact, nothing has happened to me. I am healthy and feel, blessed be God, in top condition. I have everything, do not lack for anything. At the end of July, we had a battle. The Japanese advanced on our right flank and our regiment repelled them in such a way that they are thankful to be alive. Since then, it has been so quiet for our regiment that you can't imagine. The officers treat us as if they were our own brothers. So, beloved parents, please don't worry and don't be sad. You are squandering your health needlessly and have made me anxious as well. Be cheerful and happy and I will soon write you another letter.

From me, your son,
Yoyl Moyshe Kostetski

[i] Zhifu (Chinese), Chifu (Russian). Chinese port near Port Arthur. The dates place the letter right before the siege of Port Arthur

(August 19, 1904–January 2, 1905), which resulted in a big Japanese victory. The brivnshteler appeared in 1904, before the conclusion of the battle. The manual's subtitle, "With Important Letters from Manchuria and Japan," nicely showcases an attempt to reflect current events.

◦⅌

PARENTS AND CHILDREN: AMERICA

Introduction

The brivnshteler in Eastern Europe focused on parents anxious about their children's well-being. In America, it is children who are anxious about their parents.

From the first moments of their arrival in New York, the goal of most brivnshteler children is to make their parents feel better. The American brivnshtelers of Shomer and Ben-Zion Eisenstadt devote considerable space to this aspect of writing home, probably because they anticipated their readers' desire for it. In Eisenstadt's manual, a newly arrived immigrant named Zusman Lipshits writes to his parents to tell them about his first impressions and also about how much he loves them. The whole voyage, he tells his mother and father, he thought about their "hot and boiling tears" and awaited the moment when he would finally be able to tell them he had arrived safely.[21] Zusman's second letter describes more of his journey (for instance, seasickness encountered and overcome). But here too, absent parents play a prominent role, and not only for Zusman. While still on the ship, he made friends, and when they said *le-khayim* ["To life!"]—the happy group, apparently, had time for more than one drink—they toasted their "warm and devoted families in Russia."[22] One more detail, though perfectly plausible, is no less suited to assuage parental fears: Zusman is boarding with Moyshe Finkelstein, a landsman.[23] Even life on the ship and in the big city has its familiar aspects.

Leah, a character in Shomer, takes the same approach. "If only my letter had wings and could get to you in a few minutes—I know how anxious you are about me," she writes in her first letter.[24] Like Zusman, she lets her parents know that she is in familiar hands, picked up from Ellis Island, "the place where all immigrants from third class go now" by a blank space to be filled by the name of "a friend (or relative)." Leah's parents should not worry because she will be fine: "Like thousands of other girls, I'll earn money."[25] The next letter is a response from Leah's father. He reiterates his anxieties, and notes, like the father of the young draftee into the tsarist army we met in the previous section, that paternal sufferings are nothing compared to those of the maternal heart: "As a man, I could keep all my pain inside," he writes, "but about your mother, don't ask."[26]

Leah's second letter continues to assuage parental fears. "When you arrive in New York you see so many acquaintances from home you think you're still in the shtetl,"[27] she says, echoing the conceit in the second half of Sholem Aleichem's *Motl, Peysi dem khazns* (Motl, Peysi the cantor's son; 1907–8), where half the population of Motl's shtetl seems to have turned up in New York. Leah once again assures her parents that she will work—working in America is no *shande* (shame)—and make money. Leah's optimism is crafted for her parents: as we will see in her letter in "Imagining America," she also provides a much darker picture of immigrant life. But that letter is intended for her girlfriend.

Concerned children continue to reassure their parents even beyond their first days in America. Letter 1 ("Children in America Ask for Pictures of Their Parents in Europe") is one of a pair of letters written long after the children have arrived in the United States: Eliezer notes that his sister Khane hasn't seen their parents in eight full years. In his first letter, Eliezer asks his parents to send photos of themselves—only then will his single room feel like home. The second letter effusively thanks the parents, with many references to kisses and tears.[28]

In Eisenstadt's brivnshteler, logically enough, only the children write letters: his manual was published in New York with Jewish immigrants in mind. Shomer dispenses with this convention, despite the somewhat unlikely scenario of a father in the old country making use of a brivnshteler published in America. It is possible that he envisioned selling his book in Vilna.[29] But he was also a novelist, and in his parent-child correspondence, the voices of parents establish an emotional context, and remind children what their mothers and fathers are thinking. "Your letter," writes one of Shomer's fathers, "makes us remember how you were ripped away from us and carried off so far away to a foreign and unknown world. . . . We have seen how the best children have become foreign to their parents. . . . My good, dear Markus, don't learn from such children!"[30]

Money is a major theme of parent-child relations, just as it was a major push toward emigration. In Eisenstadt's world, a happier place than Shomer's, children tend to be reliable and thoughtful. We see in Letter 2 ("This Is for Me as Sacred as a Tithe") how Aleksander Gordon held off writing for a few weeks because he wasn't working and didn't want to cause his parents anxiety. Now that he has a job, he happily explains that his pay is called "wages" (he uses the English word), his boss is honest, and he anticipates a raise. He will send his parents half his pay to thank them for their devotion to his education and his future.[31] In the very next letter, he encloses forty rubles.

Not all children are, or remain, so good about sending money home. Shomer provides a letter from "an old father" whose Dovidl has forgotten him, doesn't write, and doesn't send money. "I write out the three words, 'Dovid my son,' and tears flow from my eyes." The son, writes the old man, not only has a duty to help his father, who is too weak to earn a living, but should keep in mind that he too will grow old.[32] The occasional exchange has a nasty tinge. A pair of letters in yet another American brivnshteler (reprinted in a manual published in Vilna five years later) features a son in Chicago and a father in New York. Ezriel Pozen complains to his son that he hasn't written and hasn't sent money. The reply from Shloyme is not in the least contrite. Why didn't his father say he needed money? How is he, in Chicago, supposed to know what is going on in New York? What is he, a prophet? He is sending fifty dollars.[33]

Problems with money arise between parents and children in real family letters as well. In the Zimman family correspondence, the grain merchant Tsvi Dov complains to his son Meyshe Abbe (known as Morris in America), that another son, Yitskhok (or Izzie), has not yet reimbursed him for funding his voyage to America:

> But please, dear Morris, speak with him, and tell him that he should reimburse us little by little for the travel expenses. Let's not be worse than the peasants. Every *sheygets* [non-Jewish boy] reimburses his parents for his travel expenses in the very first year. And [Izzie] is already 3 years in America. But he sends us only jokes and writes like a smart aleck in every postcard.[34]

Another problem is marriage. The children are getting married, and the parents are not present. The pain of separation is echoed on both sides of the correspondence. In Eisenstadt, Yankev's heart is broken because his parents will not personally escort him to the *khupe* (wedding canopy); he asks them to send a written blessing.[35] Yoysef Harkav tells his parents in detail about his engagement, in which their presence is invoked. His description is full of familiar details and hints at the wealth and prominence of the family he is joining:

> A fine and intelligent group of people gathered in the home of my fiancée's brother, who is one of the most respected Jews in Brooklyn, and celebrated, quite genteelly, until two in the morning.

> All of our relatives and *landslayt* [people from our hometown] who were present at the *tnoyim* [engagement ceremony] lifted their silver cups and said a loud le-khayim for your health, dear parents. Sight unseen, they blessed you with the threefold blessings in the Torah.[36]

Letter 3 ("A Daughter Informs Her Parents of Her Engagement"), from Shomer, covers similar ground. Bella announces that she's become a bride, and wishes her parents a *mazel tov*. Who is the groom? Bella may be in America, but her husband-to-be is Lazar Grinblum from Bobruisk. Her parents can check out his family with their Bobruisk acquaintances, where they will find every precondition satisfied: not only is Lazar's father a rabbi, but he was at one time (the past tense presumably necessary to explain the son's presence in America) a very wealthy man. Bella's parents can be joyful over their daughter's marriage, even though, as they are quick to mention in their reply, they will not be leading her to the wedding canopy.[37] Of course, knowing the person your child is marrying is not guaranteed to make a parent happy. "Never before have you caused me such pain as you have with the letter that I received from you yesterday," writes a different father. "You write that you are in love with Kheykl Borgman's daughter and that you are engaged to marry her. The news hit me like a thunderbolt. . . . You are well aware of the difference between your family and Borgman's."[38]

When daughters are unmarried, the well-known moral hazards of America create a different sort of concern. Eisenstadt's Rokhl Rabinovits tries to reassure her father, telling him that even in "free America" ("free" in this sense meaning libertine) she maintains his honor by only associating with the most honest and best people.[39] A more complicated picture emerges in Letter 4 ("We Hear That You Are Frequently Seen at

Dances and Picnics") from Shomer. There, Yitskhok Funk tells his party-loving (*freylekhe*) daughter Reyzele that her parents' hearts are broken. Following the pattern already familiar to us, someone has informed on her: a "trustworthy person" has seen her at "dances, masquerades, and picnics." Yitskhak Funk goes to some lengths to establish his credentials as a modern man. He "is not one of those people who say a girl is forbidden to speak a few words to a man"; indeed, he concedes a woman's right to enjoy herself outside the family. But young men have something else on their minds and can drag a girl "into a swamp."[40]

Like the authors of European brivnshtelers, Eisenstadt and Shomer are mostly concerned with grown children. While Shomer refers to a bar mitzvah boy and Eisenstadt provides a model for a bar mitzvah speech,[41] these acknowledgments of American practices don't focus on bringing up children. The single exception is Letter 5 ("Advice on Child-Rearing"). The text, which we can understand as representing Shomer's own beliefs, dispenses altogether with the East European emphasis on education. The putative writer is a grandmother responding to her daughter's complaints about her wild child, Yankele, who runs around on roofs and fights in the street. Asserting that a boy has to know how to fight, advising, even, that he take up gymnastic exercises, the grandmother combines diminutive-heavy Yiddish with an unexpectedly clear grasp of the realities of New York streets.[42]

Letters

1: Children in America Ask for Pictures of Their Parents in Europe[i]

My dear parents!

It's already been several times, dear parents, that in my letters I have asked you to do me a big favor and send me your beautiful pictures (photographs).[ii] I was also asking for this on behalf of dear sister Khane, may she live, who hasn't seen your radiant likeness for 8 years, and I don't know and can't begin to understand why you don't respond to me about this in your letters to me, my dear parents! If to you it is a mere trifle and an insignificant matter, which, in your opinion, isn't worth writing about (and isn't worth the paper, ink, and time), well, for me and also for dear Sister, it is a matter of the greatest interest. Imagine the happiness it would bring me, if every day when I got out of bed, I could look at your dear pictures. I would no longer consider myself lonely in this big, wide country; I would feel at home if my dear, beloved parents' pictures decorated and illuminated my lonely little room.... The same goes for my dear sister, who would probably take great delight in the pleasure of having your beloved pictures in her house. And so, why won't you grant the wish of your children, whom you love and whom you want to be happy?

We hope that this won't take long and that we will have, in our homes, two beautiful and refined guests; that is, dear parents, your beautiful pictures, which are impatiently awaited.

Eliezer Kahan

ⁱ Eisenstadt, *Der moderner briffenshteller,* 46–48.
ⁱⁱ Here two different Yiddish words are used, with one in parentheses. The author uses the word *fotografyes* (photographs) to gloss the Yiddish word *bilder* (pictures).

2: "This Is for Me as Sacred as a Tithe"ⁱ

Dear Father and devoted Mother!

Even though I promised in my first letter to write you another letter immediately, I waited a few weeks because I really didn't have anything to write to you about until now, and if I had written you a letter telling you that here I came to the golden land and was going around unemployed, wasn't yet engaged in anything, and hadn't gotten a job, it would have no doubt caused you pain and sorrow. And so that's why I didn't hurry to write to you until now. Last week, thank God, I got a job, and today, the eighth day, I finally got my salary, or as they call it in America, "wages,"ⁱⁱ 9 dollars for the first week. And I hope to earn even more later because the virth (boss)ⁱⁱⁱ is a fine and honest man and treats his people very honestly.

Being aware of the great effort you, my dear parents, have expended on me my entire life, and not forgetting the great interest you have always taken in my future, educating me more than your circumstances and material resources merited, I have fulfilled my great duty, and from the money I have received for my work, I have taken half of it and put it aside for you, devoted parents. This is for me as sacred as a tithe and it really doesn't belong to me, but to you. I hope to save something for you every week, my dearest ones, and to send it to you every month.

Write to me, dear parents, about how you are doing and what has been happening since I left home.

Your most dutiful,
Aleksander Sender Gordon

[i] Eisenstadt, *Der moderner briffenshteller*, 43–45.

[ii] The English word "wages" is used.

[iii] The German word *Wirt* (owner) is given in misspelled, transliterated Yiddish and glossed as "boss" in English.

3: A Daughter Informs Her Parents of Her Engagement[i]

My dear, beloved parents!

At long last, I can send you the good news which you have so impatiently awaited.

I can send you the news that I have become the fiancée of a very respectable young man.

Mazel tov to you, dear parents!

I can imagine how surprised you are by my news and that you want to know who your son-in-law will be, and so I regard it as my responsibility to write to you about everything.

My fiancé's name is Lazar Grinblum and he is from the city of Bobruisk. You can inquire more about his family from your acquaintances in Bobruisk and you will soon be convinced that you don't need to be ashamed of your in-laws. His father, Rabbi Shmuel Grinblum, was once a very wealthy merchant and played a big role.[ii]

My fiancé is a young man, twenty-five years old. I wouldn't say that he is a heartthrob,[iii] but for me he is handsome enough.

He is a gentleman in the full sense of the word, considerably educated and a capable businessman.

He is employed in a lucrative business as a "salesman."[iv] That is, he travels around the nearby cities selling the merchandise that his principal[v] manufactures.

I met him at a dance and right away, the moment we met, we were attracted to each other with a pure, fiery love.

Father, Mother, I feel very lucky.

My fiancé is sending you a letter. He already loves you even though he doesn't know you in person.

You can rest assured that your devoted daughter will be one of the happiest people in the world.

Bella Bronshteyn

[i] Shaykevitsh, *Shaykevitsh'es nayer briefenshteler*, 70–71.
[ii] The author doesn't say in what.
[iii] In original: *bildshehner manspersohn*.
[iv] The English word "salesman" is used.
[v] The fiancé is a manufacturers' agent, representing specific manufacturers (principals) in a sales capacity.

4: We Hear That You Are Frequently Seen at Dances and Picnics[i]

My dear, devoted daughter . . .

From what I can see you have once again forgotten that you have parents, or you count yourself so lucky and are so happy with your new friends and acquaintances that for you, your parents no longer have any worth.

We, however, cannot forget that you are our daughter. We can't simply erase you from our hearts.

You don't want to write to us, you're too lazy to send a letter to the people whose blood flows in your veins.

But despite the fact that you don't write to us, we know what you are up to and how you are living. We know everything . . . and our hearts are broken, crushed, and bloodied.

Reyzele! A trustworthy person, one of our friends, has told us that you have been seen going around late at night with young men. You are seen very frequently at dances, masquerades, and picnics.

I won't tell you that it is sinful to go around with a young man or that it is wrong to go to a dance or other places of entertainment.

No, my daughter, you know me very well, and you know that I am not a fanatic. I don't belong to that class of people who believe that a woman's place is always at home and that she is forbidden to speak a few words to a man.

A woman has as much right to enjoy herself in the world as a man does. She doesn't need to flee from a man as if from a bloodthirsty beast.

But she must be much more cautious than a man in the way she lives and in society.

For, of course, nature has fashioned a woman differently from a man. Humankind has always accepted the rule that a woman must be virtuous, and that a woman who falls under suspicion is immoral. She is despised by everyone and decent society won't have anything to do with her.

Every pretty girl is surrounded by young men. To our great regret, the majority of young men are extremely depraved in this regard. They have destructive things on their mind and for them it is an easy matter to drag a naive girl into a swamp that she will never be able to escape. ... The same young men who shower a pretty girl with compliments and treat her to champagne and fancy treats despise a girl who lets herself be dragged into their net.

"Give the devil a hair from your head and you're putting your whole head into his hands," the world says and this is very true. Just let a girl show a young man too friendly a face, give him one finger, and she will fall entirely into his net.

And woe, a thousand times woe to the girl who has already fallen into the net of a heartless young man.

I don't need to tell you, my daughter, what awaits this girl. That these circumstances can bring her to the point where she becomes the murderer of her own child—this alone is already enough to frighten a smart child into fleeing from a sweet-talker as if from the fires of hell.

Will my words have any effect on you, Reyzele?

If yes, you will make us very happy. You will give new life to your worried parents, especially to your devoted father,

Yitskhok Funk

[i] Shaykevitsh, *Shaykevitsh'es nayer briefenshteler*, 116–118.

5: *Advice on Child-rearing*[i]

My dear, sweet daughter!

I received your dear letter with the greatest joy. You write me that you, your beloved husband, and your dear children are, thank God, healthy and happy. May God always make happy with such letters.

But one thing you wrote me about, my daughter, displeases me.

You write that your oldest boy, Yankele, may he live, is quite a scamp. He likes to climb up on roofs and fight with his comrades in the street and therefore you and your husband don't spare him any beatings.

This really upset me.

First of all, I regard it as the greatest stupidity when parents want to turn their small children into either peaceful doves or timid lambs. Man is neither a dove or a lamb. Man has been created to accomplish something in the world, and in his life, encounters all sorts of circumstances which demand that he display strength, make use of his own hands, and he is also sometimes forced to creep into dangerous places. And if he doesn't develop his strength in childhood, if he doesn't get used to creeping, jumping, and climbing into dangerous places, he will grow up to be a weak, timid creature, and later he will be afraid of his own shadow.

On the contrary, intelligent parents must accustom their children to fighting and to doing various gymnastic feats.

Imagine the situation of a person who falls into dangerous waters and doesn't know how to swim, or the predicament of a person who finds himself in a burning house and has to jump out of a window or jump over onto another roof. When people like this find themselves in unfortunate situations, they are lost, whereas a good swimmer or good jumper can easily save himself.

About the beatings that you don't spare your Yankele, I must tell you, children, that in my opinion, it is the greatest injustice for parents to hit their children in order to improve their behavior.

Beatings will only make a child nervous and arouse stubbornness in him. Kindness will improve even the worst child's behavior. When you treat a child kindly, a strict word will have much more effect on him than a hundred blows.

I hope that you will understand that I have given you some good advice and that you will heed the word of your devoted mother, who wishes you, your husband, and children only the best of luck,

Sonye

---

[i] Shaykevitsh, *Shaykevitsh'es nayer briefenshteler,* 119–120.

COURTSHIP AND MARRIAGE: RUSSIA

Introduction

A prime battleground of both emotion and modernity was courtship. By the middle of the nineteenth century, the institution of arranged marriage was beginning to modernize. The very early marriages characteristic of elite families (and bitterly resented by maskilim) were giving way to marriages contracted when the brides and grooms were in their early twenties. Rates of divorce and remarriage, both much higher among Jews than in the surrounding population, were in decline. ChaeRan Freeze, whose book on Jewish marriage and divorce is indispensible for understanding this important part of private life, notes the growing Jewish acceptance of the idea of "companionate marriage." Men and women coming of age toward the turn of the twentieth century sought affection and compatibility—in other words, love.[43]

The expectation of love, a precondition for courtship in general and brivnshteler courtship in particular, was a novelty not universally shared. In the opening scene of Avrom Goldfadn's musical satire *The Two Kuni Lemls*, written around 1880, the father of the marriageable heroine complains to his wife, "Just tell me this, my dear wife, before we got married, did we also play at—what do they call it—at these love games? May God protect and defend me! I'm telling you, I didn't love you then, and I don't love you now either."[44] The satire depends on the audience sharing the notion that the father's attitude is hopelessly outmoded. The memoirist Puah Rakovska reports more seriously of her own father's response, around 1888, when she announced that she wanted a divorce. "And who ever heard of a wife who doesn't want to live with her husband, especially when you have two children with him—because you don't love him? A strange motive: Yashka and Stashke love each other, but Jews? . . . You get married, you have children, and you live."[45]

Suppressed as it may have been in practice, romantic love did find expression in literature that Jews knew well. Love, and even passion, plays a role in Bible stories. A more secular view of romance is displayed in Elye Bokher's *Bove- bukh* (The book of Bovo, 1541), a Yiddish recreation of an Italian epic replete with battles, palace intrigue, and a love scene in the forest.[46] The *Bove- bukh*, popularly called the *Bove-mayse*, was one of the few secular books that, as David Roskies notes, was commonly found in people's homes before the explosion of Yiddish popular literature in the mid-nineteenth century.[47] People didn't accept Bovo's adventures as real or relevant to their lives, as witnessed by the Yiddish expression *bobe mayse* (grandma's tale), a dismissive reinterpretation of the title—but they did read them.

It fell to Yiddish popular literature to combine romance with characters who are demonstrably Jewish, particularly when the settings become close to being, or actually are, contemporary. The novelist Ayzik Meyer Dik was the master of what Roskies calls the "bourgeois romance," which featured the triumph of true love over parental opposition.[48] Women were the primary audience. Abraham Mapu's Hebrew novel *Ahavat Tsiyon* (Love of Zion) exerted a similar fascination for educated men, or, as Olga Litvak puts it, "The libidinal appeal of the plot unbuttoned the mind of even the most abstemious reader."[49] In his memoirs, the educator and brivnshteler author Avraham Paperna is more circumspect about the book's erotic potential. But even many years later, his recollections of the novel are intense: "All the trials, all the suffering of Amnon and Tamara only strengthen and intensify their love. And we, the readers, share their sufferings; we grieve with their grief and cry with their tears. But God is merciful, 'Indeed, with Him, there are no untruths,' and in the end our 'dear and sweet' lovers, to our joy, unite for unending bliss."[50]

Another source for knowledge about romance was literature in German and Russian. In her book *Reading Jewish Women*, Iris Parush notes the wide-ranging acquaintance with foreign languages and literatures among elite women, even those from religious families.[51] A survey of Jewish library use in St. Petersburg in 1905 showed that the interest in Russian literature was not confined to wealthy people: seamstresses and other non-elite but obviously literate workers were borrowing novels by Tolstoy, Turgenev, and Dostoevsky, as well as poetry by Pushkin.[52] Writing at the turn of the twentieth century, the memoirist Pauline Wengeroff recalls that as a girl, she read the *Bove bukh* (which she calls "Bobe-meisse," though she supplies the explanation "Bove the Prince" in parentheses) and the *Thousand and One Nights* (*Tsenture-Venture*, another classic of Yiddish translation). But by the time of her engagement in 1848, she and her girlfriends were enthusiasts of the supremely romantic Schiller.[53]

How this romantic reading played out in a mid-nineteenth-century Jewish arranged marriage can be seen in a different part of Wengeroff's memoirs. Her sister became engaged in 1848 and immediately became the recipient of correspondence that Pauline assessed somewhat acerbically: "The letters were not without a certain inner sympathy, attachment, and love, but they were hardly effusive."[54] Presumably she wanted more for herself. A year later, when a match was contracted for her as well, the devotee of Schiller was primed for feelings of love.

Historians of Jewish private life have noted similar psychological states among young people during this transitional period. David Biale points to the maskil Avraham Ber Gottlober, who writes that he fell in love with his future bride during their "exchange of formulaic letters" even before they met.[55] Marion Kaplan, examining the correspondence of engaged couples in late nineteenth-century Germany, comments that "romantic notions may have been easier to conjure up when partners hardly knew each other."[56] As for Pauline Wengeroff, so important to her was the first letter that she received from her husband-to-be that even as a grandmother, after the marriage had gone painfully bad, she copies it (or reimagines it) in full.

People with the linguistic and cultural skills to write their own courtship letters clearly did so. Puah Rakovska, for example, not only carried out a Hebrew correspondence with a fiancé she disliked (the idea, promoted by her family, was to display her erudition to his family), but also a secret correspondence with a young relative whom she loved.[57] Other people were less secure. They got their help from the courtship section of brivnshtelers, which, from the time of their appearance in the nineteenth century, served as yet another democratizing tool for those who aspired to live up to upper-middle-class mores. One Yiddish folk song has a working-class young man assuring the object of his affections that he will soon be sending her better love letters because he has purchased a brivnshteler. She is happy to hear it because her mistress's daughter has "the same book."[58]

The kind of help the letter manuals offered can be seen in the letters presented here. Letter 1 ("Highly Esteemed Bride!"), from 1890, is intended for a groom-to-be to write soon after the engagement ceremony. Passion is present, but kept decorously in check: while the word comes up three times in one form or another, it is combined either with "innocent" (once) or "friendship" (twice). The focus on friendship ("Oh dear friend and bride!") reflects the triumph, or at least the acceptance, of companionate marriage. Readers sensitive to cliché will note the metaphor of the feeble pen that cannot express the writer's feelings, which also appears twice. But the letter is conscious of some specific Jewish complications as well. In all the intensity of his love, the young man would prefer it if the bride and groom could meet in person to get to know each other before the wedding.

The expectation of romance and the ideal of a companionate marriage form the subtext of a lot of courtship correspondence. In *E. Miller's nayer brifenshteller in tsvey theyl* (1911), Sore Shneurzohn is surprised at how coldly her fiancé Dovid behaved to her during his visit. While "coldness" comes up often in non-Jewish letter manuals that chart the progress, or deterioration, of courtship, Sore doesn't seem to be evoking that particular scenario: she seems simply to have expected a conversation more in line with the idea of passionate friendship. More troubling is that she found Dovid's conversation trivial. The only way out of that dilemma is the brivnshteler solution of a well-written letter. And indeed, after expressing her doubts, she reassures Dovid that his letter (signed "your best friend") has cleared everything up. She understands now that he is a strong character who doesn't like to speak of what is in his heart.[59]

While Sore may have made her peace with Dovid, *E. Miller's nayer brifenshteller* also provides a template for a different kind of solution. In the very next letter, a would-be groom named Yerukhem Fishelzohn apologizes to Fraulein Zonenshayn for not writing. Her father, he says, told him that in his very first letter he must declare his intentions, and he couldn't make such a life-changing decision. He suggests they meet again. She agrees. Despite her great respect for her father, "as a daughter of the 20th century" she can't accept that meeting two or three times is sufficient for such an important decision.[60]

A step beyond companionate marriage would be a declaration of burning passion for a young woman imagined as a kind of angelic being, a balm for the tormented masculine soul. To express that in written form it helped to have a model, which could come only from non-Jewish sources. Those sources were easy to come by. European and—closer to home, Russian—letter manuals specialized in romance at all its stages: declarations of love, proposals and responses to proposals, and reproaches for coldness. In the section "What Makes the Brivnshteler Jewish" we quoted one typical Russian love letter. Here is another one, from a different letter manual:

> I have long wanted to tell you about the burning attachment I feel for you, but every time, as soon as I open my mouth to confess to you, the words die on my lips and I become incapable of uttering a single word. But today, unable to hide any longer the passion that you have ignited in me, I entrust my pen to express my burning, sincere love for you. Yes, I love you, I adore you, and from the moment I met you I have had but one desire: to please you and to not be unworthy of casting at your feet my admiration and attachment. From your answer I await either my happiness or a sentence to a life full of bitterness and regret, because if you reject me there will be no comfort for me. . . . The indescribable charm of your speech, the rare qualities that Nature bestowed on you, the moral virtues united within you, all this made a profound impression on me. Every day I think only about you.[61]

The model put forward in this letter—the male in a life-or-death crisis; the woman as a paragon of virtue—owes a lot to European romanticism. It crosses into the brivnshteler, as it does into maskilic fiction, in varying degrees and combinations.[62] In Fridman's *Der nayer praktisher brifenshteller* (1889), Avrom writes to Rokhl: "It would be better if I could answer you with kisses and hugs. You are no earthly creature; you are a heavenly phenomenon. Your words are as sweet as honey, your language a string of pearls, your thoughts a well of life. I stand abashed before you, dear Rokhele! You are too exalted, too sublime for me."[63]

Fridman is not the only brivnshteler author to merge a modern, sentimental courtship with the language a young Jewish man might be comfortable using. In his 1901 bilingual manual, Gorodinski plays something of the same game. The opening letters of his "bride and groom" section begin in a modern way, assuming that the young man and the young woman have met somewhere on their own, perhaps even often. As in non-Jewish manuals on both sides of the Atlantic, the young woman is presumed to be unaware of the young man's feelings. He, on the contrary, is in the grips of something close to the romantic trope of love as madness. His opening line declares that he no longer has the strength to restrain his heart. Why not confess that he loves her forever? The Russian on the facing page adds that he loves her "madly." The Yiddish is not quite ready for madness, though it does mention love "to the grave" later on. In both versions, the young man emphasizes his failing struggle to control himself: he runs from place to place, but everywhere he meets her gaze.

Gorodinski's romantic hero may barely be in control, but his intentions are traditional. He is not proposing love itself, as is sometimes the case in Russian manuals, but marriage. Will she say yes? In the next letter, she does. In harmony, once again, with the conventions of non-Jewish manuals, her letter is more restrained. But one Jewish element slips past—the anxiety that is a specific feature of brivnshteler emotional life. In this case, while the young woman agrees that fate has brought the two of them together, her assent is colored by doubt: "may God forbid that we ever regret this."[64]

Not all letters presuppose a traditional match. Letter 2 ("Victory over Our Enemies") refers to obstacles that a young couple had to overcome—apparently, parental opposition. The triumphant groom uses the language of battle: there was a "terrible war," with "opponents" and "enemies" on all sides. But heart's desire has carried the day, and because of what bride and groom suffered together, the two of them are united in an "eternal bond." In other cases, relatives interfere in a more explicit way. Letter 3 ("Warning to a Sister Not to Take the Attentions of a Rich Boy Too Seriously") is a bit unusual in its revelation of class divisions, as a brother warns a sister not to get carried away about a suitor who is too rich. Another letter in the same manual has a young man trying to forestall his brother's match by telling him the young woman isn't rich enough.

While not all brivnshteler marriages are modern (arranged marriages are mentioned frequently), almost all references to the *shadkhn* (marriage broker) are satirical (Letter 4: "A Shadkhn Writes to a Widower about a Match"). Only in America, paradoxically, will the shadkhn be provided with model letters to ply his dwindling trade: here in the old country, brivnshtelers follow the longstanding Jewish tradition that declares him a figure of fun. Paperna's 1897 manual features a matchmaker proposing a bride with all the virtues (good, kind, religious, and due to inherit) to a man whose five children are all daughters.[65] While this is an old joke and its satire is underwhelming, later manuals can be brutal. The 1910 *Nayer Bloshteyn's briefenshteler* presents a ruthless exchange between Azriel Shvaynman (swine-man) and a matchmaker who says he's heard that Reb Azriel is offering a dowry of 30,000–40,000 rubles for his daughter. Is that because there's something wrong with her? And must the groom also have money? Shvaynman replies that he couldn't write earlier because his bookkeeper wasn't in and he himself can't write well. In other words, not only is he a rich boor—he is deficient in the one skill that the brivnshteler values most highly.[66]

Among the few serious matchmaking exchanges in an East European brivnshteler is a set of letters written between friends. Checking up on a matchmaker's work, Khayim asks his friend to have a look at the proposed in-laws. Depending on what he finds, the friend can choose among three alternative replies: (a) looks good; (b) can't say anything good so won't say anything; and (c) guess what? The girl's family has asked him to ask about you. The third reply, with its implication that a matchmaker has done something of value, suggests that such a happy outcome is atypical: "One has to admit, that once in a while a matchmaker can propose something reasonable."[67]

Where there is courtship, there are, inevitably, problems. Bernshteyn's 1912 brivnshteler takes up the typically Jewish problem of a young man who has gone to the city, leaving behind not only the shtetl but his shtetl sweetheart. She writes to him, but he doesn't respond. When eventually he feels he must respond to her, Bernshteyn provides him with some ideas:

> Dear beloved Rokhl!
>
> I can't find the words with which to defend myself—you are absolutely correct. It is true that I have received two letters from you and that I haven't answered them. But it would not be very clever on your part to conclude from this that I have become completely disinterested in my home town and my small-town girlfriends. Believe me, dearest, that the whole time I have lived here in the big city, I still haven't met a single person with whom I can be so close in life as I am with you.[68]

Scandal and divorce are rarely mentioned in brivnshtelers. Letter 5 ("She Is Not for You") is an exception. The son-in-law to whom the letter is addressed has abandoned the writer's daughter and their child and squandered her dowry. There are also modernizing issues: her family, with their traditional Jewish clothes, will never be "aristocratic" enough for him. Letter 6 ("To a Lover Who Has Gone Away"), from a 1904 bilingual Russian-Yiddish manual, takes the shock value up a notch. A young woman writes to her beloved "Mozes" (a very fancy name), who has left town and failed to write for two whole years. Mozes has just divorced his wife of three years, presumably because of the allure of his new cor-respondent. The would-be bride employs both threats (a match is being proposed for her) and a string of romantic clichés—she is, for example, so weakened by her troubles that she "barely has the strength to sign her name." Mozes responds with a declaration of undying love, but the reader interested in the outcome of this romance would find his answer predictive of trouble ahead. Though the "Bintl Brif" had not yet been invented—the scandal-filled advice column from the New York *Forverts* began appearing in 1906—a letter like this anticipates its unconstrained airing of domestic crises.

While husbands and wives often found themselves living apart, with the one exception of emigration to America, brivnshtelers don't provide many model letters for them. Letter 7 ("Congratulations on the Birth of Our Son") stands out for its portrayal of uncomplicated love within a marriage. In this short note, the husband writes a tender note to his wife after the birth of a child and asks that she write back to him "in her own hand."

Letters

1: Highly Esteemed Bride!ⁱ

Skvira, February 8, 1890

Highly esteemed and dear bride Miss Khane, may she live,

As I take my pen in hand to write you these lines, I think of the unspeak-ably happy seconds we spent together on the night of our engagement. I say "seconds" because every hour seemed as fleeting to me as a second. Oh, dear friend and bride! I am now about to write to you, or better said, converse with you in writing instead of in person, but I highly doubt that my feeble pen is capable of expressing my feelings. The results are quite different when such passionate, good friends have frequent op-portunities to talk to one another, exchange their thoughts. Then, they can get acquainted with each other's characters. But unfortunately, for us all of this is impossible and we must remain satisfied with writ-ten communications. Although this is indeed a tough challenge, dear bride, for both of us, because how is it possible with a pen to express the feelings and the pleasure that two such passionate yet innocently lov-

*ing friends can enjoy from a face-to-face conversation? It's impossible,
and therefore, we must, against our wills, compensate for our need with
letters. So, highly esteemed bride, I hope that I will at least have the
pleasure of frequent letters from you, which I hope you won't deny me.
But I also want to ask you to please give me your word that in your letters to me you won't strain and search for unusual expressions. May it
not be hard for you to honor my request. Just write in plain, ordinary
language and let me know about your dear state of health and how you
are spending your time. In a word, write me about everything, but just
plain and simple.*

Your highly esteemed bridegroom,
Dovid Kviker

[i] Goldshteyn-Gershonovitsh, *Yudish-daytsher morall brifenshteller*,
40–41. The author glosses daytshmerish terms for "bride," "lines,"
and "engagement" with equivalent words of Hebraic origin.

2: Victory over Our Enemies[i]

Highly esteemed bride!

*Forgive me, my dear, for not writing you a letter as soon as I arrived
here, as I promised you. The great good fortune that I met with last
week when I got the greetings from your parents and their assent to our
engagement surprised me so much that from great happiness and joy I
became quite absent-minded and forgot my promise.*

*And as you know, what a terrible war we had from all sides with
our opponents and enemies until we managed to attain our goal! It's
true, we have now become bound together with an eternal bond, so significant that one could be taken by surprise. For aside from the fact that
we carried out our hearts' desire, we also had another strong victory
over our opponents, who tried by various means to thwart us from at-
taining what we wanted.*

*Be well, cheerful, and happy, and fill your heart with hope that you
stand on the brink of a good future and that on every step of your life's
journey you will be accompanied by your eternally loving*

Shloyme Kokh

[i] Miller, E. *Miller's nayer brifenshteller in tsvey theyl*, 77–78.

3: Warning to a Sister Not to Take the Attentions of a Rich Boy Too Seriously[i]

Dear Sister!

Your letter confirmed for me what I have been hearing from various people for a few weeks now. The whole time I didn't pay any attention to it because I took it for one of the many lies that get spread around by deceitful tongues. But is it really true that you have started to do business with young Taytelboym? This I never would have expected from my brave, serious, and smart sister.

I won't reproach you here about how this young man made such a deep impression on you so fast. He is, indeed, a handsome young man who speaks very enchantingly and presents himself as elegant and polite in his behavior with women. And I also won't say that the young man has any bad intentions and that he isn't sincere in his love—I can't look into his heart. Besides, I am well aware of your good qualities and your bewitching looks, and so it doesn't surprise me that you have made a new conquest of a young man's heart. Ask yourself, though, Berte, what will come of it? The young Taytelboym is the only son of a rich father who considers everyone who isn't wealthy creatures of little worth. Maks has only recently come to you in the office to get some experience in business administration prior to his father's giving him responsibility over his big factories. There is no doubt in my mind that the elder Taytelboym has already picked out "a bride with all the virtues," or more accurately said, a bride with a rich inheritance. Can you really imagine that this old miser would allow his son to marry a girl who doesn't have a dowry and works in a store? If you really think so, you are making a terrible mistake. And maybe you believe so strongly in Maks's love? Maybe you believe that for your sake he will oppose his father and jeopardize his brilliant career? From what I know of father and son, this will never happen. He was brought up in coziness and comfort and as soon as he is faced with having to give them up, he will wash his hands of his frivolous love. All of this is what's making me very nervous and I ask you, please, dear sister, you should consider well and stop yourself from taking this false step. Guard your good name dearly and keep in mind the pain of our parents when they find out that you have had something to do with Taytelboym's sonny boy.

> *May my words find an echo in your heart and may you receive*
> *them as the advice of a devoted brother who can't remain silent when he*
> *sees that his inexperienced sister is embarking on a slippery road.*
>
> *Your brother, who is certain of your consideration . . .*

[i] Bernshteyn, *Bernshteyn's yudisher brief-lehrer,* 26–27.

4: A Shadkhn Writes to a Widower about a Match[i]

To the wealthy, well-known, etc., shining star of his generation,
Moyshe Khayim Shpira, may his light shine:

Dear good friend,

I have heard that on account of our sins, your wife has departed from
the world and that she was an important woman, a pious woman, and
a woman of valor. May her piousness protect her. But as you know, I
am an old shadkhn and a great friend of yours and of your house. In
order that your modest possessions don't come to nothing, I have a
dear woman for you. She possesses, in the old-fashioned way, an an-
cient wisdom. She has her own tavern and is a great business woman.
Two hands and two feet are not enough to accomplish everything she
does. No, here she is, at the inn, in the kitchen, doing laundry, doing the
dishes. There she is, cooking, roasting, receiving guests, before dawn,
during the day, and late at night. She goes alone into the forest, she
brings back wood. Such a mistress of the house you rarely see. She's a
totally respectable woman. To be honest, a little advanced in years, not
very strong in character. I can't tell a lie, she has childhood pockmarks,
but not too many, and the measles have left her with yellow, brownish
spots on her face. But her greatest value is in her success in the home
and in the tavern in terms of household goods: long tables, big benches,
iron pots for cooking for ordinary people, useful copper cookware for
respectable people, lots of tin plates, and even clothes, all in the old-
fashioned styles, underwear left over from her youth, so much that it's
torn up and used for tinder, waists made out of solid lace, one of red
satin, of damask, and also silk dresses. If only I had this, the clothing
and the underwear that she sends to grandchildren, to poor brides. She
has long, well-used curtains, furniture upholstered in calico. She serves
customers on tablecloths that she sews herself, and gives donations.
If only I had her portion of the world to come!

*She also has a few rubles which she is holding onto for a husband,
for her intended one. I can't tell a lie, she approached me and swore to
me that she has even made provisions for when she's over a hundred
years old. She has paid for and has prepared what would be needed to
the very last. . . . Today, there is her hospitality to guests, provisioning
of the poor. She prepares a special meal and under the tablecloths, there
are coins for the poor people, as is right and proper. And often, with her
wagon, the poor people are taken to a tavern, too. I won't write you anything in detail. What a great good fortune this is. For G-d's sake, send
me a response right away because there is a lot to negotiate. There are
old and young that want to take her, etc.*

Your good, best, dear friend.[ii]

[i] Alek, *Oytser mikhtovim* [*Otsar mikhtavim*], 88–89.
[ii] Moyshe replies that he is interested in the match but wants the shadkhn to let the prospective bride know that he has enemies. But also he
has his own good points: he's strong and healthy, is experienced in the
marketplace, and plays the fiddle "as well as the best klezmer."

5: "She Is Not for You"[i]

Kherson, 1893

*To my darling son-in-law, dear to my soul, shining star of his genera-
tion, Kalmen, may he flourish,*

*Beloved son-in-law! I will ask you in as friendly a way as possible:
what sort of grudge do you have against my child? I'm not questioning
your complaints and I won't say that you are wrong, but just want to
know one thing: what do you want from the poor soul? When you were
pretending that you were going off to buy wine barrels you took 280
rubles. In the end the barrels remained with the cooper and he doesn't
know who you are or you him, and the wine and the money are with the
tavern-keeper or with your good buddies.*[ii] *I've supported you for two
years; you've brought a child into the world and don't want anything to
do with it. But about all this, I'm not complaining. First of all, because
it's a done deal, and secondly, because I don't want to be your teacher or
take students like you under my wing. All I want is that you don't make
her unhappy. I'll admit it, she is not for you. You are an aristocratic
young man; you can play the violin; while she is a plain and simple little*

Jewish wife. She'll never be an aristocrat because you don't see me or anyone in my family wearing a frock coat, only long kapotes. And so I ask you to be a real aristocrat and demonstrate that you have a decent character by letting her go. The cost of the divorce and the child, may it live, is not your concern. This way, you can come and go, as you wish.

From me, your father-in-law,
Sholem Oshomirske

 i Yoysef Arukh, *Arukhs brifenshteller,* 57–58.
 ii In original: *di gite bruder.*

6: To a Lover Who Has Gone Away[i]

Dear, darling Mozes,

How quickly did the wheel of our fortunes turn. How quickly, without our noticing, did misfortune come running, unexpectedly. Darling Mozes, we didn't get to have much enjoyment from our happiness. A person's life is like the sun. Sometimes a cloud hides it and it gets dark and sometimes it becomes bright. Like you, my dear Mozes. As soon as I saw you it became bright. But then came a bad person and our fate was disrupted and darkened. He wants me to take his son. And for me, this would be worse than death. I'm afraid that I won't be able to survive this. Therefore, darling Mozes, have compassion for your bride to whom you swore eternal love. Don't delay too long. Write me a letter and you will keep me alive. Since you went away, nothing in the world is any consolation to me. All the time, when I go walking in the garden and come to the place we met, it consoles me a little bit and reminds me of the happier time when we would both go strolling. But immediately I am reminded that this was, indeed, only a dream. Always, the greatest, happiest things happen in a dream. Dearest Mozes, it's already been two years since you left and you haven't written to anyone, not even to your parents, and you have forgotten everyone. So I ask of you, please swear to me by all that is sacred in the world that you are coming as quickly as possible or at least write, even if all it says is that you can't come. And have compassion for your frail beloved who barely has the strength to sign her name.

 i Poliak-Gilman, *Der nayer obraztsover brifenshteller,* 36. A reply from Mozes notes that he left his wife for the correspondent but that he became discouraged by the cold tone of some of her letters to him.

7: Congratulations on the Birth of Our Son[i]

To my beloved wife Dvoyre, may she live.

*I just now received a letter from your dear father wishing me mazel tov
and telling me that you have, thank God, made it through, and with
good fortune, have given birth to a son. I wish you, my dear wife, a mazel tov, and hope that we will live to have pleasure from our newborn, as
well as from the other children. Please, my dear wife, when you feel better in a few days, write in your own hand to your husband,*

Yitskhok Zak

[i] *Eyn nayer brifenshteler in dray obtheylungen,* 41.

COURTSHIP AND MARRIAGE: AMERICA

Introduction

In American brivnshtelers, courtship is more than ever the domain
of young people, who try to balance what they knew growing up with
their heart's desire and what they see around them. Battles with parents
are no longer a looming issue, though family members in America can
also complicate matters. Romantic passion is mostly assumed. But the
high-culture Russian and European model of love as madness has been
left behind.

Trying to reflect the local mood and local needs, the American brivnshteler authors Shomer, Eisenstadt, and Harkavy reconcile the freedoms
possible in the New World with the uneasiness that came with the abandonment of traditional practices like arranged marriages. Alongside
letters depicting young people taking matters into their own hands are
examples of men contacting shadkhonim and American shadkhonim
marketing themselves.

In the courtship letters of Russian brivnshtelers, the standard take
on the shadkhn was unrelentingly satirical.[69] Writing in America, both
Shomer and Eisenstadt revive this figure in letters that are not satirical
at all, though some are a little defensive. In one of Eisenstadt's shadkhn
letters, a potential client who signs himself A. Shtroys addresses matchmaker Herr Yankev Mintz with undisguised embarrassment. He has

heard of the shadkhn "by chance." He has met the young lady on his own. Why contact a shadkhn, then? He needs an intermediary to press his case because the pair lack mutual acquaintances. He goes on to provide details:

> In New York, at 301 Madison Street, on the second floor, lives a family by the name of Shvarts. They come from Russia. I met this family a few weeks ago at an engagement party on Broome Street and the whole family seems to be very intelligent and decent. I especially noticed their oldest daughter, a brunette, whose calm, serenity, and fine, respectable language I really liked. From what I understand, I also caught her attention, and almost the entire time we spent at the engagement party, we held a conversation and discussed various matters.
>
> And so I would, esteemed sir, ask you to try and go to the above-mentioned house and explain to the family and also to the girl that I would be happily honored if I could hope and expect that Miss Shvarts will be my intended.[70]

Shomer's American brivnshteler has two sets of shadkhn letters. In the first, the shadkhn introduces himself to the father of a young woman (this is another letter in which parents, unusually, are in America with their almost grown children). Shomer spends several paragraphs charting the shadkhn's circuitous route through the variety of occupations that led him to his present profession, on the theory, apparently, that being a shadkhn requires some explaining. Finally the shadkhn gets to his point, which is a match for the recipient's daughter.[71]

In Shomer's second set of letters, (Letters 1–2: "Young Men Today Are Embarrassed to Utter the Word 'Matchmaker'"), the shadkhn is still on the defensive. Responding to a young man who has sought his assistance, he argues against the idea that his profession is obsolete. "It is entirely possible," he writes, "that you belong to the class of young men who don't hold with old-fashioned things" like getting married through a shadkhn. But what if a friend were to introduce you? How is the shadkhn any different? While Shomer is all for modernity, he envisions a role for traditional Jewish values and customs in America in an updated form.[72]

Courtship letters that involve a shadkhn are predictably conservative in the way they evaluate potential matches. In Shomer's first set of letters, the shadkhn admits that his client, the prospective groom, has a minor defect (he's not particularly good-looking) but "he makes the best impression." With that out of the way, the matchmaker goes on to list the young man's exacting standards for his future bride. Perhaps because his job and salary make him a winner—he's a "cutter" who brings home $25 a week—the young man is alert to the signs of American licentiousness in a potential wife. He doesn't want the kind of girl who goes to picnics and dances and "doesn't take off her girdle even at night" (presumably because she is too concerned with her appearance). Love is not on offer here.

In his response to the shadkhn, the would-be groom is very demanding. He lists seven numbered conditions that the bride needs to fulfill. The lucky girl will have to be pretty, from a good family, able to cook and sew, and "not too educated." For his part, the groom hopes to do well, but if it's God's will that he ends up poor, she'll have to put up with it. Letter 3 ("Knock the Idea of Higher Education Right Out of Your Head"), in which a woman advises a girlfriend to give up her dreams of education for cooking and sewing, shows the same ideas aired between women.

Aside from matchmakers and matches between widows and widowers, the courtship world of the American brivnshteler is awash in romance. A congratulations letter in Shomer applauds a friend ("Bravo! Dear Max! You could be a hero in a novel.") for overcoming unidentified, but likely not parental, obstacles in becoming the groom of Miss Goldberg. The writer's only wish is that Max's love for Miss Goldberg and hers for him will never weaken.[73]

But what words should an ordinary working man use to express romantic sentiments? Eisenstadt, whose preface presents him as someone who "always uses a plain and pure prose style that reads the way people speak,"[74] addresses that problem in a letter from a man, Avrom, answering his fiancée's complaints that his letters have been too short. It's not because he can't write. Back in Lithuania he was a shrayber who wrote letters for other people, where he became "familiar with all the happy and embittered hearts and even wrote many, many letters from grooms to their fiancées." But writing to her is a different story altogether, because of the problem of romantic sincerity. Adopting the banal language of love—the hackneyed style of brivnshteler romance, though he doesn't say that directly—would make him sound like "a farmer's son." He gives an example and declares it false to both of them:

> "My beloved, sweet, delicious, beautiful, clever, good, good-looking, dear, diamond and gem." Imagine what would be said if I continued to seduce you with language about nature, about forests and fields, about gates, seas, and

> deserts. I have mercy on you, because why should I seduce you to such an extent and wear you out? I won't creep up into the sky and won't sink into the ground and I will let the angels rest above and the peaceful below.

Instead, he decides to talk about more prosaic things: "I will tell you about my landlady ['*Mrs.*'] and the neighbors, their conversations, squabbles, and arguments, may they be healthy and may their husbands take it out on them."[75]

Shomer does not avoid romantic banalities (neither does Eisenstadt later in his book) but he does keep in mind the social awkwardness of the type of people who use brivnshtelers, and suggests language that would be appropriate for them. His very first courtship letter addresses the situation of a man who has fallen in love with someone at work. There is no shadkhn; he has to press his own case. How to begin? Shomer proposes something like this: "You might be asking yourself, what kind of business does Herr [*space left blank*] have with me? Why is he writing me a letter? But there are moments in a man's life, dear lady, when he is forced to express his feelings."[76]

Further on, Shomer's love letters express ardor through simile: the writer compares himself to a "fire-spitting mountain"[77] or to Adam in the Garden of Eden, "who could not be happy until he caught sight of lovely Eve."[78] A careful reader might, however, avoid comparing himself with Adam. Of the two replies that Shomer provides for this particular letter, the first is an assent. But the second points out that Adam and Eve had no choice, while "you, dear Sir, aren't in a Garden of Eden and can find women who are prettier and better than I am."[79]

Harkavy's women would not think of availing themselves of this sort of retort. We saw earlier how his character Joseph Marks (aka Mr. Fred Hill from an American model letter book) protests Miss Abrahams's coolness toward him. As Joseph's future hangs in the balance, Miss Abrahams is provided with two options for reply. The positive response announces that she has already shown "his kind and manly letter" ("friendly and brave" in the Yiddish version) to her parents. In the negative one, the letter is again referred to as "kind and manly"—or "friendly and brave"—but Miss Abrahams regrets that the sentiments expressed are, unfortunately, not reciprocated.[80]

The one letter in Harkavy's book that breaks this genteel American pattern is labeled "from a young workman to his sweetheart,"[81] and seems to be original rather than plagiarized from an American letter-writer. While American manuals do provide an occasional love letter from a servant or a sailor, Harkavy's young workman has little in common with those stock characters. He writes about going with his beloved to the theater—definitely a pastime of working-class Jews. And instead of calling at her house or the home of her employer, he asks her to leave a note at his "lodgings": they will go to the park and talk about their future over coffee and cake.

Where there is courtship there are courtship problems. Several letters in Shomer refer to coldness or the gap between the suitor's romantic prose—taken, perhaps, from a brivnshteler—and his conduct in person: "Nathan, my good angel! Do you really love me as passionately and earnestly as you write?"[82] Jealousy is an issue in Letters 4–5 ("From a Jealous Fiancé"), from Shomer, but is vehemently denied in the reply. In Harkavy, Esther Goodman writes a curt note to her fiancé, Mr. Morris Cohen: "I was both shocked and surprised yesterday at seeing a letter from you to Miss Stone, written within the past week and making the most ardent protestations of undying love." Following American preferences for brevity, in the remaining two paragraphs, each one sentence long, Miss Goodman cancels the engagement:

> Since it is utterly impossible that you can desire to fulfil [sic] your engagement to me with such sentiments in your heart for another, I raturn [sic] to you your gifts and letter, and release you from your bondage.
>
> I shall require of you to return my souvenirs, and the letters written in the belief that you were faithful.[83]

In Eisenstadt, an exchange between Yakov Levinzohn and Lina Rozenblatt goes on for eight pages. He thinks she has been cold to him; she complains that he has said cruel things and has complicated her relationship with her cousins. Still, she loves him. He is thrilled and wants to see her the next day, no matter what anyone says: "Let no one stop us, let no one make us anxious."[84]

Not everyone rushes headlong to the marriage canopy. In Letter 6 ("What Value Does the Life of an Unmarried Man Have?"), from Shomer, a man offers a friend some good reasons for getting married. But another letter, also from Shomer, is less upbeat: this time, a friend in love is advised to proceed with open eyes, because you can go around with a girl for a year, but she will show her true character only after marriage.[85] This slightly misogynist bent, however, is not the general rule.

A novel feature of American brivnshtelers are letters between husbands in America and wives back home who believe, rightly or wrongly, that they have been abandoned. Bad marriages and absent husbands were hardly unknown in Russian Jewish life, but brivnshtelers ignored the phenomenon, as they did much else. Non-Jewish letter manuals, both European and American, never touch it. But both Eisenstadt and Shomer take up the problem of wives whose husbands on a different continent are not writing and have perhaps left them altogether.

Letter 7 ("An Abandoned Wife Writes to a Rabbi in Minsk") from Eisenstadt is unusual because the wife is in America with her three children, while her husband has apparently been seen in Minsk. Because she is writing to a rabbi in Minsk, her language is more subdued than the kind suggested for women writing directly to their errant spouses. An example of the latter is Shomer's Hinde Gutman, whose husband Anshel is rumored to have an American girlfriend. Hinde does not mince words. Anshel is squandering the money "with which you could save us from death" on the pretty girl. She herself has been left a withered flower: "Why did I fade so quickly? Where has my beauty—which amazed you a few years ago before our wedding—gone so quickly? You yourself know the answer. . . . If a flower has rain, dew, sunshine, and air, it retains its beauty. . . . But if even the prettiest flower has no rain, dew, sunshine, and air, it fades quickly."[86]

Shomer gives two alternative replies for Anshel or someone in his position. The first begins "Every word of your letter pierced my breast like a sharp knife"—a suggestion, common enough in brivnshtelers, that a good turn of phrase will awaken love (or in this case, reconciliation). America is an alien world, and Anshel hasn't yet been able to set aside money. But for him, Hinde is not a withered flower; she is "the freshest and most beautiful." The alternative letter reflects a situation in which Anshel actually does have a girlfriend. In the apartment where he is boarding, the young and beautiful "missus" treated him very warmly, and he strayed. But his wife's words have pulled him out of his drunken stupor.[87]

In Eisenstadt, Sore Turman has not heard from her husband Yoysef for quite a while, and there are also rumors about his conduct. She writes "not with black ink but with the last drops of blood."[88] Yoysef also gets two letters to choose from as a response. In the first variant, he professes his undying love and encloses every bit of his earnings since coming to America, $5,000. In the alternative (Letter 8: "Letter from a Husband in a Sanatorium"), he declares that he has tuberculosis and is in a sanatorium in Colorado.[89] He may or may not be dying, but Eisenstadt has assuredly provided him with the last word.

Letters

1: Young Men Today Are Embarrassed to Utter the Word "Matchmaker"[i]

Worthy Herr Goldsmit.

It is entirely possible that you belong to the class of young men who don't hold with old-fashioned things: getting married by way of a matchmaker. I realize that the great majority of today's fashionable young men are embarrassed even to utter the word "matchmaker." They have been educated to think that it is a disgrace for a young man to become a bridegroom by way of a stranger and that every groom must find his bride himself and that every girl must seek out her intended on her own.

But, my dear sir, just consider the subject and you yourself will admit that this is just a fantasy.

First of all, I believe that you yourself are already thoroughly convinced that, indeed, the great majority of matches where the groom and the bride marry out of love are the ones that do not end well.

I won't say to you that all such matches are unsuccessful. There are always exceptions.

Secondly, I'll give you an example: suppose you're unemployed and you're looking for work or a job somewhere and someone comes to you and says that he can direct you to such a job, where you have prospects of being happy. Wouldn't you grab it? Would you, instead, answer him: no, I must find a job myself?

It's the same with a match. You look for a bride after your wishes, but in the meantime, you haven't managed to find anyone like that. And then I come to you and want to show you a girl who more than matches your wishes. Nu, would it be smart of you to answer: no, I must find a bride after my wishes myself?

How do you know that the girl I want to show you is not what you're looking for?

Maybe you don't believe me? This would be very reasonable of you. When it comes to these kind of things, one doesn't take things on faith. I'm not at all asking you to believe me. See with your own eyes, do some research, make as many inquiries as you can, and if you discover that this is not suitable for you, I won't, of course, force you to go the altar with the girl.

But I assure you that you will find her very pleasing because in my opinion she is exquisite.

Her name is _____ and she is twenty years old, very educated with all the most lovely attributes. Her father's name is _____. He lives _____.

If you want, I will introduce you to her as early as tomorrow and I am sure that with her passionate eyes she will kindle the fire in your heart that is called "love."

Awaiting your reply, respectfully yours,
Dovid Teykhgang

ⁱ Shaykevitsh, *Shaykevitsh'es nayer briefenshteler*, 110–113.

2: Young Men Today Are Embarrassed to Utter the Word "Matchmaker," reply

Worthy Herr Teykhgang.
I have received your letter, and I can assure you that I am not one of those idiots who would be embarrassed to marry a beautiful girl by way of a matchmaker.

I must tell you that I am very happy with the opportunity you are now giving me to have an intermediary in such an important matter.

About the match that you have proposed to me, I must tell you, worthy sir, there is no way that I will decide to take even a single step forward until there is honest clarification about the following points.

1) Whether the bride is really beautiful.
2) Whether she possesses, in fact, the necessary training that every housewife must have. I'm not looking for anyone highly educated. First of all, in my opinion, a woman doesn't need to be too preoccu-

pied with books; secondly, she should consider housework her prior-
ity rather than higher education.

3) *Is she a good housekeeper? Can she cook and sew?*

4) *Is she not too fond of ostentatious finery?*

5) *Does she fantasize about a life of luxury? Because no man can guar-
antee it; that depends on good luck. If I become rich, of course, I will
see to it that my wife has every delight, and if, God forbid, I'm poor,
she should be content with what her husband has.*

6) *Does she really come from a good family?*

7) *Whether her parents will at least provide her with a fine dowry.*

*If you assure me that all these seven conditions are met, I will start to
work on it.*

Respectfully,
D. Goldsmit

3: Knock the Idea of Higher Education Right Out of Your Head[i]

Dear, beloved friend Liza.

*I received your long letter and it gave me great joy, as well as great
pain.*

*It gave me pleasure to hear that, first of all, you are, thank God, in
good health, and secondly, that even though we haven't seen each other
for a year, you have, after everything is said and done, remained the
same friend as before.*

*What caused me pain in your letter is that you have decided to
become a highly educated miss. You want to know everything and study
everything, so that (as you put it) you won't be ashamed to enter a circle
of educated individuals.*

*You can get mad at me, dear Liza, but I must quite openly say that
this is an empty, even stupid, conceit.*

*Ask me, I'm a married woman, and in the three years that I've been
married I've had enough experience in delving into what education
means for women like us.*

*Just like you, as you know, I once fantasized that a woman must
know and be erudite about everything.*

When it came to the phrase, "know and be erudite about every-thing," I meant knowing several languages, excelling in mathematics, geography, history, and all the other disciplines.

I don't have to tell you, you know that I don't need to be ashamed of myself in comparison to any educated man because up until I was twenty years old I diligently studied the above-mentioned subjects.

But since I became a married woman, I've often been very angry at myself. Instead of mathematics, geography, and history, it would have been better if I had thoroughly learned cooking and sewing.

Ach, dear friend, how unacceptable is the woman who doesn't know how to do both of these things.

My husband does not care about all my academic expertise. A good lunch makes him much happier than any mathematics prob-lem and I think he's right. All day long he works, and when he comes home, he wants to eat and enjoy the food. But I myself couldn't cook and had to hire a cook. I was almost driven crazy by these cooks. I would say a harsh word to one of them and she would leave and then I would have to find another one, and until I found another one, all of us starved.

God has bestowed two beautiful children on us who, week after week, need one trifle after another, such as shirts, dresses, and other such important items. I myself can't sew and must buy everything. Un-fortunately, things aren't going well for us and it causes me the greatest pain that I am not in the position to sew for myself and my children all that we need.

Where do I stand now when it comes to education? I'm happy if I can soothe my children and keep everything in the household in order.

I have told you all this, dear friend, so that you will knock the idée fixe of higher education right out of your head.

Better to learn how to be good housewife. Whatever academic expertise you have acquired is more than enough for you. Take classes in cooking and sewing. You can't imagine how useful this will be to you later on, and I am sure that you will therefore be eternally grateful to me, your true, devoted friend,

Bella

[i] Shaykevitsh, *Shaykevitsh'es nayer briefenshteler*, 165–167.

4: From a Jealous Fiancé[i]

My dear Rashel!

I am sitting here and reading one of the letters you wrote to me before our engagement.

Among the other sweet words in the letter I also find these words.

"Forever and ever, I will love you, my dear good Volf. Just as the heavens are unending, so will my love for you remain unending. This I swear to God and by all that is sacred."

When I read these words for the first time, I gulped down every word. Every word from these lines refreshed me as if they were the most precious balm.

Now, however . . .

It is very hard for me to openly speak with you about such a matter, but it doesn't matter. I have no choice but to unburden my heart because I feel as if I will suffocate under the heavy load that constricts my breast.

Rashel! Is it true that you have secrets with Herr Bernard Goldberg?

I don't want to believe this. I'd give half my life if I could be convinced that this isn't true.

But facts, hard facts incriminate you, dear Rashel.

Is it not true that this week you've gone around twice in the woods with Herr Goldberg?

Don't deny it, Rashel. Several trustworthy individuals have told me about it.

You, Rashel, you stroll around late at night in the woods with a strange young man?

I want an explanation. I want to know what it means.

Maybe you have decided that Herr Goldberg is a better match for you. So why should you make this a secret? Tell me honestly, set me free, and I certainly won't stand in the way of your happiness.

> *Your fiancé, who awaits your*
> *explanation with impatience,*
> *Volf Kroysman*

[i] Shaykevitsh, *Shaykevitsh'es nayer briefenshteler*, 143–145.

5: From a Jealous Fiancé, reply

My angry, jealous Volf!

If I didn't honestly love you, if you weren't so dear to me, I would answer your accusations in such an angry tone that the desire to look upon me once again would for sure desert you.

But my love for you is too strong. I can't be furious with you, I can't be angry at you, so all I will do is defend myself.

The people who told you that I went strolling with Herr Goldberg late at night in the forest are common liars. Let them just say this to my face and the spit I will give them will drown their low-thinking ways.

It is true that this week I have twice met with Herr Goldberg, not in the forest, but here in the street. I was coming back from the pharmacy (you know that my mother is sick). I was running at night to the apothecary to buy her the pills that the doctor prescribed and just then Herr Goldberg was coming from the club. He greeted me and asked me where I was going so late and since I told him I was coming from the apothecary with medicine for my mother, he escorted me to our house.

Do you finally understand what kind of love affair I'm having with Herr Goldberg? What should I have done in a case like this, chase him away so that he wouldn't escort me home? Or was I supposed to pick on him for being polite and not wanting to let a girl walk alone in the street late at night?

If you call this a sin, you can be as angry as you want. I won't care because my conscience is clear.

I am sure, however, that after these words, your conscience will trouble you and you will come in person to beg forgiveness from your guiltless bride.

Rashel

6: What Value Does the Life of an Unmarried Man Have?[i]

My lucky friend Yozef!

Even though I am very busy, I feel obliged to forget about all my businesses for a few minutes to send you my best wishes and express the joy that I've been feeling ever since I got the invitation to your wedding.

These days, there are plenty of pessimists who want to deny all the necessities of nature.

These pessimists have the nerve to say that marriage is unnecessary, even burdensome. They say that along with marriage one takes upon one's shoulders a terrible yoke because one must support a wife and children, and that from the majority of women, one only has trouble and that children bring more pain than pleasure and that after you expend all your resources on their behalf, they are ungrateful.

If I thought that spitting in the faces of these pessimists would drown them in my spit, I would definitely do it.

It is not great art to turn white into black, to find defects in the most beautiful thing. One can even finds spots in the shining sun.

Every intelligent upstanding person knows that a human being can never be happy living alone, without loving people and without loyal friends.

Your life can't be pleasant if you don't care about the world.

And who is more loyal to us, who loves us more than our own wives and children?

How good one feels when one knows that there are individuals to whom our lives are as dear as their own. Individuals who constantly beg God on our behalf, who share joy and suffering with us.

And these individuals are none other than our own wives and children.

A head of household who must support a wife and children has an intense interest in life because he knows that he is working for his loved ones. He wants to make them happy and to provide them with everything good. Therefore, nothing is hard for him and if he succeeds in bringing them pleasure he feels fortunate and happy to the highest level.

And what value does the life of an unmarried and childless man have?

His best friends are only his friends when they can get some use out of him, or when he doesn't need to ask them for any favors. Let him become impoverished, however, and all the friends will fly away like flies when one drives them away from a sweet thing. They hide from him and won't recognize him.

What kind of interest can an unmarried man take in life?

All pleasures, even the best of them, become boring, and he finally looks around and sees that he is lonely and helpless.

But to convince somebody how necessary it is for a man to get married is the same as trying to produce evidence that two times two is four.

Therefore, I am very happy that you, my friend, have recognized the necessity of marriage. I am sure that you will feel fortunate in the constant company of your loving, beautiful wife. I am sending you both my best wishes along with a small gift. I hope that you will enjoy receiving both because they come from your best, most loyal friend,

Mikhael Melnik

[i] Shaykevitsh, *Shaykevitsh'es nayer briefenshteler,* 44–46.

7: An Abandoned Wife Writes to a Rabbi in Minsk[i]

Worthy Rabbi Yankev Meyer Grodenski, Minsk.

Hearing of your good and renowned name and that you are loyal and devoted to your sacred religious work, I am sure that you will certainly have compassion for a lonely woman like me whose husband left her with three children two years ago and who hasn't heard from him or gotten any information about him the entire time. But 2 months ago, I learned from a letter sent to me by an acquaintance in Minsk that my husband, whom she also knows, is in Minsk and that she ran into him there strolling in the Governor's orchard (garden),[ii] and that he, so it seems, tried to hide from her. But of course she stopped him and asked him what he was doing in Europe right now. He gave her some sort of evasive reply and then disappeared.

Please, honorable Rabbi, publicize this in the synagogues and in the Minsk newspapers. His particulars (simonim)[iii] are: his name is Moyshe Rubin, he is 41 years old, not tall in stature, a brunet, and he is a heavyset man, with a trimmed beard (and maybe by now, he has completely shaved even this off). If this costs anything, write to me and I will gladly send you the money on the next occasion.

Yours,
Tsivye Rubin

[i] Eisenstadt, *Der moderner brieffenshteller,* 105–106.
[ii] An alternative word is supplied in parentheses in the original text.
[iii] The Yiddish word is given and glossed in Hebrew.

8: Letter from a Husband in a Sanatorium[i]

My dear Sore!

You have issued me an ultimatum and so I must reveal it to you. I can't hide it any longer from you, my dear, because your letter intensified my wounds and increased my pain. It wasn't because of good times that I didn't write to you and it wasn't because I forgot about you, my dear, that you didn't hear from me for such a long time.

I have already been (may this never happen to you) sick for five years. I have already turned to every doctor and have lain in various hospitals, but I must reveal to you that my help comes only from God. The great doctor of heaven can cure my illness, while the human doctors are not, as it seems, in the position to bring this about.

I wasn't able, my dear, to write to you because I knew of and valued your pure love for me. But because of your most recent words to me, I must finally reveal to you the secret that I have been keeping to myself.

I am quite distant from our townsmen. In fact, I am in an institution for tuberculosis patients in Colorado, and only your or my worst enemies could have dreamed this up for me.

Beseech God for me, my dear wife, and tell my dear children to beseech God for their helpless father, who hovers between life and death. Maybe God will have mercy on their behalf. Maybe their tears will have an effect on the gates of heaven so that they will open and accept my request to live.

Your despondent husband who hopes only for help from God,
Yoysef.

---

[i] Eisenstadt, *Der moderner brieffenshteller*, 64–66.

BUSINESS

Introduction

While all letter manuals in Europe and America devote a lot of space to business letters, and almost all include sample IOUs and other templates considered useful for business, the brivnshteler focuses on the specific needs of Jews, including, on occasion, rudimentary instruction in bookkeeping. With small-scale trading often the only profession open to Jews, the Jewish market for business forms was disproportionately large. Like all business owners, Jews needed to generate IOUs, receipts, and other commercial documents, but were often in no position to hire help. For them, as Joseph Bar-El has pointed out, brivnshtelers took the place of trained clerks.[90]

Pointers on what makes a good business letter were standard fare in both Jewish and non-Jewish letter manuals. Goldshteyn-Gershonovitsh's 1913 *Der praktisher zhargon-russish-daytsher briefenlehrer, un briefenshteller in zeks theyl* (The practical Zhargon-Russian-German letter primer, and brivnshteler in six parts) gives the usual kind of advice: first of all, a business letter should be short (businessmen are very busy and don't have time to read pages and pages). Its message must be clearly stated (after all, it is money that is being dealt with: a good reason to avoid a misunderstanding). Letters should be written on good paper with high-quality ink. Finally, it's not a big deal in ordinary correspondence if you don't reply right away, but procrastination in business could lead to negative consequences.[91]

Though Gershonovitsh was a teacher, he lived in a world of small business, which likely engaged many of his friends, family, and associates. To make a living, many brivnshteler authors probably had to resort to small-scale trading at some point in their careers—or at least contemplate the possibility. A brivnshteler from 1910–1911 acknowledges this situation in a letter from a young man who once dreamed of studying philosophy in university and of pondering "Jewish problems" but has been forced to become a merchant and live "a practical life." Nevertheless, he continues to subscribe to all the Hebrew and Yiddish periodicals.[92]

Because the needs and lives of businessmen were familiar territory to brivnshteler authors, model business letters focus on the commodities in which Jews were most likely to trade: grain, agricultural produce, lumber, tobacco, and haberdashery or women's clothing. The rhythms of buying and selling seasons, the ins and outs of credit and loans, and the need to travel between markets in different cities or even different countries are also frequently covered. Letter 1 ("A Businessman Requests a Loan") is an example of a "typical" business letter from the early to mid-nineteenth century, this one dealing with the buying of flax, honey, and beeswax, and business trips to Pest and Leipzig.

A common category of business-related correspondence is a letter from a job-seeker, or a letter of recommendation for a job-seeker. Not particularly distinctive in content, such letters lay out the applicant's qualifications for the desired position, stressing education—particularly proficiency in foreign languages—and job experience. Letters 2–3 ("Request for a Job in a Business Establishment") provide instruction not only on how to write a job-hunting letter but also on how to respond politely that there are no open positions in one's place of business. The focus on Russian, French, and German marks their provenance in the Russian Empire. American brivnshtelers either stick with Yiddish, for business dealings in the Jewish world, or (as in Harkavy's manual) switch to English.

While American brivnshtelers continue the focus on business, they update the content to reflect the new business environment. The 1902 *Harkavi's amerikanisher briefen-shteler* (Harkavy's American brivnshteler) has more than fifty pages of business letters. His businessmen deal almost exclusively in dry goods, the manufacture and sale of which was the most common occupation for Jews in New York in the 1890s.[93] They have Americanized Jewish names (Morris Goodman, Hyman Blank, Albert Newman) and correspond with other businessmen, Jewish and non-Jewish (R. Smith, H. Williams), about the purchase and sale of cloth, the receipt of shoddy merchandise, mistakes in billing, and announcements of the opening of new dry goods establishments. There are almost no letters in *Harkavi's amerikanisher briefen-shteler* related to employment in factories, sweatshops, or peddling.[94] This may reflect an unwillingness to portray lower-class life, or it may simply reflect the fact that letter writing was not a job requirement of either factory work or peddling.

Harkavy's readers may have "arrived" in the sense of having amassed enough capital to open their own businesses, but this new status was precarious. Many letters deal with requests for credit and for deferment of payments on loans. Harkavy's letters, like those in American English-language manuals, handle the topic of debt in a calm, neutral, business-like style. Quite different are the loan and debt letters in the brivnshtelers of Eisenstadt and Shomer, which are emotional and personal, full of appeals to friendship and kinship. Consider, for example, how a tenant who is delinquent in his rent writes to his landlord in *Harkavi's amerikanisher briefen-shteler:*

From a Tenant, Excusing Delay of Payment

Sir:—I have now been your tenant above ten years in the house where I now live, and you know that I never failed to pay my rent quarterly when due.

At present I am extremely sorry to inform you that from a variety of recent disappointments, I am under the necessity of begging that you will wait one quarter longer. By that time I hope to have it in my power to answer your just demand, and the favor shall be ever remembered by

Your obedient servant.[95]

Letters 4–5 ("Please Forgive Me for Not Paying the Rent on Time") from Eisenstadt's manual portray a similar situation, but in a much more emotional vein. Eisenstadt's delinquent tenant makes a bid for his land-lord's sympathies, not hesitating to mention his sick children, and he announces his insolvency without apology. Harkavy, by contrast, is as impersonal as a form letter. He eschews emotion, and we can all but hear the writer clearing his throat in embarrassment when he speaks of his "recent disappointments." Like many of the letters in Harkavy, this one is likely to have been pirated or lightly adapted from an existing English-language letter-writer, with changes in the names of the correspondents and an added focus on the garment trade as the only nods to the ethnic identities of its intended readership.[96] The assumption seems to be that to properly Americanize, one must step out of the confines of one's ethnic community and shed one's cultural style as well as one's language.

In Eisenstadt and Shomer, letters about credit and debt are exclusively between Jews. Often the creditor and debtor are old friends as well as business associates, and the letters are not only emotional, but angry and very personal, as in the exchange between Mordkhe Zeligson and M. Aleksandrov, his debtor (Letters 6–7: "A Storekeeper Demands Re-payment of a Debt"). These correspondents have a long history and don't hesitate to use their intimate knowledge of each other's ups and downs to make a point. In Letters 8–9 ("Complaint about Merchandise and Re-quest for a Discount"), Zalman Berman in Cherkassy essentially tells Efroim Oksman in Zhitomir that he is an idiot. The personal anger of the first set of letters would be unthinkable in a French, German, American, or Russian letter manual in any context other than romance: even when a mid-century Russian calls someone out for a duel, the preferred tone is icy restraint. The sarcasm of the second set is unimaginable in any model letter book not written in Yiddish. In both cases, the no-holds-barred discourse is a direct cultural carryover from Jewish behavior in Eastern Europe, where brivnshtelers, as we have seen, considered emotional outbursts in correspondence to be normal and appropriate.

A fair number of business letters focus on business downturns or the sheer struggle needed to establish one's self and make a living. In Dov Arye Fridman's manual, published in Berdichev in 1891, Avrom Dov Kuperman writes a heartrending letter to his wife Rokhl after a year of wandering "in a strange land" barely making a living, and reduced to sleeping on the floors of train stations (Letter 10: "I Am a Wanderer in a Strange Land"). Shomer in particular seems to take into the account the possibility that some of his readers might encounter a real reversal of fortune and end up destitute. The introduction to his section on "Friendship Letters" in his American brivnshteler establishes a specific category for correspondence between former friends who are no longer in the same social class because one has risen or the other has sunk.[97] In two different letters, men down on their luck beg for financial assistance from wealthy acquaintances. Both quote from the Bible as they make naked appeals not only to the potential benefactor's generosity but also to the shared Jewish kinship of both parties. In one of the letters, Mordkhe Rozenthal writes to an old friend who is doing well financially, asking him for a job, a letter of recommendation, or a loan:

> I won't bother you by describing my sad situation in detail. I will only tell you that *Bo'u mayim ad nofesh*[98]—the water is already rising up to my soul, and we might all, God forbid, be extinguished due to our lack of all that a living human being needs. . . . Loan me a little money so that I can do a bit of business and if God helps me, I will return your *gmiles khesed* [interest-free loan] with the utmost gratitude at my first opportunity.

> The tears are pouring from my eyes and I can't write any more. So I am ending my letter with the hope that my words won't be *ke-kol koyre be-midber*[99] [like one who cries out in a wilderness].[100]

Few overt mention of economic restrictions against Jews ever appear in the pages of Russian brivnshtelers. The exceptions come, not surprisingly, in the context of the more lenient atmosphere that prevailed after the revolution of 1905. The 1910–1911 *Bernshteyn's yudisher brief-lehrer* (Bernshteyn's Yiddish letter primer) includes several letters in which a young man laments the lack of opportunity for Jews in the Russian Empire. The subject is also candidly discussed in *Nayer Bloshteyn's briefen-*

shteler (New Bloshteyn's brivnshteler), where Leon Finkelshteyn writes his brother from Courland (part of Latvia, in which the imperial government permitted Jews to live). He complains that he is unable to make a living because there are non-Jewish competitors and some businesses are forbidden to Jews (Letter 11: "Times Are Bad in Courland").

Letters 12–13 ("You Could Make a Good Living Here") from the same manual are rare examples of letters involving a woman in business. Roze Rozentsvayg, a seamstress in Ekaterinoslav, is having a hard time making a living. She wonders if things might be better in Liepaja (like Courland, in Latvia), where Lina lives. Lina makes inquiries and says if Roze can produce documents attesting to her skills and experience that she will have no shortage of customers in Liepaja.

A mid-century brivnshteler by Hirsh Lion Dor presents an unusual maskilic critique of Jewish economic life. Letters 14–15 ("A Critique of Money-Lending") present an exchange between a groom and his future father-in-law. The letters touch on a wide variety of brivnshteler preoccupations: in the opening letter, the young woman is praised for writing well; in the reply, the young man's Hebrew prose style is analyzed and also praised. One remark, however, is cause for concern: the future groom has suggested that the wedding date be postponed until the dowry is invested. But the bride's father, as a matter of ethical principle, does not want the money invested at all. He condemns money-lending and the practice of charging interest on loans in a maskilic internalization of the non-Jewish world's attitude about this classic Jewish economic niche. The young man, his father-in-law counsels, should stay away from people who make their money this way, which leads to corruption and avarice. Reform, in Lion Dor's brivnshteler, is not only about education but also about how a modern Jew does business.[101]

Letters

1: A Businessman Requests a Loan[i]

Noble friend!

I am now forced to ask you for a favor. For three months, I have sold various products in Pest and am owed ten thousand guilder[ii] for them. I have also sent my people to Leipzig with flax, but they haven't yet come back. And now it is the best season to buy honey and beeswax but one

*needs real money to pay for it and I have no kreuzer at hand. Therefore,
I ask if you would please be so good as to lend me two thousand guilder
for one month. Of course, you know me very well, that I am an honest
man and you are well aware that I am wealthy enough. We've been doing business with each other for twenty years and up to now we have
never had a single conflict. And you can be sure that the money will be
paid back on time or maybe even ahead of time. And since I hope that
you won't refuse my request, I am thanking you in advance. I remain
your friend,*

Shmul Shtriks[iii]

  [i] *Khalifas igroys* [*Halifat igrot*] (1850?), 37–38.
 [ii] Guilder (singular: gulden) was the currency of Hapsburg lands
between 1754 and 1892. There were 60 kreuzer to a gulden until 1857,
and 100 kreuzer to a gulden thereafter.
[iii] His friend replies granting his request for a loan, noting that he is
flush with cash because his son has just returned from a successful
business trip to Frankfurt.

2: Request for Job in a Business Establishment[i]

Esteemed friend!

*I was very happy to hear that you are working in Herr Trakhtenberg's
commercial firm and that you hold a high position there. You are not
unaware of the circumstances which force me to see to my needs now,
nor are you unaware of my proficiency in Russian, German, and French.
Aside from that, I have acquired a beautiful and readable penmanship.
May I not now rely on our years-long friendship in order to request a job
in your place of business? I will be grateful to you from the depths of my
heart for this big favor and will never flag in my devotion to you. Trust-
ing deeply in the goodness of your heart, I await your favorable answer,*

Your best friend.

  [i] Gorodinski, *Der hoyz-korrespondent*, 70–72.

3: Request for Job in a Business Establishment, reply

Dear Friend!

*My business, which occupies me all day long, doesn't leave me much
time to chat with you, however much I might wish to. To your question*

I can only reply that unfortunately I can't help you out at all in this matter or even give you any hope of getting a job in Herr Trakhtenberg's commercial firm. We already have many, almost too many employees. However, my friend, I can assure you that I will always remember our long friendship, and that as soon as a job is available, I will immediately let you know, and that you will have an advantage over others. With assurances about this,

Your best friend.

4: Please Forgive Me for Not Paying the Rent on Time[i]

Esteemed Herr Landa!

Please forgive me this time for not paying the rent[ii] on time. As you are no doubt aware, I have not worked for almost the whole month, and in particular, my two dear children were very sick this month, and this has put a lot of pressure on me. I hope that such a refined man as yourself, who has also has sympathy for the plight of another person, will patiently and calmly wait until next month, when I expect to obtain work. The first money that I receive I will bring in to you, with gratitude.

Your friend,
Yoysef Berman

[i] Eisenstadt, *Der moderner brieffensteller,* 23–24.
[ii] The English word "rent" is given and glossed in Yiddish.

5: Please Forgive Me for Not Paying the Rent on Time, reply

Esteemed Herr Berman,

Your apology was completely unnecessary. In the five years that I have known you, I have found you to be a highly respectable man who does not ask anything of strangers, and when you didn't give my agent[i] the rent this month, even he didn't say a word to you about it. I believe that he too has a good impression of you.

I hope that things will improve and become easier for you.
I remain your friend.

Respectfully,
Yankev Landa

[i] The English word "agent" is given and glossed in Yiddish.

6: A Storekeeper Demands Repayment of a Debt[i]

Herr Aleksandrov!

I have decided to write to you a third time. I always prefer the calm and peaceful way over quarreling, and you know that I have supported you during bad times, and that I gave you credit during the period when you were out of work because I had compassion for you. But you know that I am not a wealthy man and that I am a poor storekeeper, who slaves away with his last, feeble strength from morning until late at night in order to make a living. Very little of it has come from you. You owe me 65 dollars. For me this is quite a bit. You've been working for a year already and are making a fine living. I have written you about the debt a few times already and you have ignored me.

    I must now write to you for the last time to say that if you don't reply to this letter, I will take you to court[ii] and will seek justice.

    I hope that you will decide to avoid strife.

Mordkhe Zeligson

[i] Eisenstadt, *Der moderner brieffensteller,* 29–31.
[ii] The Yiddish word is given and glossed in English.

7: A Storekeeper Demands Repayment of a Debt, reply

Esteemed Herr Zeligson!

I don't understand why you write and express yourself in such a harsh and angry tone. You, like all my acquaintances, know that I, thank God, have not taken money from strangers, and that's the way it is too with the debt I owe you. Every last penny of it will be paid back, but it takes time.

    Who told you that I'm making a fine living? Though I am working, more than half the time I remain unemployed. Moreover, in the last few months, I have continued to have severe illness in my home, which has resulted in such severe financial pressures that I can't even come up with anything for our basic necessities.

    But rest assured that in the course of the next 2 months, the debt to you will be paid off, and you don't have to get so angry.

Sh. Aleksandrov

8: Complaint about Merchandise and Request for a Discount[i]

Tuesday, Torah portion Bo,[ii] 1894, Cherkassy

To my friend, Herr Efroym, may his light shine, Oksman,

Who ever heard of such a thing? Is this your first year as a merchant? Is this the first time you've dealt in this sort of merchandise? Surely, there is a big difference between a householder who purchases wood from you in order to build a house or some other building and a wholesaler who buys in order to trade. First of all you didn't send me the merchandise as specified in my order. That is, instead of a hundred 6-arshin[iii] boards, as I directed, you sent 130. So what sort of math is this? The beams, too: you didn't send what was in my order. And aside from this, you charged me prices that I can under no circumstances accept. And so, my dear friend, I will appeal to you, as an honorable man, and ask if you can give me at least a 5% discount on your prices. If so, I will accept the merchandise. All I ask is that you immediately fill the attached order. If I have the opportunity I will sell the merchandise retail. And regarding the money you wrote about, I will ask you to send me a revised invoice, and G-d willing, I will not delay in sending you payment in the coming month with the large proceeds. In any case, I ask you to send me a proper reply right away.

Your friend, who awaits your reply,
Zalman Berman

[i] Gorodinski, *Gorodinski's korrespondent: Der nayer brifenshteller. Der postalion*, 49–51.

[ii] Exod. 10:1–13:16.

[iii] An *arshin* was a Russian unit of measurement equal to about 28 inches.

9: Complaint about Merchandise and Request for a Discount, reply

Sunday, Torah portion Besholekh [Be-shalakh][i] 1894, Zhitomir.

To my dear, renowned shining light of his generation, Zalman, may his light shine, Berman!

Reading your letter, one might imagine that you have suffered who knows what kind misfortune, God forbid. Surely you realize that between one type of merchandise and another there is a big difference, and along those lines, other people might be able to give you a discount. I could too, probably. But let's take one thing at a time. You are asking me to give you the merchandise for 5% cheaper. Believe me, many a time I myself would have been happy with a 5% profit. In particular, this type of merchandise, boards and beams, is easy to sell. Therefore, it's too much to ask for on your part. As you yourself must certainly understand, I can't agree to this under any circumstances. I am filling your order and ask you, as an honorable man, not to have such an opinion of me, because I have, G-d be thanked, been a dealer for many years now and have never, God forbid, dealt with anyone dishonestly. The maximum discount I can give you is 2% on the prices you are paying now, and I expect that you will be very pleased with the merchandise. Enclosed, I am sending you the bill and the merchandise and hopefully you will receive them without a hitch. All I ask is that regarding the money, do as you wrote me in your letter.

Your friend forever,
Efroym Oksman

[i] Exod. 13:17–17:16.

10: I Am a Wanderer in a Strange Land[i]

Lodz, August 18, 1888

To my dear wife Mrs. Rokhl, may she live

Dear Rokhl,

This Rosh Hashanah I wept a great deal. My heart broke, and my tears flowed constantly like a river. I couldn't restrain myself because every second I was thinking about you and my dear children and what has happened to us in the space of a year. A year ago we were together even though things weren't so cheery. But our little bit of blood wasn't scattered to the winds. But what has happened to us this year? I am a wanderer in a strange land,[ii] among people I don't know at all and don't understand. And they don't understand me. To them, I seem like a wild man, like a beast of prey, but out of pity, they let me make a few groschen,[iii] and from these couple of groschen I must support myself and also send you something to live on. And so you can understand what kind of life I could possibly manage to lead here. An entire year where you do nothing but work like a beast of burden, and at night, when you come to the station, you fall down like a stone on the bare floor. There is no time to dwell on your troubles. But on this holy day, on Rosh Hashanah, when everyone tosses aside worries about livelihood and starts coming to terms with where he stands; on this day you understand how unfortunate you are. But I won't lose hope, I am deeply convinced that God will have mercy on me so that I can soon return and once again lead a happy life with my children. Be well and may God inscribe and seal you for a good year. Best wishes from your husband who longs to see you again.

Avrom Dov Kuperman

[i] Fridman, *Der nayer praktisher brifenshteller*, 28–29.
[ii] The allusion is to Exod. 2:22.
[iii] A groschen was a coin in circulation in many European countries beginning in the Middle Ages. The name remained even after the coin disappeared. A reasonable equivalent for the time of this letter would be "penny."

11: Times Are Bad in Courland[i]

Mitau, October 9, 1903

Dearest Brother!

Forgive me for not writing for so long. Unfortunately, I couldn't write. The reason is that I didn't have any good news to write you and I simply didn't want to write to tell you about my vile life, about my poverty and troubles. I know you wouldn't get any pleasure from hearing about that . . .

A couple of years ago, when I got permission to reside[ii] in Courland,[iii] I thought that I was more than lucky. But this was an empty fantasy. Everywhere now, shops have opened which are competing with Jewish businesses. Jews are completely barred from many businesses, and expenses are high . . .

And this is the only reason I didn't write to you until you wrote me about how worried you were.

Your brother,
Leon Finkelshteyn

[i] Bloshteyn, *Nayer Bloshteyn's briefenshteler*, 45–46. This letter also appears in *Briefenshteler in shraybshrift*, 40–41.
[ii] The Russian word *pravozhitel'stvo* (residency permit) follows in parentheses.
[iii] A province of Latvia, then part of the Russian Empire.

12: You Could Make a Good Living Here[i]

Ekaterinoslav, April 5, 1903

Dearest sister Lina!

Last week I had regards from you via Fraulein N.N. She told me that you are making a good living and are happy. This made me very happy. May God grant that you will always be happy and well.

Here, I am living quite alone. Here in Ekaterinoslav no one knows how to live a normal life. From morning until evening one slaves away to earn one's piece of bread. Write to me if I could make a living working as a linen seamstress there in Liepaja. I have thoroughly mastered the work. But here, unfortunately, it doesn't bring me much in the way of an income.

If this sounds feasible, write to me and I will come over there, where I will make a living and won't be lonely.

Your sister,
Roze Rozentsvayg

[i] Bloshteyn, *Nayer Bloshteyn's briefenshteler*, 48–49.

13: You Could Make a Good Living Here, reply

Liepaja, April 10, 1903

Dearest sister Roze!

I received your letter. I consulted with my dear husband and he is also of the opinion that you could make good living from your work here. So, write to us about whether you are completely secure in your work, if you have a certificate from a firm for which you've worked, and if you are able to run a workshop.[i] One can't achieve happiness from one's own ten fingers. If you open a workshop, however, we hope that you will earn a good living. You will not lack for customers.

Your sister,
Lina Rozenboym[ii]

[i] The Russian word *masterskaia* follows in parentheses.

[ii] A subsequent letter in the cycle urges Roze to come soon so that she won't miss the beginning of the vacation season and its influx of potential customers.

14: A Critique of Money-Lending[i]

To my dear mekhusn,[ii] the renowned rabbi, shining light of his generation Ezriel Getsil Blumenshteyn.

Dear Mekhusn,

I received by post your letter written on August 5 with the dear greetings from my bride, and also the package with the gift from my precious, lifelong friend. Every line of her letter brought forth great joy in our house and gave joy to me because her letter is very succinctly and very clearly written, and especially because of her pure language. It is most remarkable. In my letter in Hebrew, included here, you will read of my pleasure.[iii] On behalf of my father and mother I send warm regards to you all and please pass on a special greeting and thank you to my dear bride for the honor she has given us. My parents hope for loving friendship and an eternal bond in the future!

My father is now on a business trip abroad and told me before he left to write to you that he will remain there for a certain amount of time and might be delayed, and aside from that, the time of the wedding should be put off so that the dowry money can be transferred somewhere where it can earn interest in secure hands, which he has already discussed with you in a letter. And if you can arrange this, please send me a letter by post and I will clearly write to my father right away and then if everything is in order, I will write to you on behalf of my father and will wait for a reply by post from you.

Your loyal and loving groom,
Lipman Zerakh Grayzil

[i] Hirsh Lion Dor, *Eyn nayer brifn shteller*, 67–69.
[ii] Usually co-parent-in-law (masculine); in this case it means father-in-law.
[iii] The Hebrew letter is not included in the original text.

15: A Critique of Money-Lending, reply

My dear child, I have received your letter with the pleasant regards and your lovely, sweet letter from the 19th of this month via the post. Not only your bride, but also many of our good friends, learned people, read your letter in Hebrew and Yiddish.[i] It provided an evening of beautiful social-

izing for us. Everyone was surprised, especially by your Hebrew letter, how beautifully it was written with fluency and very noble language, with nothing repeated; extremely concise, but full of significance. There were no pretentious words; everyone who read it understood it, and everyone enjoyed it, especially your bride. Thank you, my child, for persevering in your scholarship and education. May God, blessed be He, lengthen your life so that you can keep on with Torah and secular learning.

About the dowry money and giving it away to earn interest: Oh! My child, this doesn't please me at all, especially the two words: money lender! And what's more, those who charge a lot of interest—see here, my child, don't get involved with them, and don't even think of it. Investing takes you away from studying, takes away a person's conscience, deprives you of friendships, of bonds with other people. Certainly, my child, to be wealthy is good, but wanting and demanding wealth is inappropriate. I'm older than you, I have more experience. Such habits inadvertently lead to people losing their sense of compassion. That's the way it is. The first time you charge a small amount of interest, and later you charge more and more interest, because you are providing yourself with rationalizations! Please, my dear child, don't get involved with it. Better to stick with scholarship and education or to conduct yourself honestly in business. Money takes over a person's character. A person makes a name for himself with money by doing business honestly. From scholarship and education come the branches of wisdom and from honesty in business a pure groschen.

Please, my child, send this letter off to your father. It seems to me that he too will agree that I'm right. Adieu and live well.

ⁱ Idesh-daytsh.

JUDAISM AND JEWISH IDENTITY

Introduction

While it was standard for brivnshtelers to include templates for *tnoyim*[102] and *ketubahs* (marriage contracts) in their back pages, reference to religious practice or Jewish holidays is largely confined to High Holiday greetings or the occasional invitation to a *bris* (circumcision ceremony).

The High Holiday greetings in Letter 1 ("Rosh Hashanah Greetings to a Fiancée"), from a groom to a bride, are a particularly flowery example. The lack of focus on Judaism only serves to emphasize the main role of the brivnshteler: it was a guide to secular life, not Jewish religious life.

Even though Judaism does not take up much space in brivnshtelers, anxiety over assimilation and Jewish identity occasionally makes an appearance in manuals published in the early twentieth century. A man in Letter 2 ("Bar Mitzvah Greetings"), from 1911, congratulating a brother on the bar mitzvah of his son, expresses the hope that the boy will grow up to be true to the Jewish people and not a Jew only in name, as noted on his birth certificate and other official documents. In Letter 3 ("A Gymnasium Student with Jewish Heart") from the same book, a man assures his father that his grandson has maintained his Jewish identity even though he is a student in a Russian gymnasium, spending day after day among Christians. Letter 4 ("A Jew Living Outside the Pale of Settlement") is written from the perspective of a Jew who makes his home within Russia, but far from traditional Jewish life. He tells his friend that most of the Jews among whom he is living are extremely assimilated and that he misses a "Jewish atmosphere."

This cautiously worded regret over the dilution of Jewish life is an anomaly in the world of brivnshtelers, which, as a rule, do not express disapproval of Russification. Letter 5 ("A Sister Excoriates Her Brother for Attempting to Russify Himself"), from an 1892 manual, goes much further, openly and passionately attacking an assimilated Jew—a brother who has changed his name—for being ashamed of his origins. Letter 6 ("Fire in the Ringtheater") is taken from a 1904 brivnshteler, but is probably a reprint from much earlier. Its warning against assimilation and the temptations of secularization come in the form of an old-fashioned, sensationalist story. A young man studying in Vienna remained pious and resisted the temptation to attend the theater. Because of this, he avoided being caught in a fire that broke out there (a real event that occurred in 1881, with 650 casualties). His friend, who lacked such scruples, was killed.

American brivnshtelers depart from their Russian counterparts by devoting far more space to religion and Jewish identity. In melting-pot America, which lacked the communal framework of the shtetl and the constraints of tsarist restrictions, remaining Jewish was much more of a choice. Children had access to public education, and, within less than a generation, many immigrants found themselves living lives not exclusively focused on Jewish tradition or community. Few Torah sages had immigrated, and those who did found that the rhythms of American life were not conducive to study and scholarship.

The authors of the American brivnshtelers realized all of this. Even as Shomer stresses the need for a "modern" outlook, letter after letter urges readers not to turn their backs on Jewish tradition altogether. Letter 7 ("A Defense of an 'Old-Fashioned Custom'") scolds those who scoff at bar mitzvah ceremonies. Another letter conveys a father's objections to his son marrying a girl whose family is without *yikhes* (lineage).[103] But Shomer reserves his real enthusiasm for Jewish identity expressed through secular Jewish culture. In answer to a friend's question, "What is the state of Yiddish literature in America?" Shomer's Yankev Moyshe Vebman writes that it "is a joy to see how our *zhargonishe* [Yiddish] literature has developed in America. There have never been as many good writers and excellent poets in our poor language as there are today." Yiddish literature in America can hold its head high, Vebman continues. The major English newspapers frequently print translations of stories and articles from the Yiddish press, and the Yiddish writers in New York have even formed a union. And who would have believed that in New York City alone there would be five Yiddish daily newspapers, not to mention monthlies, annuals, and five Yiddish theaters?[104] Shomer's somewhat apologetic tone about Yiddish—the vehicle for his fame as a writer—acknowledges the low regard with which it was held by many in the Jewish intelligentsia. But it does not obscure his enthusiasm for the future of a Yiddish-based Jewish culture in America.

Eisenstadt spends much more time than Shomer on the topic of Jewishness in America. His brivnshteler is chock-full of letters related to Jewish communal life and even includes a selection of letters written in Hebrew, as well as a couple of sample bar mitzvah speeches to be delivered by the boy's father and teacher. But at the same time, he is aware that his readership includes Jews of all stripes, not only the steadfastly Orthodox but also, as Jenna Weissman Joselit puts it, Jews "who were highly selective in their approach to ritual behavior and cultural identity" and were given to "ignoring, retaining, modifying, adapting, inventing, reappropriating, and reconstructing tradition."[105]

Eisenstadt's position is that Judaism can and must survive in America, though he seems more than willing to acknowledge that Jewish practices might, at least on the surface, need modifying to suit new lifestyles. While Shomer portrays Jewish ritual as deserving of respect but old-fashioned, Eisenstadt promotes the combining of Jewishness and religious observance with the everyday realities of life in America. His model letters project a world in which there are synagogues and Jewish educational and communal institutions, albeit in a different form from those in Eastern Europe. Indeed, the types of letters he supplies—invitations to a benefit picnic for the "Brooklyn *lines-hatsedek*" (aid society for the indigent sick), a reminder from the *shames* to a member of a *shul* about his father's *yahrzeit*[106]—are not to be found in any Russian brivnshteler and reflect circumstances that would have been alien to religious life in Russia and Poland. In the last section of his brivnshteler, a set of Hebrew letters envisions an America that is not completely devoid of a Hebrew-speaking intelligentsia. One letter is from a *prenumerant* (an advance subscriber to a forthcoming book); another invites a rabbi to deliver a speech in honor of a *siyem toyre* (celebration to mark the completion of the writing of a Torah scroll) in a synagogue in Brownsville, Brooklyn; yet another asks a dignitary to deliver an address at a special event in honor of the opening of the Ninth Zionist Congress. Eisenstadt includes several sample invitations to bar mitzvahs and three bar mitzvah speeches, one in Hebrew and two in Yiddish, reflecting the new prominence of this ritual in American Jewish life.[107]

Throughout his book, Eisenstadt seems intent on dispelling the stereotype of America as a place devoid of Jewishness. Letter 8 ("A Son in America Reassures His Father in Europe That He Has Remained as Steadfast in His Judaism as He Was Back Home") is a case in point: a son reassures his father back in Russia that he has remained religiously observant. But lurking in the shadow of Eisenstadt's optimism is the fear that America poses particular challenges to the continuation of Jewish life and identity, not only for the untutored masses but even for those with a highly refined Jewish education. This anxiety finds its fullest expression in an exchange of letters in which one friend accuses another of permitting a Christmas tree in his home (Letter 9: "A Man Accuses His Friend of Having a Christmas Tree in His Home"). Following the script for brivnshteler sons berated for misconduct, the accused friend replies that it is all a false rumor spread, perhaps, by his "enemies." He remains as pious and Sabbath-observing as ever. Like the happily resolved exchanges between parents and children (the young man was not sick, or has recovered, or did not go on the wrong path; it was all a malicious rumor), Eisenstadt has succeeded in both raising the specter of Christmas and, for the present, dismissing it.

Eisenstadt's approach can be contrasted with that of Shomer, who does not articulate a strong alternative vision of Jewishness in America. Instead, when a father writes to a son who he has heard is contemplating conversion to Christianity, the best deterrent Shomer has to offer is Zionist in tone: Jews are persecuted now, but one day, when they have their own land, they will be as respected as other peoples.

But Shomer does not turn his back on Jewish tradition. We have already encountered one of Shomer's business letters, in which a poor man, begging an acquaintance for financial assistance, uses Hebrew words, phrases, and biblical citations in order to emphasize their Jewish bond and the wealthy man's religious obligations. All the Hebrew words are glossed in Yiddish in case the reader was not educated enough to know their meaning. Here and in many other places, Shomer's inclusion of Hebrew give letters a more educated, high-class tone. But the Hebrew also serves as a reminder that charity and mercy are religious obligations.

Letters

1: Rosh Hashanah Greetings to a Fiancée[i]

Warsaw, August 15, 1888

To my dear bride, the enlightened Miss Feygil, long life to her.

Dear Feygele!

Tomorrow it is Rosh Hashanah for us Jews. On this sacred day, everything that will happen to a person for a whole year is inscribed in heaven, but do you know why we celebrate the sacred holiday on this particular day? Why the Jewish new year comes specifically at the end of the summer? I will explain everything to you. A human being is like a flower that grows in the field. The flower grows beautifully in the summertime, emits a pleasant aroma, and spreads out lovely petals. It's a pleasure to behold her. But when the end of summer arrives, the petals drop off, she spoils and withers, and nothing more remains of her. And so it is with the person: in his youth he blooms like the flower, and he is healthy and strong, but when he gets to old age, his strength diminishes, his legs grow feeble, his hair white, and from day to day he gets weaker and weaker until he dies. And that's why Rosh Hashanah was set for this particular time so that the human would learn from this example. But dear Feygele! For us, this day is even more important because we must now go out into the fresh, living world. We must now begin to tread a new path, a path that is full of temptation, thorns, and briars and barbs.[ii] A path that leads a person blindly so that he doesn't know where he is going. Sometimes, it leads him off to a meadow with beautiful grass; good air; fresh and cool water, so that the person is refreshed there and his heart freed. But sometimes it leads him off to pits of snakes and scorpions, of evil and mischievous creatures, where the person becomes most unhappy. Therefore the responsibility rests on both of us, dear Feygele, on this holy day, to raise our eyes to heaven, pour out our hearts to our beloved God and ask him to support us with his guidance; open our eyes so that we will tread the straight, righteous path; destine for us good, happy years; lighten our hearts with his light; and turn away from us all misfortune. May he seal our union with his signature, in which the holy word emes[iii] is engraved, so that we will out our lives in happiness, without battle or strife. I will certainly take this responsibility upon myself and will beseech God not only for myself but for you, too. Be well and strong. May you be written and sealed for a good year. [iv]

Yours, with love,
Yankev

[i] Fridman, *Der nayer praktisher brifenshteller*, 26–27.
[ii] In the original: *mit derner, mit shamir vashayis*.
[iii] Truth.
[iv] Traditional Rosh Hashanah greeting: *Ksive vakhasime toyve*.

2: Bar Mitzvah Greetings[i]

Dear Brother!

I deeply regret that I am unable to travel to take part in your joy, in the celebration of the bar mitzvah of your son Avigdor. I am full of joy that God has assisted you in the upbringing of your son and his education

*right up until the present day. You've given him a real Jewish education,
which, in these times, is accomplished with great difficulty. I hope that
God will help you to further guide and educate him to follow the same
path and that you will merit seeing good results from all your effort.
And when he gets older, may he be a loyal son, not only toward you, but
also toward our people. May he not only have respect for his parents
and loved ones, but also for all our precious national treasures, and may
he call himself your son not only in birth certificates and other official
documents, but also in terms of his deeds.*

Your brother,
Mordkhe

ⁱ Miller, E. Miller's nayer brifenshteller in tsvey theyl, 44–45.

3: A Gymnasium Student with a Jewish Heartⁱ

Highly esteemed Father!

*I don't know if you will recognize the young boy who now stands before
you and places this letter in your hand. This is my son, Emanuel, who,
during the long time in which you haven't seen him, has changed a great
deal. But I imagine that as soon as you enter into conversation with him,
you will immediately recognize that he is a son of mine, a limb from
our family, and that he is worthy of your esteem and love, as much as
if he were your own child. For even though he is clad in the uniform of a
gymnasium student and speaks Russian, he has a Jewish heart, and
his sentiments are the same ones that you disseminated among your
children your entire life. Even though he is one of the best students in the
gymnasium and is very busy with his classes, he finds the time to read
lots of Hebrew books and newspapers, and there is scarcely a new Hebrew book that he hasn't read and whose content he doesn't know thoroughly. Even though he is among Christians all day, or among Jews who
are alienated from Judaism, he himself is loyal and devoted and, with all
his heart, bound to all that is sacred, all that is precious to our people.
And, thank God, here in our city, he has a reputation that not everyone
is privileged to have. I believe that you will really enjoy his visit.*

Your son,
Naftule

ⁱ Miller, E. Miller's nayer brifenshteller in tsvey theyl, 31–32.

4: A Jew Living Outside the Pale of Settlement[i]

Dear Friend,

You asked me in your letter how I felt in this Russian city outside the Pale? About this, I can categorically answer: bad. True, from a commercial standpoint it is a lot easier for me than at home in our city. Here, the competition is not so bad. Business opportunities abound and await a capable entrepreneur who will understand how to exploit them. And with Christians it is also very easy to come to an understanding—I have already even acquired a few true, good friends among the local merchants—but I don't feel good. There is no Jewish atmosphere here, or Jewish street and Jewish population, which, in the end, is dear and beloved to me. There are a few Jewish families here, residents, but these Jews can't compare with our Jews in G. Maybe they are Jews in their hearts, but in appearance, language, and habit, they are true Russians. And this is enough to alienate me from them.

I feel particularly lonely during the Jewish holidays. Then I feel alienated from both the Jewish city, where I spent the best years of my youth, and the Russian city, where I find myself now, it seems, completely by accident.

But the most pressing issue for me is this: my children are growing up, beginning to develop and form their character for their entire life. How can I ensure that they grow up Jewish? On the other hand, I am afraid to return to G., where five years ago I lost everything I owned.

I consider everyone who has tried to establish himself in a Jewish city a lucky person, because life depends not only on making a living.

Give my regards to all the friends of my youth and tell them that lucky is he who can be among Jews . . .

Yours, _____

[i] Bernshteyn, *Bernshteyn's nayer yudisher folks-brifenshteler*, 121–122.

5: A Sister Excoriates Her Brother for Attempting to Russify Himself[i]

July 18, 1882, Tarotin[ii]

To my beloved brother, the wealthy, shining star of our generation, Shloyme, may he flourish,

My tears flow like a river and this letter is washed by my weeping.[iii]
Oy, dear brother! Things are bad for me, I am in darkness, I am bitter!
More than once, I have written to you about my bad circumstances,
but my letters, as far as I can tell, have moved your good heart about as
much as a steamboat would move on dry land. Tell me, please, why you
have so quickly forgotten me, your sister, who has given you more than
enough help? Why don't you remember the suffering and torment you
caused me until I managed to bring you back from America? Oy! I have,
alas, done everything for your sake, and now that things are tough for
me, you have decided that it is all right to forget me! But, dear brother!
Please don't resent this; it just might be that you haven't even read my
letters, because from what I hear, you are now, a total, what's the word,
"aristocrat," you have changed the name that you were born with. You
are no longer called Shloyme ben Zvi, but "Solomon Grigorovitsh," and
your wife Tsharni and your children, may they live, also have differ-
ent names. And since I write to you only in plain Jewish[iv] *(to my dear*
brother, shining star of his generation, Shloyme) and address your wife
as Tsharni, you are angry! And truth be told, you are entirely right,
since you are now such a great man, and here I come with my letters
showing you up as just a simple Jew[v] *and that you were also once a pau-*
per! It's the truth! You're right, in your situation, I myself wouldn't be
any better, but dear Brother! You have had little in the way of a Jewish
education,[vi] *but you must know that our sages said: Don't judge your*
friend until you stand in his shoes. Believe me, I didn't realize that when
someone becomes wealthy, he has to be ashamed of a Jewish name. I
remember, and I believe you do, too, unless you want to forget it, that
when I had money, I wasn't ashamed of my name, and I helped out as
much as I could, not only friends, but even strangers, too, but maybe
the key to becoming wealthy is changing one's name? No! This I didn't
know about, but after all this, I want to know. It's the truth! You are al-
ready an "aristocrat," but can you already speak Russian? I don't know
how you would have learned. Also, I would like to know, so that you
won't be angry with me, what is your wife's name? I know that once one
was allowed to call her Tsharni and I've already asked several people
what it would be in Russian, but everyone says something different.
Some say that one can't change Tsharni[vii] *into Russian, and if that's so,*
this would be a tragedy. But you, a nouveau riche, have figured out how

to do it, so write to me and tell me so that I can at least write a letter with everyone's names. Oy, you foolish man! How long will you keep on being such an idiot? How long before the gatekeeper opens your eyes? Don't be deceived, don't be blind, figure it out! Carefully consider who you are, what you are, what it looks like, when you think that you snap a long whip, and are educated in several languages. But how do others see you? What! You think that they don't recognize you? Wouldn't it be nicer and better if each and every one of us at the very least knew and understood that the entire world is nothing more than a big roadside inn and that we are the travelers who arrive there for a certain period of time? Furthermore, when the guest returns home, he takes with him in all his luggage only what he brought with him, but the foolish person doesn't take any of it with him. Therefore, is it not better—God helped you, you can travel in first class very nicely, travel in good health, live, be happy—to see to it that your brother at least has a ticket for third class so that he won't have to lie under the seats and get dragged out and arrested by the conductor? But you! Do you travel first class? You think only of increasing your capital. No! This is not the way to live in the world. Oh, why should I keep complaining so much? I've said enough and I know that in particular, Ha-shakhar,[viii]* blessed be its memory, also wrote about this, but it didn't do any good. And especially, a foolish Jewish woman like myself is also not going to have any effect, but it doesn't matter: when the heart aches, one speaks. It will probably get easier. That's it, have pity on your sister, daughter of your people, because my situation is bitter.*[ix]* So don't be angry that I scold you. Believe me, it's my troubles that are speaking, and I ask you to be helpful to me. There is no additional news. Very friendly regards to your family.*

From me, your sister,
Sore Feldshteyn

[i] Yoysef Arukh, *Arukhs brifenshteller*, 32–34.

[ii] This may be the Yiddish version of Tarutino or Taratino. There are several different similarly named towns in Russia and Ukraine.

[iii] Original text in Hebrew.

[iv] *Yudish.*

[v] *Prost yudeli.*

[vi] On the other hand, the letter writer, a woman, seems to be educated enough to quote in Hebrew.

^{vii} Tsharni, or Tsharna, is a name derived from the Slavic root *chorn*, black (Russian *chorny*; Polish *czarny*). Since it was already Slavic, no Russian equivalent could be devised, though it was a name popular only among Jews and virtually unheard of among Russian-speaking non-Jews. The writer is being sarcastic.

^{viii} *Razsvet* (Dawn), edited in Odessa by Osip Rabinovich (1817–1869), the first Russian-language Jewish periodical. It began publishing in 1860 but soon went out of business. The author, Arukh, refers to it by its Hebrew name.

^{ix} Hebrew.

6: Fire in the Ringtheaterⁱ

Dear, beloved Father,

Thank you for teaching me to travel the good road and to guard my faith. I remember well your words before my departure for Vienna. I wrote them down and they are more precious to me than gold, pearls, or all other precious things in the world. I read them every day as if they were the best book. And these words have really come in handy and make me realize what a sage you are: First of all, that I should every day, morning and night, offer praise to Eternal God and observe the Sabbath and holidays, and not eat any treyf. Secondly, that I shouldn't associate with bad company, since a bad friend leads one down bad paths. Thirdly, that I shouldn't go out at night if it isn't necessary, or go to a theater or circus or such things because this does not lead to the good road. And I make sure that I observe these rules as far as possible. My dear father, sometimes it is very hard to do this in such a big city like Vienna and being in a foreign country, to boot. But I try as much as possible. And all this went to good use. As you will hear and perhaps read about, and as my dear mother and brothers and sisters should also hear, right after I arrived in Vienna, I became acquainted with a respectable young man. He was also from Berdichev and was also studying in Vienna. We would look out for one another in terms of food, lodging and teachers, and would go walking together. In my eyes, he had every virtue. On one particular evening, he was about to go out and asked me to go with him to the theater. They were going to show things never before seen since the creation of the earth and never to be seen again. He tried to convince me but I took out my diary, in

which all your sayings are written. When I showed them to him, he had
a good laugh and said, "Your father is from the old world." Then he left
and never came again. The next day, I had the fortune or misfortune to
seeing him lying among the asphyxiated victims, and then they took all
of them and dug mass graves where they laid them all, Jews and Christians together. The story is that in Vienna there is a Ringtheater, which
can accommodate endless numbers of people, and during a performance of novelties, there were so many people, almost as many as are
in Berdichev altogether. My friend was also drawn there. The theater
was on the second floor, up high, inside, and was lighted with gas. But
you have to know how to handle the gas lamps. When you want to ex-
tinguish them, you give the pipe a turn with your hands. And when you
want to turn them on, you give the pipe a turn the other way and light it
with a wooden match. If you forget to light it with a match, the pipe lets
out too much gas with fumes. And no one noticed that someone forgot
to turn it off, that the janitor forgot to turn off one of the pipes. A day
and a night went by and a lot of fumes accumulated on the ground and
it was as dangerous as vitriol.[ii] But no one knew about it. Just as the
audience assembled, someone threw something. It was a lighted match
which skipped onto the floor. And the clothes of many of the people
caught on fire. Many also died of asphyxiation from the smoke. Many
tried to escape but didn't know where to turn. Many jumped from the
windows. A few survived because people almost right away threw down
feather beds underneath. The fire department took a long time to get
there because no fire was visible from the street. You can imagine how
grateful I was to you. It was just as if, dear father, you had foreseen
that it would be this way. Please, my dear father, write to me the story
of the fire in the circus and don't mince any words.[iii] You will revive
me because I can't rest until you write about my brothers and sisters
and friends, about everything in detail, because the tragedy has put all
of Vienna and the whole world in an uproar.

[i] Poliak-Gilman, *Der nayer obraztsover brifenshteller*, 18–20. This
letter also appears in Kresin, *Der berihmter zhargohn loshn koydesh
russisher brief korespondenter* (1903).

[ii] Sulfuric acid.

[iii] Possibly he wants his father to comment on the tragedy. Or he may
have in mind another disaster, a fire that broke out at the Circus

Ferroni in Berdichev in 1883, which killed hundreds of people. The cover of the other book in which this letter appears, Kresin's *Der berihmter zhargohn loshn koydesh russisher brief korespondenter,* advertises that its contents includes letters about "the Vienna theater and the Berdichev circus."

7: A Defense of an "Old-Fashioned Custom"[i]

Dear, good friend!

The report that you are celebrating the day of your son's bar mitzvah has brought me much joy.

Today's modern sages laugh at such festive occasions. They regard a bar mitzvah celebration as an old-fashioned custom, but an ordinary person like myself has great respect for this celebration.

How should parents show their joy about having lived to see their dear, dear son enter his fourteenth year of life?

At the age of thirteen, the youth begins to understand, that it is finally time for him to cast off childish pleasures and take up something more serious.

The first thirteen years of a person's life are the hardest for his parents, because that is when his development begins and they must get him through various illnesses and mishaps, and the parents constantly tremble with fear and worry over their dear child.

Up until his thirteenth year of schooling, the youth thinks that everything is permitted to him, because he is still a child.

Therefore, it is the responsibility of the parents to remind him that he is no longer a child and that the time has come when he should look at the world in a different and more serious way.

A thirteen-year-old child already understands what you say to him and intelligent words can finally make the right impression on him.

And so, the day of bar mitzvah is a festive occasion in two ways.

First, the parents rejoice that the danger-filled years of childhood have finally come to an end, that their child has made it safely through all the illnesses and mishaps.

Second, the day of bar mitzvah is the station at which the child is asked to climb out of the baby carriage and is shown a new, true path which can lead him to much good fortune.

And since you, my friend, have lived to celebrate this beautiful, festive occasion, you must feel happy.

I hope that you will live to celebrate your son's wedding and that he will always walk on the straight, honest path that you will show him.

You know how dear you are to me and how heartfelt my congratulations are, because your happiness is also the happiness of your eternal friend,

Elkone Ayzenshteyn

[i] Shaykevitsh, *Shaykevitsh'es nayer brivnshteler*, 40–41.

8: A Son in America Reassures His Father in Europe That He Has Remained as Steadfast in His Judaism as He Was Back Home[i]

Dear Father!

I received your dear letter and it made me very happy to hear that dear Mother, may she live, has been completely cured of her rheumatism and that she was finally in good enough condition to travel to see my dear sister in Minsk for a few weeks.

It is completely unnecessary, devoted Father, to advise me in your letter to observe the Sabbath, in particular, and to observe Judaism, in general, because you know me, dear Father. You know that I have always trod one path. Whether sitting in Kiev or Odessa, Warsaw or Moscow, I steadfastly continued to observe Jewish customs, especially the Sabbath, which is one of the greatest and strongest fundaments of Judaism. I have never traded Judaism for money, not even for riches and wealth.

I can even tell you that in my present occupation, I was offered a job for which I could get 3 dollars more a week than I do now. However, it would have involved me having to do business on the Sabbath and on the Jewish holidays and so I didn't take it, because for me, the peaceful and holy Jewish days are much dearer than money.

I am also a member of a beautiful shul where I go to worship every Sabbath and holiday.

Hoping that you will stay well and be happy, your son,
Ruvn Fink

[i] Eisenstadt, *Der moderner briefenshteller*, 50–51.

9: A Man Accuses His Friend of Having a Christmas Tree in His Home[i]

My worthy friend Avrom Lib Khishin!

You know that I am one of your best friends and therefore I hope that you will excuse me for writing you this letter. I believe that as a practical man you will take into consideration that, indeed, it is only because I am your true friend that I feel that I have to write this letter.

I don't mean to preach at you, my dear friend. I'm not one of God's Cossacks. You know me—I don't wear a mask, and I don't adorn myself with colorful clothes.[ii] Nonetheless, I must now, my friend, comment on a blunder you made, quite recently, this week, on Christmas day.

There is, blessed be G-d, a world full of blunders big and small, which one sees and hears and one must also keep quiet about, but this blunder, that you have made, dear friend, cannot pass by without comment, especially from a true friend who holds your honor dear and your name in love and respect.

I have heard from a reliable source, that in your house, where there is a library with our best Jewish pearls; where there are many, many of the best Jewish holy books; in your Jewish home where mezuzahs hang on the doors and beautiful pictures of our greatest spiritual giants decorate and adorn the walls[iii]—in that same house, you permitted the Christmas rituals to be observed in all their holiness (may it not be so) and in your house you allowed the display of a tree around which your children partied in an entirely goyish way. My dear friend! Consider carefully what you have done. It might seem like nothing but child's play, an occasion for having fun and nothing more. But it smacks of something completely different. And my feeling is that if such a Jewish Jew as you, a man like you who was brought up among passionate and warm Jewish loyalists, could allow this to be done in his own house, then what, in the end, will the simple and ignorant masses do?

It is possible, dear friend, that maybe it was done without your permission, that maybe no one asked you. We know the children of today: they don't often consult their parents. It's possible that it was the so-called "modern" and "civilized" children, the ones who constantly imi-

tate the Christians, who brought the "green crucifix" into your house, and that their kosher hands planted the non-Jewish plant completely without your knowledge. But I believe, dear friend, that an educated and learned man such as yourself should have known how to handle such a situation. You should have known that this kind of child's play always ends in the worst, most terrible and saddest tragedy of "assimilation," which is, in reality, not just the death of yiddishkeit,[iv] but also a very, very shameful and ugly death. You should have known that in the final result these sort of "playthings" bring no honor into the Jewish home, but only degradation and spiritual malaise.

Yes, dear Avrom Lib, I am wondering a great deal about you. I've known you for many years, as a loyal citizen of the Jewish city, as a true friend of your religion, and how astounded I was to see that in your middle age you have begun to exchange your beautiful way of life. You, dear friend, who has so extensively studied and researched Jewish Wissenschaft and education[v]—who knows better than you the magnificence of Jewish laws, Jewish traditions, and everything that is Jewish? You would certainly be considered a member of the Jewish intelligentsia—who more than that intelligentsia knows and sees the pure light and beautiful rays of our true faith? Today, I ask you, what has led you to such an absurd and disgraceful, or better said, foolish incident like this one?

One simply does not want to believe it, even though I don't doubt the veracity of the report, which comes from a reliable source. I still want to hope that you, dear friend, will solve the riddle for me, and set me straight, and how happy I will be to find out that I have been mistaken and that what I was told isn't true, and that you, dear friend, are far, far away from evil.

Your honorable friend,
Moyshe Zusman

---

[i] Eisenstadt, *Der moderner briefenshteller*, 99–103.

[ii] Meaning, perhaps that he isn't wearing a Cossack hood (*bashlyk*) or colorful Cossack clothes.

[iii] Presumably, portraits of important rabbis. The author, Ben-Zion Eisenstadt, was known for his biographical works on Orthodox religious leaders in America, including *Oytser temunes* [*Otsar Tmunot*] (1909), a book of photographs of rabbis.

^{iv} Yiddishkeit: Jewishness, encompassing culture, behavior, and
certain patterns of thought.

^v *Wissenschaft des Judentums,* a nineteenth-century movement that
promoted the use of secular European academic methods for the
study of Jewish history and culture.

IMAGING AMERICA

Introduction

The heyday of brivnshtelers coincided with the height of the mass immigration of East European Jews to the United States. Yet comparatively
few model letters in manuals published in the Russian Empire concern
themselves with emigration to America, and some that do regard it nega-
tively. What are the possible reasons for the brivnshtelers' relative neglect
and distaste for this mass communal phenomenon?

The duty of reforming Jews and Jewish life in keeping with maskilic
ideals was presumably never far from the minds of brivnshteler authors.
But their focus was either on the reformation of Jews and Jewish life
in situ, in the Russian or Austro-Hungarian Empires—or, by the turn
of the twentieth century, on a Zionist solution, the dream of building a
new, modern Jewish life in Palestine. America did not fit neatly into this
agenda. Worth noting, too, is that while some brivnshtelers included non-
letter material of practical utility, such as instructions on how to address
letters in Russian, lists of Russian *guberniias* (provinces), and templates
for IOUs and marriage contracts, none included information related to
emigration, such as passport application forms. In this case, brivnshtelers
did not do a good job of keeping up with the times. There was a discon-
nect between the standard templates they continued to reprint and what
was required by the estimated 1.6 million Jews who immigrated to the
United States from the Russian Empire in 1881–1914.[108]

When America does make an appearance in model letters, it often
does so in a negative way. Letters 1 and 2 from 1900 ("You Squandered
Your Youth") link a son's emigration to America to the young man's failure to live up to maskilic educational ideals. This association is not uncommon in Russian brivnshtelers, which, because of either the ideologies

of their authors or a fear of portraying Russian Jewry as disloyal, tend to imagine America as a purgatory for those who have committed the sin of being uneducated or unskilled. It is a punishment for young men who have not pursued a secular education—the preferred solution to the problems of modern Jewish life—and thus are ill-suited to survive in the changing economy. Castigation of an unsuccessful son is, as we have seen, a familiar brivnshteler genre. It has been updated in this case to include exile in a strange land as an additional punishment for neglecting one's studies and failing to heed the sage advice of one's elders.

Another criticism of America comes through as horror over its fast pace and reputation for hard work. In a letter from a brivnshteler of 1911, Avsholem presents his emigration as a kind of exile:

> God has cast me out in a distant land where life is very hard—the busyness, the frantic pace of work is terribly intense, indescribable. No one who hasn't seen this sort of life with his own eyes can imagine what a hell it is; life itself goads and chases you, forcing a person to work like our ancestors in Egypt, beyond one's capabilities, and there is no time to take a breath.[109]

While a look at real family correspondence can provide only anecdotal evidence for Jewish immigrant attitudes toward America, reading just a few letters is likely to reveal sentiments starkly dissimilar to those expressed in brivnshtelers.[110] In real letters written to immigrants in North America, families acknowledge that adjusting to a strange new world is hard for their children and express their longing to see them again, but America is generally depicted as an opportunity, not a misfortune. For most of those who emigrated, formal higher education in the sense that it was envisioned by brivnshtelers did not appear to have been an option, nor was its absence a motivation for emigration. Real family correspondence is often explicit about the more likely reasons that millions of Jews left for America: lack of economic opportunity, the desire to avoid military service, and, occasionally, the need to flee in order to avoid punishment for anti-tsarist activities.[111] The first two reasons are mentioned in the following letter, sent by Meyshe Abba Zemkropski from the Lithuanian town Butrimonys (Baltrumonts) to his brother Izzie, who had emigrated a couple of years earlier and for some unexplained reason does not seem to want his brother to come to the United States:

Dear brother, I have written to you about how I am planning to come to America . . . but you have not replied at all. I really don't understand why you are angry at me, why you don't write to me. After all, we are brothers. My coming to America won't cost you a single kopek but because army service is coming up and I'd have to do four miserable years of duty and only then be able to come to America, well, you can certainly see the situation I'm in. As you know, Father won't spend a single kopek on me and I don't mean anything by this, I feel no resentment toward him. He can't spend anything on me—he is a sick man and has no business that would enable me, as a young man, to stay in Baltrumonts [Butrimonys] . . . Fayfke Khayim Shuel is also going to America today because there is nothing to do here. . . . It feels as if in Baltrumonts we go to sleep from Friday night to Saturday night, and afterward there is nowhere to go anyway.[112]

Airing the Jewish desire to avoid army service would, of course, have been off-limits to brivnshteler authors—one good reason that the emigration phenomenon was not confronted honestly in model letters. But America was also a political topic for another reason: the civic equality that Jews enjoyed there. In Letter 3 ("I Thought That Gold Rolled Around in the Streets"), from an 1890 brivnshteler, an advertisement for America is slipped in between lamentations about how homesick the newly arrived immigrant is for Russia.

The characterization of the United States as a country where Jews had full civil rights is an implicit, if not explicit, criticism of the Russian policy, and it is interesting to consider whether, in this case, the censor wasn't paying attention. One of the few other positive portrayals of America in a Russian brivnshteler appears in Letters 4–7 ("Here, No One Is Ashamed of Honest Work"), all from a single manual of 1891. Here, the author avoids criticism of Russian policy toward the Jews by substituting a social critique of the Russian-Jewish community, which is described as averse to taking on menial or physically arduous work and uninterested in training young men to be craftsmen. Twenty years later, Letter 8 ("I Too Have Decided to Go to America") demonstrates that even in the Russian Empire, by the second decade of the twentieth century, America could be presented as a viable option for young Jewish men seeking greater opportunities. Written after the 1905 revolution, on the eve of the First World War, it openly discusses discrimination against Jews.

The letters in brivnshtelers published in the United States take quite a different tone from their European counterparts, for most part portraying America in positive terms. Shomer's 1905 *Shaykevitsh'es nayer briefenshteler* (Shaykevitsh's new brivnshteler) and Eisenstadt's 1910 *Der moderner brieffenshteller* (The modern brivnshteler) were written with a Jewish immigrant audience in mind. While many of their letters deal with specifically local situations, offering wording for American versions of courtship, business, and Jewish communal life, they also provided guidance on communicating with family and friends left behind in Europe. Shomer and Eisenstadt went so far as to furnish letters useful for their readers' first days after landing in New York Harbor, despite the unlikelihood that someone just off the boat would have prioritized the purchase of a brivnshteler (Letter 9: "From a Son Newly Arrived in America"; Letter 10: "In New York, You Think You're Still in the Shtetl"). Both authors suggest that merely stepping foot on American soil effects an immediate transformation of the East European Jew into someone who, in comparison with those back home, is already a sophisticate, a man or woman of the world.[113]

Despite these advertisements for America, Shomer and Eisenstadt pull back from endorsing everything about American life or from touting America as an option for every single Jew in Eastern Europe. Eisenstadt has Yoysef Bernshteyn giving his friend Avrom cautious advice:

> You ask me whether it would be worth it for you to come to America. And believe me, I can't give you one correct answer to such a question. America is like the whole world: everywhere one must have a bit of luck. People who are entirely common and ordinary come here and work themselves up to being wealthy, but, on the other hand, one also sees here intelligent and educated people who are not very well-off.
>
> Naturally, there is more room to make a living in America than in another country, but a lot depends on one's capability for work and even more on getting the right job.[114]

Shomer, too, warns those back home about having too rosy a view of life in America. In Letter 10 ("In New York, You Think You're Still in the Shtetl"), Leah, just off the boat, tells her parents only positive things. Everyone is helpful; she's already working; and above all, contrary to what they think in the shtetl, America "is no Gehenna." But writing to her girlfriend (Letter 11: "In America, Girls Don't Need a Dowry"), she debunks a different shtetl myth. In the shtetl, "they think that gold can be scraped up from the street with shovels because Khayim Yekel the tailor, who couldn't earn a piece of dry bread in our shtetl, sent no less than two hundred rubles to his Khane Dvoyre in his first year in America."[115] In New York the same ten dollars that would constitute a Russian fortune does not go far, especially if a girl wants to dress fashionably and enjoy a few luxuries.

The brutal pace of work in America is the drawback of life in the New World that is most often cited. While some immigrants arrived with tailoring skills and experience of city living, many others had to learn their trade on the job, in sweatshops and factories where work hours and other conditions differed markedly from those of the small-town workshops they were used to. In Letter 12 ("A Brother Warns His Sister Not to Come to America"), Eisenstadt's Avrom Kaplan tells his sister that she shouldn't come to America, pointing to the terrible effects of factory work on the health of young women.

Shomer, too, focuses on the particular hardships for women in the workshops and factories of America, but his view of their prospects is considerably less bleak than Eisenstadt's. In Letter 11 ("In America, Girls Don't Need a Dowry"), Leah tempers her criticism by citing some serious advantages. She makes it clear that she emigrated because of economic desperation. And this was justified: in America, girls can work just like men, and they don't need a dowry to get married.

Shomer's Letter 13 ("America Is the True Garden of Eden") lists other ways in which life in America is superior to life in the Russian Empire. America is described as a modern Garden of Eden, a place that combines the sights and sounds of progress (automobiles! elevated trains!) with a fantastic array of social services. Girls and orphans are protected. Anyone can go to a hospital. But most of all, America is a land of opportunity where the poorest Jewish nobody can make a fortune, or join the ranks of doctors, lawyers, and scholars.

Letters

1: You Squandered Your Youth[i]

New York, May 24, 1897
Esteemed Father!
Forgive me for not writing until now. It was all because I didn't have any good news. You can imagine how it is for me, in a strange city with-

out friends or acquaintances, with no education and profession, not to mention the strange language. It is very hard for me to get by. I have taken advantage of everything that has come my way, but haven't had any luck at any of these enterprises. I can't find any business from which anything would come of it for me. Therefore, dear Father, I am writing to ask you if I can come home. Maybe I will be able to get some work from people you know. Stay well and happy as per the wishes of your son who awaits a friendly response.

Efroym Zilbershtayn

[i] *Eyn nayer brifenshteler in dray obtheylungen*, 18–19.

2: You Squandered Your Youth, reply[i]

Vilna, June 5, 1897

Dear son Efroym, shining star of his generation, may his light shine,

I received your letter. You complain about your bad circumstances, even though I know that you yourself are responsible for your bad situation. As your father, of course, I deeply regret this, but how can I help you? You yourself know the truth, that I, on my part, have done everything I could for you. I have paid teachers to teach you everything essential and I have demonstrated and explained to you how education brings a person good fortune and how unsuccessful an ignorant person is. He is useless to himself and even more so to others, and most of all, he is a superfluous person in society. Useless people become a burden and have to live on the accounts of others. I have told you this so many times, but you didn't want listen to me. Now it is bad for you! You can't find a profession for yourself because you can't write or do arithmetic, and you also didn't want to learn a craft, so what are you good for? It's no wonder. You squandered your youth, didn't listen to parents or teachers. Now your eyes are opened to everything. I understand, my dear child, that you now realize full well, but too late. Nonetheless, if you truly have regrets about your bad behavior, all is not yet lost. You can come home and I will do everything on your behalf. These are the words of your father,

Your father

[i] *Eyn nayer brifenshteler in dray obtheylungen*, 19–20.

3: I Thought That Gold Rolled Around in the Streets[i]

New York (America), October 30, 1890

To my dear and pious mother Mrs. Rokhl, may she live, may you live to age one-hundred-and-twenty.

First of all I want to let you know, dear Mother, that on December 20 [sic] I arrived safely in New York and immediately looked around. And what a bad deal I made because I didn't take your advice and let myself be misled by superficial people and believed that in America gold rolled around in the streets and one only had to bend down and pick it up. In the end, I saw that it is not like that at all. Of course, this is a very free land where the Jew has all same the human rights as any other nationality, but in order to cross over into such a distant part of the world he must store up more than just patience, in order to come to the decision to become separated almost forever from the land of his birth, where every bit of land, every blade of grass, every tree is beloved, and to never again have the opportunity to see his parents and acquaintances. Not to mention all the hardships: one must learn the language spoken in every neighborhood, and also learn to specialize in a profession. But it is so particularly bad for me right now that I can't write to you, dear Mother, about my situation at all; first of all, because I don't want to cause you too much suffering, and secondly, because I don't have the time right now. Only, dear Mother, I ask you to please have mercy on me and forgive me for my impulsiveness and give me some advice about how I can come back to Russia. And please write me a reply immediately.

From me, your son who awaits your reply,
Arn

[i] Goldshteyn-Gershonovitsh, *Yudish-daytsher morall brifenshteller*, 17. This letter can also be found in *Eyn nayer brifenshteler in dray obtheylungen*, 20–21. There, the son's name is Khayim and the mistake about the date of his arrival has been corrected to October 20.

4: Here, No One Is Ashamed of Honest Work[i]

New York, Mates [Matot][ii] 1888

To my wife Mrs. Khane, may she live,

I am writing to tell you that I have arrived safely in New York. I suffered a great deal on the ship, just like everyone else who is unaccustomed

to the sea air. I am now based at your brother-in-law's, and after I
have rested up a bit, I will also begin to look around for a way to make
a living. I hope that God, blessed be He, will help me and that I will,
if G-d wills it, find something at which to make a success here. I have
run into Khaym Yekl, Grune's son. You wouldn't recognize him at all;
he is quite the aristocrat, goes around in a fine coat and a top hat, and
already speaks German and English. He earns bars of gold. Borekh[iii]
doesn't have it too badly either. True, one must slave away beyond one's
strength, but something can come of it. I also won't be lazy. I won't be
embarrassed to do anything, because here one isn't ashamed to do any
sort of work. Only thievery is a disgrace. But honest hard work is free
and open to everyone, and that's what's really good about America.
If only back at home, people wouldn't be ashamed to do everything, it
would be America by us, too. But among us, the only thing that matters
is whether someone is a person of good family, a high-class person, and
that is why people starve to death. I don't have any news to write you; in
the meantime I am sending you a money order for 15 rubles that I borrowed, and that I will, if G-d wills it, pay back, because I know full well
that I left you without a kopek.

> Your husband, who wishes you much happiness,
> Khayim Yoyne

[i] Fridman, *Der nayer praktisher brifenshteller,* 58–61. These are the
second–fifth letters in a five-letter cycle of letters between Khayim
Yoyne and his wife. The first letter is written from Hamburg, where
he is about to board the ship to America. He had to leave Russia
because creditors were sucking his blood "like leeches," but he is
nervous about his decision to go to America because he has heard
that there is already a glut of immigrants there.

[ii] "Tribes." Torah portion for that week: Numbers 25:10–30:1.

[iii] Presumably, Khane's brother.

5: Here, No One Is Ashamed of Honest Work, reply

Mezhibozh, October 15, 1888
*To my husband, the shining star of his generation, Khayim Yoyne, may
he flourish,*
Your letter saying that you have arrived there safely has given me
great pleasure and I received the 15 rubles, but what good will it do?

What should I pay first? Rent needs to be paid, the children must be clothed, and we have to eat, too. And about paying off our debt I won't even speak. But why should I pour salt on your wounds? God will certainly have mercy on us and will send us his aid, but you must not forget God; you must serve him with all your heart, and then he will certainly help you. I tell you, if only you had listened to me, you wouldn't have had to go to America. You could have lived here, too. We could have eked out a living here. People don't make a fortune in America either. A lot of people come back from there empty-handed. May G-d grant that you will not regret it and that you will earn a lot of money and will soon come back to your home safe and sound.

From me, your wife who wishes you life and happiness,
Khane
Yankele and Khayele sent you their warm regards.

6: Here, No One Is Ashamed of Honest Work, another letter from Khayim Yoyne

To my wife, Khane, may she live,

I am sending you a money order for 40 rubles which I have, thank God, honestly earned. May it only be no worse later on. Here, one must bitterly slave away. If you could see the big packs that I shlep on my shoulders and must carry up to the sixth floor, I am sure that tears would flow from your eyes. But despite this, I am happy. However, the skilled workmen do much better here. They sit there at peace and earn real money. Our people of good family, the yudlakh,[i] Abraham, Isaac, and Jacob's grandchildren, who don't want their children to learn any craft, now they should see how they ruin the luck of their children. They eat each other up and remain paupers, poor men, lying in dirt and living in muck and thereby darkening their years with chaos. If you could see how clean and tidily one lives here, you would say that the Americans are angels compared to the Russian Jews. The lowliest peasants live so cleanly that their floors shine like mirrors. And the clothing they wear! How cleanly and beautifully they dress when they go out! That's why they are also strong and healthy, because cleanliness is halfway to health. I tell you the truth, that sometimes it occurs to me, deep in my heart, that I should send you a ship's ticket and bring you and the chil-

dren here. But I am afraid to encourage you to do so, because you won't want to leave your parents and everyone you know. And this is certainly no sin, one must respect and love one's parents. What do you think, Khane? Could you agree to come here? If yes, I will indeed immediately send you a ticket. Because one doesn't have to pay it off immediately but can do so over time. I await your answer.

Your husband,
Khayim Yoyne

ⁱ Little Jews, derogatory.

7: Here, No One Is Ashamed of Honest Work, reply

To my husband, shining star of his generation, Khayim Yoyne.
My dear husband!

I see that you are still the same Yoyne that you were here at home. You always want to catch the fish before it is in the net. It hasn't been long since you arrived in America and already you want to bring your family there. Believe me, I also wish that we could live together, and about what you wrote, that I won't leave my parents, you are greatly mistaken. Even though I love them very much, don't you know that one must go with one's husband, even across an ocean? But what is the use of all this and all this empty talk when it is not yet the right time? First you must sock away a bit of capital so that we can survive there; then we can start to talk. But not now! So drive those thoughts right out of your head. If G-d wills it, when you feel that we can live decently there, I will fly to you on wings.

Your wife,
Khane
Your children send you their warm regards.

8: I Too Have Decided to Go to Americaⁱ

Dear friend!

Before your departure, you promised to write me often with your impressions of your new country, where you are among foreign people and a foreign culture, and to give me a detailed report of the life of a Jewish emigrant. How does a member of the Jewish intelligentsia feel when he arrives in America and has to take on ordinary physical labor? And I was really waiting for this, because you would have been the one to provide me with a greeting from all the friends of my youth who have ended up on the other side of the ocean. Half of the young people from our shtetl have left for America and most of them are in New York. Consequently, America has become for me and for almost every Jew in Russia a sort of "new home," one that we've never seen, but which is nonetheless dear to our hearts.

I am floundering around here just like almost all young Jews, without a plan or life. For a while I was an auditor,[ii] *and sat for exams several times but didn't succeed in passing them. Later, I gave lessons. I've already tried to get into business but this didn't succeed either. . . . In a word—this isn't it!*

For all of us, the fault is that we aimed very high, built sand castles in the air, trusted too much in our own capabilities, and failed completely to take into account the difficult conditions in this country or of the lamentable situation of the Jews. We all but forgot that we are Jewish children, that we shouldn't compare ourselves to young Christian men, that even if we have wings, they can't bear to let us out of our cage.

Now we stand at the crossroads, with goals unattained, but torn away from the old world, where a Jew can still find a way of supporting himself. There is really one remaining way out: to go to America and restart one's life anew there, from the very beginning. True, it is hard in one's riper years to sit one's self down on a stool and maybe even get a lash of the whip occasionally. . . . But there is nothing to be done about it. As you can see, my friend, I too have decided to go to America. Before I take this step, I would like your opinion because the two of us have plenty in common, and I have no doubt about the validity of what you think. Your experience in America will serve as an example for me about what might happen to me too there. I await your letter with impatience.

Yours . . .

[i] Bernshteyn, *Bernshteyn's yudisher brief-lehrer,* 6–67.

[ii] Word in original: *eksteren.* Someone who was not officially enrolled as a student but was permitted to sit for exams. A frequent position for Jews who, because of the quota system, could not get into high schools, universities, or other institutes of higher education. In 1909, the quota system was extended to *eksterens,* thereby closing the loophole.

9: From a Son Newly Arrived in America[i]

My dear parents!

In my first letter, I promised to write to you about everything without delay, and my word is dear to me, especially when it involves your pleasure and happiness, dear parents. And then my promise is also sacred, because I sense that for you, a letter from me equals health and life, encouragement and joy. And to create this for you, I am always ready, with my best and last strength.

My journey on the ship was difficult at the beginning. For close to two entire days, I didn't eat and was constantly nauseated from the tossing of the ship. On the third day, I was already used to it and the weather was calmer and I finally started to feel better and better. I talked to my ship comrades who I knew from Rotterdam, and every time we made a "le-khayim," we cried out, "le-khayim to our passionately devoted families in Russia," and I had you, dear parents, very much on my mind.

Due to poor weather and storm winds which began on the ninth day of the journey, the ship was delayed by two days. There was also almost an entire day when a dark cloud and a thick fog reigned, and the ship kept on tooting, and from time to time gave terrible alarm sounds which threw a pall of fear upon all the passengers. But, thank God, we overcame everything, and as soon as we saw the Statue of Liberty in New York Harbor, it became light before our eyes.

We were deeply inspired by the American symbol as expressed in the image of an angel standing in the middle of a vast and stormy sea holding its hand outstretched and inviting everyone who is lonely and homeless to turn to it so that it can take them under its wings and protect them and stretch out a helping hand to them.

In the meantime, I have arranged for a place to live with our townsman Moyshe Finkelshteyn. He received me with much friendliness, and I hope to start working next week.

Stay happy and healthy. Best wishes, your
Zusman Lifshits

[i] Eisenstadt, *Der moderner briefenshteller*, 40–42.

10: In New York, You Think You're Still in the Shtetl[i]

My dear, beloved parents!

Not for nothing does the world have the proverb: "The devil is not so ugly as he has been painted." This is very true. In our small shtetlakh,[ii] it is believed that traveling to America is a sort of trip to Gehenna. You imagine the most terrible things about this journey, that you constantly hover on the brink of danger and that with every step you might meet with misfortune.

But it's not so terrible, dear parents. Thousands of people—men, women, and children—make the journey over the stormy ocean and don't come to any harm. And if you meet with misfortune on the sea, you shouldn't forget that great misfortunes also occur on dry land, if, God forbid, you're destined for misfortune, even in the safest of places.

The journey on the ocean is at first unpleasant. But later, you get used to it and it becomes pleasant. You get to know a lot of people on board the ship, and it is noteworthy that on shipboard everyone becomes friendly with one another. You feel somehow connected with each other.

When you arrive in New York you encounter so many acquaintances from home that you think you're still in the shtetl.

There is hardly a shtetl in Russia, Austria, and Romania that hasn't sent a few families to America, and so a new arrival, or as it is called here, a greener, won't be lost. His landsmen help him with advice (and sometimes actually do something for him).

Blessed is America for the fact that here, working is no disgrace. Everyone works: old and young, men and women, and as long as one wants to work, there is no lack of work in New York.

Even though it hasn't yet been four weeks since my arrival here, I have also found work. I have been hired by a handshuhe factory (called "gloves" here)[iii] and in the first weeks have earned only two dollars a week because I'm not yet acquainted with the work. I hope that I will learn the art quickly and will begin to earn more.

I don't lack for anything, thank God. I eat, drink, and sleep well.

You don't need to worry about me, dear parents. You will yet live to hear very good news from your devoted and passionately loving daughter,

Leah Goldberg

ⁱ Shaykevitsh, *Shaykevitsh'es nayer brivnshteler*, 59–60.

ⁱⁱ Shtetlakh: plural of shtetl, small town; in practice, small town with a large Jewish population.

ⁱⁱⁱ The English word "gloves" is used.

11: In America, Girls Don't Need a Dowry ⁱ

My dear friend, Rokhl!

I promised to write you a letter from America and acquaint you with the world here, and I will keep that promise. I'm now sending you my first letter.

First of all, I want to tell you, dear friend, that I really miss you and all of our friends, and even really miss our small shtetl, which is a flea compared to New York City.

I must admit that New York is worth marveling at. If a person had a hundred eyes, they wouldn't get sated from looking at the exquisite things that can be seen here. But a person who has to break his head over making a living, a person who is lacking even the most essential things, doesn't think of looking at even the most beautiful, most precious and exquisite marvels.

You know what kind of situation I left back home and with what a bitter heart I parted from my dear parents and from all my relatives and acquaintances.

You know, dear friend, that I didn't leave for the new world for fun, but out of need. I didn't want to be a burden on my parents any longer. I couldn't watch them suffer, and so I decided to seek my fortune by going to America. Maybe I will be able to earn money and support them, my impoverished parents, as much as possible.

You know what kind of ideas our shtetl residents have of America. They think that gold can be scraped up from the street with shovels because Khayim Yekel the tailor, who couldn't earn a piece of dry bread in our shtetl, sent no less than two hundred rubles to his Khane Dvoyre in his first year in America, and Khasye the shopkeeper's daughter Beyle sent her mother money for a wig and a coat.

In our shtetl, they think that everyone in America lives like kings in beautiful palaces with the most expensive furniture and that we ride around in equipages. But when they get here, they see how mistaken they were.

It is true that in New York one can earn money faster than in our shtetlakh. But one must bitterly and strenuously slave away. The working classes here don't live in palaces, but in stifling, airless little rooms.

The only bit of luck is that the American ruble (dollar) is worth two of our Russian ones and when Khayim Yekel the tailor saved up a hundred dollars over an entire year here, it became two hundred rubles in Russia.

But even though an American dollar is worth two of our rubles, in America, it isn't worth more than one ruble, and while in our shtetl one can live well on three rubles a week, in New York, one needs at least fifteen dollars (thirty rubles) to live well, because, first of all, rent is very high, and secondly, everything is more expensive than back home.

Here, girls work as hard as the young men do. All the factories are packed with girls who work there and they must work very hard for the few dollars a week they get.

When, for example, you hear that a girl here makes ten dollars a week (twenty rubles), you would think that she can have a good time with all that money or that she can save up a lot of money. But you would be mistaken. It is barely enough for her to clothe herself in a manner suitable for life in America or to buy herself a little enjoyment.

But despite all this, I must admit that America is a blessed land. Whoever wants to work can make something of themselves. America also has the advantage that the majority of girls don't need a dowry. As long as a girl is not ugly and is respectable, she can easily find a groom who will take her as she is.

I have started to work. I make very little and work very hard. Sometimes, I'm angry at myself for coming here. But seeing the progress made by other girls who came here as unfortunate as I am, seeing how many poor, lonely girls have gotten married to very respectable men and are today wealthy, I am more encouraged and I hope that I too, will attain good fortune.

I must end this letter because it's late at night and I have to get up very early in the morning to run to work.

Live well, dear friend! I have done my duty and have written you a letter. And now you must do your duty and make your true friend happy with a letter.

Leah Goldberg

i Shaykevitsh, *Shaykevitsh'es nayer brivnshteler,* 61–64.

12: A Brother Warns His Sister Not to Come to America[i]

My dear sister!

I have received your dear letter, and from what I understand, you are still leaning more toward coming to America, notwithstanding the difficulties I told you about in my previous letter. But as a brother who loves you very much, and for whom your good health is priceless, I consider it my sacred duty to advise you to think it over once again, calmly and patiently. Don't forget, dear sister, that a girl of your age will have to go work in the shops, and God forbid, you will become a wreck. Don't look, dear sister, at the pictures that the girls from our hometown send to their relatives in Europe, and which make it seem that in America, everything shines, that everything is good and fine. Don't forget, dear, that it is nothing more than a picture that has been gussied up and colored by the artistically talented workers here. I would like to point to the example of Ruvn's daughters, how gloomy and dark they are in reality, how white their faces are; they don't have a drop of blood—even though their pictures, which this summer they sent off to their parents, caused a stir in the shtetl—and then you will see what a terrible wreck America makes out of girls like you.

But, my dear sister, do what you think is right. I had to write the truth to you because you are very dear to me.

Your brother, who loves you very much,
Avrom

[i] Eisenstadt, *Der moderner briefenshteller*, 69–71.

13: America Is the True Garden of Eden[i]

Dear Friend!

You asked me in your last letter to write you about what America is and how we live here.

I had a smile on my face reading these words.

You probably think that it is a mere trifle to describe what kind of land America is and how one lives here. Yes, I can indeed write about this for you in a few words. I can tell you, for example, that America is a land of milk and honey and that life here is happier than in other countries.

Nu, will this answer make you happy? Will you not answer me: this is not what I wanted to hear from you, this I know without you telling me.

What then do you want, my friend? That I should describe for you clearly and in detail every single thing that is related to America and her inhabitants? In order to do this, I would need to live for a few more decades and order so much paper that I wouldn't have enough room for it, nor would you have enough room to receive it on your end.

Describe America!

This, my friend, is no little village or small shtetl. These are many small worlds contained within one big world. Here live people from every continent, from every country, from every city, and of every nationality.

Here, you can every day discover such wonders as you have never imagined in your wildest imagination. Here one travels on the ground, and up high over the ground, and underground. One travels here even under the beds of seas (rivers). This is a real wonder world, and if one were to describe everything that one sees here, one wouldn't know where to start and however much one would describe an important thing, it would end up not being enough.

If you could by magic instantly transport a person from your shtetl and set him down in one of the bustling streets of New York, I am sure that he would go crazy. He would under no circumstances be able to understand what was going on around him.

This is the scene he would have before his eyes:

Electric trains packed with women and men flying back and forth constantly. Aside from this, in the same streets fly automobiles with dressed-up people, equipages, and wagons with a variety of wares. And the tumult of it all mixes with the noise of the electric trains that fly up high on the railroads built in the air. The sidewalks are packed with so many people that one can hardly push through. Added to the extraordinary tumult is the resounding cry of the youngsters who sell newspapers: "Extra!"

It seems to me that I have already described at least something, but this is still not even a start because such a scene one must see with one's own eyes. The pen is too feeble to describe it.

But in just a few words I can tell you that in my opinion America is the most blessed, best, luckiest land in the world.

I won't tell you that here one sees pure beauty, pure goodness, and only good fortune. No, my friend, even here one encounters plenty of ug-

liness, plenty of evil, and great misfortune. But this is not the country's fault. This is a natural thing. Wherever there is light, there must also be a shadow.

But in comparison with the countries that I know, America is the true Garden of Eden. Here, every strong person can feed himself well. Here, every talented person can reach the highest level. Here, every unlucky person finds somewhere where they declare themselves willing to soothe his pain. The charities of New York, for example should serve as examples to the entire world. A sick person quickly finds a fine hospital with all the necessary means to cure him. For an orphan there is a good place where they take him in, educate him, and turn him into a useful human being. A widow with small children for whom things have taken a turn for the worse can find a superb place where she can leave her children for an entire day until she is let out of work. Here, there are institutes that give girls who have no parents and need somewhere to work fine rooms and fine food and treat them beautifully for a very low cost. Anyone who wants to educate himself will find here countless libraries and schools where he can study anything he wants to without having to pay a single cent (kopek).

But can one even list the many charities that exist in this one New York?

Describe America!

Once again, I have to laugh when I remember your request.

In order to describe such a thing, one would need to be an artist in every medium, one would need to be conversant with all the sciences, and know every language. In addition, one would need to set aside many years to see and consider everything.

All I can do is give you a report about the Jews in America because this, no doubt, will interest you more than anything else.

May we only live to see our Jews in their own land Palestine be as happy as they are here in America.

Don't laugh, my friend, at this wish. If you could be here and consider with open eyes the situation of the Jews in this world you would understand that I have sincere love for my people and that I can't think of any better blessing for my co-religionists.

You need only look at the main business streets in New York and you would be astonished at the fine businesses that are Jewish-owned.

*Aside from this, you would be astounded to see how fast all the Jews
who fled Russia naked, barefoot, and with only their souls, live respectable lives here. A high percentage of them are wealthy, and a small percentage, millionaires.*

*Here, in America, the Jews have demonstrated their talent and
energy.*

*Here, one can see how high our Yankele can go when he is given full
freedom.*

*The best students in all the schools and universities are our Jews.
The best doctors, professors (in medicine and mathematics) are Jews.
Who are the greatest, best lawyers? Jews, all Jews.*

*But if I were to describe everything related to our Jews in America,
I would need another couple of years in a row, and there would never be
an end.*

*Therefore, I will end my letter once again with the wish that we will
be deemed worthy of seeing our people in their own land be as happy as
they are in America.*

*This blessing comes from deep within the heart of your devoted
friend,*

Yitskhok Dov Ayzenshtayn

[i] Shaykevitsh, *Shaykevitsh'es nayer brivnshteler*, 167–172.

NOTES

1. About sentimental male friendship and the Haskalah, see Litvak, *Haskalah*, 44, and Werses, "Portrait of the Maskil as a Young Man."

2. Paperna, *Mikhtov meshulesh* [*Mikhtav meshulash*] (1889), 37–38. Yoyne Trubnik's 1886 *Zhargon-lehrer*, a primer that includes nineteen model letters, takes this one step further when a young man tells his friend that he is jealous of him for being enrolled in a gymnasium and complains that even though he himself has seen the "radiance of the Haskalah," he has been left behind in the shtetl with "foolish teachers" and "fanatics" (62).

3. An-skii, *Pionery*, 73.

4. Inditski, *Ha-metargem* (1899), 48–49.

5. Bernshteyn, *Bernshteyn's nayer yudisher folks-briefenshteler* (n.d.), 64–65.

6. Ibid., 58–60.

7. Ibid., 103–104.

8. Poliak-Gilman, *Der nayer obraztsover brifenshteller* (1904), 14–15. In the Russian translation, Shmuel says that he will have to throw himself off a bridge into the water—a rare instance in which the Russian is more histrionic than the Yiddish.

9. Miller, E. *Miller's nayer brifenshteller in tsvey theyl* (1911), 11.

10. Ibid., 35–36.

11. Ibid., 37–38. Unhappiness is also appropriate for Rosh Hashanah greetings outside the family, as when Nisn Peskovski apologizes to his friend for not writing all year. That year, he says, was a very dreadful one for him (36–37). Even a small child can articulate the fears that fill the minds of adults. In Poliak-Gilman's 1904 *Der nayer obraztsover brifenshteller,* a little boy reassures his father that he studies and writes "to the limits of his strength" and that he and his siblings obey the words of their mother as if they were "the Torah." This is a wish-fulfilling letter, but its most positive statements also display an awareness of what might go wrong. The little boy concludes: "I write this letter to reassure you, so that you will be able to keep your mind on your business and bring us food" (11).

12. Miller, E. *Miller's nayer brifenshteller in tsvey theyl* (1911), 13–17.

13. ha-Kohen, *Ksav yoysher* [*Ketav yosher*] (Vienna, 1819); we have read a later edition (Warsaw, 1859).

14. Paperna, *Mikhtov meshulesh* [*Mikhtav meshulash*] (1889), 42. The exact same text, same pagination, appears in Shalom ha-Kohen, *Mikhtov meshulesh* [*Mikhtav meshulash*] (1876). In both editions, the series runs from 40 to 71.

15. Paperna, *Mikhtov meshulesh* [*Mikhtav meshulash*] (1889), 84–112.

16. Shaykevitsh, *Der nayer Shomer's briefenshteler* (1908), 31.

17. Ibid., 31.

18. Miller, E. *Miller's nayer brifenshteller in tsvey theyl* (1911), 63–64. Aggrieved parents often tell their children how much they have done for them, like this mother in Yoysef Arukh's *Arukhs brifenshteller* (1892), 27: "Secondly, I ask you: tell me why you have such a bad character and forget your mother who has had so much grief from you. Oy! What haven't I done for you?" She sat by her daughter's sickbed and wished the illness on herself, she made her a good wedding, and so forth. *Shomer's pinkas,* 7–9, presents a fable that demonstrates the value of maternal anger. Mother bird cautions her babies not to leave the nest while she's gone and not to believe the honeyed words of the cat. One bird, convinced by the blandishments of the cat that their mother is bad and keeping them in prison, leaves the nest and, of course, gets eaten. The moral: "A mother's anger is better than a stranger's compliment."

19. Poliak-Gilman, *Der nayer obraztsover brifenshteller* (1904), 29.

20. Ibid., 9–10.

21. Eisenstadt, *Der moderner brieffenshteller* (1910), 39.

22. Ibid., 41.

23. Ibid., 42.

24. Shaykevitsh, *Shaykevitsh'es nayer briefenshteler* (1915), 54–55.

25. Ibid., 56.

26. Ibid., 57.

27. Ibid., 59.

28. Eisenstadt, *Der moderner brieffenshteller* (1910), 46–50. Eisenstadt (1873–1951) was born in Kleck, a shtetl in Belorussia, and immigrated to the United States in 1903. He was a prolific author of Hebrew works, such as biographies of rabbis (including Orthodox rabbis in America) and sermons. *Der moderner brieffenshteller* may have been his only foray into more secular provinces.

29. Shomer did publish a brivnshteler in Vilna after he emigrated.

30. Shaykevitsh, *Shaykevitsh'es nayer briefenshteler* (1915), 66–67.

31. Eisenstadt, *Der moderner brieffenshteller* (1910), 43–46.

32. Shaykevitsh, *Shaykevitsh'es nayer briefenshteler* (1915), 122–123.

33. *Nayer Bloshteyn's briefenshteler* (1910), 39–40, identical to a letter in *Briefenshteler in shraybshrift* (1905), 35–37.

34. Collection of Zimman Family, Letter 262, July 23, 1910.

35. Eisenstadt, *Der moderner brieffenshteller* (1910), 54–56.

36. Ibid., 52–53. "Threefold blessings" refers to the three-part priestly blessing of Numbers 6:24–26: "God bless thee, and keep thee. May God make His face to shine upon thee, and be gracious unto thee. May God lift up His countenance upon thee, and give thee peace."

37. Shaykevitsh, *Shaykevitsh'es nayer briefenshteler* (1915), 70–75.

38. Ibid., 120–121.

39. Eisenstadt, *Der moderner brieffenshteller* (1910), 52.

40. Shaykevitsh, *Shaykevitsh'es nayer briefenshteler* (1915), 116–118.

41. Eisenstadt, *Der moderner brieffenshteller* (1910), 134–138; Shaykevitsh, *Shaykevitsh'es nayer briefenshteler* (1915), 38–39.

42. Shaykevitsh, *Shaykevitsh'es nayer briefenshteler* (1915), 118–121.

43. On early marriage, see Freeze, *Jewish Marriage and Divorce*, 56, and Stampfer, *Families, Rabbis, and Education*, 7–41; on rates of divorce and remarriage see Freeze, 63; on companionate marriage, see Freeze, 12, 163, 168.

44. Berkowitz and Dauber, *Landmark Yiddish Plays*, 205–206.

45. Rakovska, *My Life as a Radical Jewish Woman*, 45.

46. Baumgarten, *Introduction to Old Yiddish Literature*, 163–206.

47. Roskies, *A Bridge of Longing*, 7–8, 57. For more on love and eroticism in Yiddish literature, see Roskies, *Ayzik-Meyer Dik*, 62–71, 248–249.

48. Roskies, *Ayzik-Meyer Dik*, 249–252.

49. Litvak, *Haskalah*, 137.

50. Paperna, "Iz Nikolaevskoi epokhi," 144–145.

51. Parush, *Reading Jewish Women*, 46, 75–76, 86–93, 172–206; Parush, "Readers in Cameo," 7–9.

52. Freeze, *Jewish Marriage and Divorce*, 321.

53. Wengeroff, *Memoiren einer Grossmutter*, 2:33–34. Wengeroff says that she and other young women readers shared their fascination with Schiller with young, "educated" Jewish men. In her introduction to her translation of volume 1 of *Memoirs of a Grandmother*, Shulamit Magnus notes the role of women in disseminating an enthusiasm for Western romantic literature. Our point here is that they were, through Schiller and others, also disseminating certain notions about romantic feelings and behavior (57–58).

54. Wengeroff, *Memoiren einer Grossmutter*, 1:181.

55. Biale, *Eros and the Jews*, 154.

56. Kaplan, *The Making of the Jewish Middle Class*, 86, 109. In "Based on Love: The Courtship of Hendele and Jochanan, 1803–1804," 86–107, Kaplan examines a set of romantic courtship letters written in Judeo-German. She suggests that the couple found models for sentimental prose in either German romantic fiction or German briefstellers, one of which, she notes, was used as a textbook in the Bavarian school system.

57. Rakovska, 28–31, 35. In *Eros and the Jews*, David Biale discusses how Moses Mendelssohn broke with tradition by writing to his fiancé without using a template from an igron, 153.

58. Courtship letters in brivnshtelers are a nineteenth-century phenomenon. The earliest Yiddish letter manuals, *Igeres shloyme* [*Igeret Shelomoh*] and *Loshn zohov* [*Lashon zahav*] do not have any, nor do Avraham Paperna's Judeo-German manuals of the 1880s—though the 1911 Frishman and Paperna does. Our thanks to Chava Lapin for directing our attention to the folk song, which can be seen in full in Chana Mlotek, "Opruf afn lid vegn a brivnshteler," 22.

59. Miller, E. *Miller's nayer brifenshteller in tsvey theyl* (1911), 71–3.

60. Ibid., 73–5.

61. Ivanov, *Polnyi noveishii delovoi pis'movnik*, 96.

62. See Cohen, "Reality and Its Refraction," 144–165, for a discussion of how young heroines of maskilic novels are similar to those depicted in Western literature, while married women are more recognizable as real, Jewish women.

63. Fridman, *Der nayer praktisher brifenshteller* (1891), 50.

64. Gorodinski, *Der hoyz- korrespondent*, 36–39.

65. Paperna, *Mikhtov meshulesh* [*Mikhtav meshulash*] (1889), 40–41.

66. Bloshteyn, *Nayer Bloshteyn's briefenshteler* (1910), 89–90.

67. Ibid., 91–93.

68. Bernshteyn, *Bernshteyn's nayer yudisher folks-brifenshteler* (n.d.), 44–46.

69. For a striking example of a shadkhn as the butt of satire, see Weinreich, "Levin Lion Dor's brivn-shtelers," 109–112.

70. Eisenstadt, *Der moderner brieffenshteller* (1910), 80–81.

71. Shaykevitsh, *Shaykevitsh'es nayer briefenshteler* (1915), 108–110.

72. Ibid., 110–111.

73. Ibid., 42–43.

74. Eisenstadt, *Der moderner brieffenshteller* (1910), 21–22.

75. Ibid., 77–79.

76. Shaykevitsh, *Shaykevitsh'es nayer briefenshteler* (1915), 124.

77. Ibid., 130.

78. Ibid., 126–127.

79. Ibid., 129.

80. Harkavy, *Harkavi's amerikanisher briefen-shteler*, 140–141.

81. Ibid., 150–151.

82. Shaykevitsh, *Shaykevitsh'es nayer briefenshteler* (1915), 142–143.

83. Harkavy, *Harkavi's amerikanisher briefen-shteler*, 156–157.

84. Eisenstadt, *Der moderner brieffenshteller* (1910), 92–98.

85. Shaykevitsh, *Shaykevitsh'es nayer briefenshteler* (1915), 176–177.

86. Ibid., 76–79.

87. Ibid., 80–81.

88. Eisenstadt, *Der moderner brieffenshteller* (1910), 61.

89. Ibid., 62–66.

90. Bar El, "The Yiddish 'Briefenshteler,'" 20. The inclusion of model contracts is not unique to brivnshtelers and in fact goes back to the *mahzorim* of medieval Ashkenaz. See Carlebach, *Palaces of Time*, 25.

91. Goldshteyn-Gershonovitsh, *Der praktisher zhargon-russish-daytsher briefenlehrer* (1913), 69.

92. Bernshteyn, *Bernshteyn's yudisher brief-lehrer* (1910 or 1911), 61.

93. Rischin, *The Promised City*, 52. In *A Time for Building*, 74, Gerald Sorin asserts that in 1897 more than 60 percent of the Jewish workforce in New York was employed in the garment industry.

94. The one exception is a courtship letter from a "young workman" in *Harkavi's amerikanisher briefen-shteler*, 151. His *Der englisher lehr bukh* is practical about supplying English phrases particularly useful to the businesses in which immigrants were likely to be engaged. In a chapter called "Buying and Selling," Harkavy teaches Yiddish-speakers selling unspecified items—perhaps from a pushcart—how to *handl* (bargain) in English: "I sell them [sic] 75 cents.... Sir, I cannot sell them any cheaper" (76).

95. *Harkavi's amerikanisher briefen-shteler*, 79.

96. A few of the English letters in Harkavy and the 1901 *Freynkel's english-yudisher brifenshteler* are identical, and all of the letters in the latter appear to have been copied verbatim from existing American letter-writers and then translated into Yiddish. For instance, Frankel includes and translates into Yiddish without change a letter from Oliver Brooks to his mother, looking forward to vacation from school, when he will "enjoy the celebration of the Christmas festivities in the old-fashioned manner" (*zikh frayen in kristmus vi in di gute alte tsayten*: celebrate Christmas like in the good old days, 62–63).

97. Shaykevitsh, *Shaykevitsh'es nayer briefenshteler* (1915), 85.

98. Psalms 69:1.

99. Isaiah 40:3.

100. Shaykevitsh, *Shaykevitsh'es nayer briefenshteler* (1915), 104–106.

101. Another letter in this manual (79–81) promotes modern business practices by criticizing a Jewish merchant for messing up an order of merchandise because of his shoddy recordkeeping. Orderly books are touted as the path to success, a message echoed in the several brivnshtelers that offer arithmetic primers and bookkeeping courses as appendices.

102. The term *tnoyim* ("conditions") refers to both the engagement contract and the ceremony of its signing.

103. Shaykevitsh, *Shaykevitsh'es nayer briefenshteler* (1915), 40–41, 120–122.

104. Ibid., 172–174. In this letter, Shomer makes oblique reference to his own vilification at the hands of critics. All good Yiddish writers earn a lot of money and live very well, he says, but this was not the case ten years earlier, when Yiddish writers had nothing to eat "so they ate each other," attacking the "few writers who were fortunate enough to be earning enough for a piece of bread."

105. Joselit, *The Wonders of America*, 4.

106. A shames is the caretaker of a shul, a common word for synagogue; a yahrzeit is the yearly anniversary of someone's death.

107. Eisenstadt is also the author of a few compilations of bar mitzvah speeches. Joselit writes extensively in *The Wonders of America* (89–110) about the new prominence the bar mitzvah ceremony and celebration assumed in American Jewish life.

108. Lederhendler, "America," 34. In *Bread to Eat and Clothes to Wear*, Gur Alroey writes extensively about the resources that did exist for prospective emigrants, including information bureaus and booklets about the emigration process created by Jewish organizations beginning in 1906.

109. *E. Miller's nayer brifenshteller in tsvey theyl* (1911), 18–19.

110. See examples from two family letter collections, those of the Zimman family, based in Butrimonys, Lithuania (near Vilna), and the Weinberg family, based in Warsaw. The authors of European brivnshtelers may have drawn inspiration for their negative portrayals of America not primarily from letters sent home by immigrants but from the Jewish press. See Zabarenko, "The Negative Image of America in the Russian-Language Jewish Press, 1881–1910."

111. For instance, the private family letter collection of Jaime Weinberg contains several letters from Polish Jewish anarchists and members of the Socialist Revolutionary Party writing from Paris and the United States, whence they had apparently fled in the wake of the revolution of 1905.

112. Collection of the Zimman Family, Letter 143, 17 October 1908. Other letters from this collection include stories about schemes for bribing officials and doctors to get young men exempted from the draft, about people purposely maiming or poisoning themselves to get out of military service, and about Jews who were killed in the course of army service or who attempted to flee their units.

113. Descriptions of voyages and arrivals in America were not unique to brivnshtelers, as attested to by a cycle of letters from J.C., an Irish immigrant in *The Lady's Letter-Writer* (1902), 106–107. J.C., newly arrived from Dublin, writes to her siblings that she has had a similarly harrowing voyage but that she too has arrived safely.

114. Eisenstadt, *Der moderner brieffenshteller* (1910), 121–122.

115. Shaykevitsh, *Shaykevitsh'es nayer briefenshteler* (1915), 61–62.

THREE

Beyond Letters

While model letters are the heart and soul of brivnshtelers, almost all manuals include other information that might come in handy for their readers. It is standard for the letters sections to be preceded by lists and guides, such as alphabetical lists of men's and women's names, common Hebrew words or phrases in Yiddish, common abbreviations and their glosses, salutations in Hebrew with Yiddish glosses, days of the week and months in Hebrew, and alphabets in several languages (such as Yiddish, Russian, German). Usually relegated to the back of the book is information deemed useful for business, such as templates for contracts, IOUs, invoices, and even entire courses on bookkeeping. The text for tnoyim, traditional engagement contracts, is also a common feature.

More unusual, but not unheard of, is the inclusion of short verse (often with an edifying message, such as "Pure Truth," the poem presented here) and jokes and fables. Then there are the anomalies, a few of which we have included in this chapter. These include Lion Dor's imagined "correspondence" between older and newer editions of his own brivnshteler; Bloshteyn's etiquette rules for young Jewish ladies; and Goldshteyn-Gershonovitsh's laundry list.

Letter from an "Old" Brivnshteler to a "New" One[i]

Friend of mankind and lover of education![ii] Please don't take it the wrong way if I try your patience with another letter.[iii] It's because I'm jealous that you're coming out in today's enlightened world. For sure, you haven't suffered too much yet and will laugh about how much I suffered in the old days. I will tell you a bit about what happened to me and what turned out to be my fate. You mustn't laugh at anything, though anything can happen. When I, the old brivnshteler, made my appearance in the world a few decades ago, I came off the press with my new cursive letters and everyone in the world found me useful, especially for young children. Everyone bought me. One time, a yishuvnik[iv] *came to the city and heard about brivnshtelers, and bought one for his son. He brought me home. The yishuvnik engaged a melamed for his son and asked him to use the brivnshteler to teach the child. The melamed had looked through it earlier and learned the model letters from me and started to give his student a lesson, to use me to teach him how to write a letter. The son of the yishuvnik didn't do too badly with writing the first shin from "Hello, my beloved"*[v] *but by the end had made too many unnecessary twitches and turns and the letter was full of mistakes. Who got blamed? The melamed. But the melamed wasn't at fault because he himself hadn't learned how to do this and so, mercy upon him. He blamed it on other things: the pen is bad, the ink is diluted, the paper is inferior, the table is too high to write on, the child isn't sitting right, it's too dark to write, the child's eyesight isn't good. But in the end, he said that the brivnshteler just wouldn't do. The innkeeper grabbed the brivnshteler in anger and threw it on the ground. My heart ached, I couldn't say anything. Also, the innkeeper's wife said that a brivnshteler would only confuse the child. I heard everything and laughed inside. How was it my fault that the head doesn't understand and the hand doesn't do what it's supposed to? In anger, they threw me into a pantry cupboard. I lay there for a while and finally, when the semester was over, the melamed took me with him to study. Despite all this, I wasn't heartbroken, because I had found myself a ride with the book peddler and the book seller, lying there together with great works and religious books. Many times I've been clad in thick, fat covers, and was finely bound, a gift for a bride, with gilded pages and bound in morocco leather. I've been inserted into bookshelves under other religious books. But eventually they began to use me. Young children and women began to learn from me how to write letters, spell names, and do arithmetic. They began to understand that I have a purpose in the world and, to this very day, are grateful to me. Well, how lucky you are already, new brivnshteler, that you are being published in such a beautiful, enlightened world where there are already educated and knowledgeable people. For sure, you won't suffer too much and will be honored for your efforts.*

i   Lion Dor, *Eyn nayer brifen shteller,* 51–53.

ii "Friend of mankind" is a European Enlightenment term dating from
    the early eighteenth century. It frequently appeared in sentimental
    literature to describe the "man of feeling," an individual whose
    capacity for sympathy bridges the gap between self-interest and
    benevolence. See Isaac Nakhimovsky, *The Closed Commercial State,*
    169. The "old brivnshteler" is showing his maskilic roots.

iii The book contains other exchanges between old and new brivnshtelers.

iv A Jew living in a rural village where there were few Jews.

v   *Shalom l'ahuvi,* which begins with the letter shin.

Foreword to a Brivnshteler[i]

The well-known book dealer, Herr Yoysef Reznikovski from Slonim,
sought me out in New York with the help of his grandson, and asked me
to create for him a brivnshteler called "Shomer's briefenshteler."

At first I turned down the work because it seems to me, in my opinion, that our Jews don't need any brivnshtelers, because the *zhargonishe*
language is not equal to other languages. In a living language, a brivnshteler is an important means of teaching children the language, as well
as its most essential rules of grammar, whereas no one needs to learn our
zhargon, because nearly all Jewish children can read and write Yiddish.
And there is no need to talk about rules of grammar here, since zhargon
doesn't have any grammar.

Finally, however, I decided that my opinion was quite incorrect. For
our Jews, a brivnshteler is very important. A Yiddish brivnshteler can be
useful to all classes of Jews, from children to adults, because even though
they can all speak and write Yiddish, not everyone has the skills to write
a letter. With the help of an accurate brivnshteler, every reader will acquire the skill to think and express all his thoughts on paper. Therefore,
I decided to carry out Herr Reznikovski's wish and to prepare, for the
time being, a small brivnshteler for his book dealership. And if I see that
it fulfills the needs and expectations of the people, I will in short order
create a longer brivnshteler, which will include not only letters, but also
various essays which will provide everyone with the opportunity to learn
the art of writing a literary essay.

As I have said, the zhargon does not have a grammar and so I can't
give the reader any rules for writing it properly.

But I am almost certain that every discerning reader will quickly find for himself the right style[ii] for writing a letter according to his needs.

[i] Shaykevitsh, *Shomer's briefenshteler,* 3–4.

[ii] In original: *geshmak* (taste).

Ethics[i]

1. You should always obey your parents and teacher even when you do not understand why they wish you to do one thing instead of another.

2. You should realize, my child, that your first duty is to learn from every older person, because he has already lived through your years, but you—you haven't yet gone through his.

3. You should never do unto your friend what you would not want him to do unto you.

4. You should never buy unnecessary things even if they are very cheap.

5. You should guard yourself against anger as if it were a terrible disease.

6. You should always give your friend the benefit of the doubt instead of judging him for the worst.

7. You should consider time as being very precious: the day gone by will never return.

8. You should ask yourself at the end of every day what you have accomplished that is useful for yourself and others.

9. You should remember, my child, that learning is never too late and or not enough.

10. You should realize, my child, that your parents are your best friends and that you can't buy a father or mother for a million in any currency.

11. You should remember that gossip is one of the worst character traits, which can, God forbid, bring misfortune to you and your friend.

12. You should always strive to make a living and to carefully guard what you have. Stinginess is almost a sin, but thriftiness is very admirable and important.

13. You should realize, my child, that you must thank God at every moment for everything you possess, and never assume that you are entitled to it.

14. You should always keep your things in order and then you will never lose them and waste time looking for them.

15. You should never put off till tomorrow the work that you can do today.

A Joke about Art[i]

A certain artist painted a child with a small basket in his hand, in which there were grapes. When a group of people were present, one of them said, in praise of the picture, that the grapes were painted so well that birds had pecked at them more than once. A smart peasant was listening from a distance and said to the one who had so highly praised the picture, "But really, if the grapes are painted so well that they look real, then the child must have been painted badly because the birds had absolutely no fear of him."

> [i] Alek, *Oytser mikhtovim* [*Otsar mikhtavim*] (1906), 77. This joke, which appears in several brivnshtelers, is clearly an import from non-Jewish sources. Its original source is an anecdote about Zeuxis, a fifth-to-fourth-century BCE Greek painter in Book XXXV, Section 36 of Pliny the Elder's *Natural History*. In his painting *Boy with Grapes*, Zeuxis depicted the grapes so realistically that birds flew down to peck them. But the artist castigated himself for not painting the boy, too, well enough to fool the birds and frighten them off.

A Fable[i]

A woman from Damascus was charged with a crime and was to be put to death. In the meantime, they threw her into a secure prison to stay until it was time to carry out her sentence. The prison warden found out that the woman was going to be executed in a terrible way; he had pity on her and decided that it would be better if she died of hunger than come to such a terrible end.[ii] He told her daughter when she was visiting her mother in the prison that she could come as often as she pleased, but that she shouldn't bring any food. The daughter agreed to this and came very frequently to see her mother and never brought anything with her because she saw that the warden was keeping his eye on her. When some time had passed and the woman didn't die, the warden was very surprised. He said to himself, "I must figure out what is keeping this woman alive." And so he found out that the daughter was feeding her mother with her own breast milk. And when he found out, he decided that he must make his discovery public. He let the authorities know and they assembled many people and announced this to them. And they also reprieved the woman from her death sentence on account of the love of the daughter for her mother and decided that they would both be provided with financial support from the government. On the site of the prison a holy temple was built to honor forever the memory of the mother and daughter.

[i] Alek, *Oytser mikhtovim* [*Otsar mikhtavim*] (1906), 81–82. This story may have been derived from *The Grecian Daughter: A Tragedy,* a popular play published in London by Arthur Murphy (1727–1805) in 1772, or from the same source that inspired it. In the play, the heroine saves her father, the imprisoned king of Syracuse, from starvation by feeding him with her own milk.

[ii] This may be intended sarcasm as there is no explanation of why death by starvation would be more merciful than execution.

Pure Truth[i]

When a mirror is good and clear
It makes every face in nature shine
But if the smallest fragment is missing
The reflected image is dulled.
No matter how good the pen may be,
If the writer is unlearned
It laughs at what he tries to do
And has no advice for him.

[i] Lion Dor, *Mikhtovim* [*Mikhtavim*], *oder eyn nayer brifen shteler* (1882), 19. This awkwardly worded poem, rhyming in the original, appears in a number of different brivnshtelers. A variant of this poem appears in *Briefenshteler in shraybshrift* (1905), 14. Thanks to Ellen Kellman for assistance with the translation.

Etiquette and Behavior[i]

A. In the Morning

As soon as you wake up, you should wash yourself all over with cold water and nice-smelling soap. While washing yourself, give special attention to scrubbing your face so that it will be fresh and your cheeks rosy.

You can go for a few hours before your toilette, but not later than twelve o'clock. A young woman whose fiancé is not in the same city can go around at home without her toilette until noon.

By five o'clock in the afternoon in the summertime and by three o'clock in the wintertime, you must already be in your corset and dressed up.

B. Clothing

A young lady must have as many dresses as possible. If the number of her dresses diminishes, her parents should move heaven and earth to buy her more.

Just as you must every month bless the new moon, so must you go and take a look at the latest journals every month, with the understanding that the ones from Paris are the best.

You should not rely on the seamstress: it never hurts to make your waist narrower.

You should have as many inserts and as much lace on your dress as possible.

The young lady who is in the position to do so must see to it that she is the first to adopt all the latest fashions, that is, before one sees them on Main Street.

A young lady, bride, or woman must dress herself up even if she is as ugly as the devil—it won't help her face but she will have a more beautiful figure.

A hat without a feather is like a wedding without music.[ii]

When it's snowing you must buy a hat, in the summer—a hat, in the autumn—a hat, and in the winter—a winter hat.

You must not haggle over the cost of a hat. It isn't proper and you mustn't do it.

C. Walking

You must take small steps, slowly, not pound away with your shoes, and keep your head level. In one hand (the left one) hold your dress, and in the other a parasol or small handbag in the summertime, and in winter a muff. You may also carry a book or a small package, well-wrapped.

You must go strolling every evening except when it's raining and drizzling.[iii]

You shouldn't count on having visitors.

It isn't proper to walk to a wedding—you must ride there.

You mustn't walk around for a long time with a suitor you have just met for the first time.

You can only walk with one other person, that is, no more than two at a time.

When going to the theater, you can walk along with everyone, but on the way back—only with someone you know well.

A girl who is engaged may also stroll with an older person.

While strolling, you take turns, that is, everyone turns over his partner to another and walks with that person's partner.

Respectable young ladies don't go out walking late at night.

D. Greeting

When you encounter someone you know, you must greet him; that is, nod your head.

While greeting someone you must also give a little smile.

A gentleman must take off his hat as he greets someone.

A young lady only needs to reply to a greeting; that is, the gentleman must greet her first.

To a gentleman to whom you haven't been introduced, you reply without a smile; that is, coldly.

A gentleman must greet a young lady whom he has met socially, even if he hasn't been introduced to her.

The gentleman must speak when greeting her; that is, say, "*Zdravst-vuite!*" [Russian, "Good day"], "*Bon Jour!*" or "*Moe pochtenie*" [Russian—"My respects"]. The young lady, however gives only a polite nod of her head and doesn't say anything. If, however, the young man inquires while greeting her, "*Kak pozhivaete?*" [Russian, "How are you?"], you must answer, "*Spasibo*" [Russian, "Thank you"]. It is more modern to answer in French, "*Merci!*" or "*Grand merci!*"[iv]

E. Behavior

A person should speak as little as possible. Even a fool is thought to have good sense if he doesn't say anything . . .

In the company of others, you shouldn't talk only about yourself, and it also isn't nice when you talk about someone else.

A young man may sit only halfway on a chair, while a young lady must sit fully on the chair.

The young man must be the first to offer his hand.

A modern, aristocratic young woman offers only half her hand; that is, her fingers.

When you are introduced and become acquainted, you must reply "*Ochen' priiatno!*" [Russian, "Pleased to meet you!"] or "Pleased to meet you!" [*Zehr angenihm!*].

It is not appropriate for a young man to ask a young woman to visit him, but a young woman can ask him to visit her. However, she must first be sure that her parents won't show the young man the door.

A truly aristocratic woman is forbidden to read Yiddish books, even if she understands no other language.

When something that I don't understand is being spoken about, I am very careful not to reveal it—I make sure that no one will notice . . . [v]

[i]   Bloshteyn, *Der nayer rikhtiger Bloshteyn's briefenshteler*, 130–136.
[ii] *Klezmer* in the original.
[iii] In original: *Amitshelitse*. May be related to the Polish word *mżyć* (drizzle).
[iv] The French and Russian greetings are given in Romanized and Cyrillic form. The French spelling is copied from the original. One Russian word has two misplaced letters. It is not clear why "Thank you," in any language, is a good response to "How are you?"
[v]   Change in pronoun in original.

Receipt for Laundry Sent Out, August 10[i]

Men's shirts—15	Carryover from subtotal—104
Ditto, Women's—20	Aprons—10
Ditto, children's—16	Kerchiefs—20
Ditto, from the kitchen—9	Bed sheets—11
Chemisettes—4	Pillowcases—15
Cuffs—18	Handkerchiefs—17
Pairs of men's underpants—10	Ditto, from the kitchen—6
Pairs of women's underpants—12	Pairs of stockings—20
Subtotal: 104	Total: 203 pieces

[i]   Goldshteyn-Gershonovitsh, *Der praktisher zhargon-russish-daytsher briefenlehrer, un briefenshteller in zeks theyl*, 86.

BIBLIOGRAPHY

List of Nineteenth- and Twentieth-Century Brivnshtelers

This bibliography section lists only letter manuals that contain Yiddish letters or Yiddish glosses of letters from other languages (such as Hebrew and Russian). We have chosen to exclude books not verified as being actually Yiddish even if they are identified as such in earlier bibliographies by other compilers. It presents all the brivnshtelers we were able to locate, including variant editions. (We thank Brad Sabin Hill for suggesting a format for presenting this information.)

With two exceptions (*Khosn-kale brief* and *Varn's folshtendiger englisher-yidisher briefenshteler,* which are listed in library catalogs but have apparently been lost), we have been able to access at least one edition of every title in this bibliography.

The main sources for the titles and editions in this bibliography are the catalogs of the Library of the YIVO Institute for Jewish Research, the Library of the Jewish Theological Seminary, the New York Public Library, the Russian National Library (St. Petersburg), Harvard University Library, the Yiddish Book Center, the Judaica Collection of the University Library at the Goethe University in Frankfurt am Main, Bibliothèque Medem (Paris), and Stanford University Library. Other sources include William Zeitlin's 1919 "Bibliographie der hebräischen Briefsteller" (*Zeitschrifte fur Hebräische Bibliographie* 22) and Judith Zwick's bibliography in *Toldot sifrut ha-igronim* (1990).

The list should be considered incomplete. Brivnshtelers often went into many reprintings, and title pages sometimes refer to earlier editions that did not come to light during the course of this project.

Other works consulted, including letter manuals in languages other than Yiddish (for instance, Judeo-German books by Avraham Paperna and Moshe Neumann) appear in the second bibliography section, "Other Sources."

Alek [A. L. Kartuczinski; Aharon Eli'ezer ben Mordekhai Avigdor]. *Kvutses mikhtovim* [*Kevutsat Mikhtavim*] *oder guter hebreyisher daytsher und russisher brifenshteller.* Warsaw: Fayvl Munk, 1880.

——. *Oytser mikhtovim* [*Otsar mikhtavim*], *oder brifenshteler fir yudishe kinder.* Vilna: L. L. Matz, 1895. Reissued 1896. Other editions Warsaw: F. Baymritter, 1906; Vilna: Kh. Mo. L., 1911.

Altshuler, Ezra. *Gulat mayim.* Piotrkow: A. Rozengarten, 1910. Reissued 1911.

Arukh, Yoysef. *Arukhs brifenshteller: in fier thayl.* Kishinev: Yehezkl Litvak, 1892. Another edition Kishinev: E. Shliomovicha, 1893.

Avrukh. *Khosn-kale brief.* Warsaw: n.p., 1931.

Berliner, P. Dr. *Berliners moderner yidisher brivnshteler.* New York: Star Hebrew Book Co., 1926.

———. *Moderner yidisher folks-brivnshteler* [Dr. *Berliners moderner yidisher folks-brivnshteler*]. Warsaw: P. Kantorovitsh, 1930.

[Bernshteyn]. *Bernshteyn's nayer yudisher folks-brifenshteler: mit a baylage. Der yudisher kaligrafisher briefenshteler.* Warsaw: B. Shimin, 1912. Reissued 1913; [19-?]. Another edition Warsaw: Ya. Kelter, n.d.

———. *Bernshteyn's yudisher brief-lehrer: mit a kurtser yudisher gramatik.* Warsaw: Gatsefira, 1910 or 1911.

Bloshteyn, Oyzer. *Der nayer fielbeserer ales Bloshteyn's brifenshteler: mit dem zhargonlehrer tsuzamen* [*Bloshteyn's briefenshteler*]. Warsaw: Cajlingold, 1917. Other editions Lublin: n.p., 1922; Warsaw: Y. Y. Raynerman, 1924–1925.

———. *Der nayer rikhtiger Bloshteyn's briefenshteler.* Warsaw: n.p., [189-?]. Another edition Warsaw: Cajlingold, ca. 1905.

———. *Nayer Bloshteyn's briefenshteler.* Vilna: Romm, 1903. Reissued 1910. Another edition Warsaw: Cajlingold, [19-?].

Briefenshteler in shraybshrift. New York: Hebrew Publishing Co., 1900. Reissued 1905.

Eisenstadt, Ben-Zion. *Der moderner brieffenshteller.* Brooklyn: Morris Shapiro, 1910.

Eyn nayer brifenshteler in dray obtheylungen. Vilna: Hd's, 1900.

Frankel, Aaron H. *Freynkel's english-yudisher brifenshteler.* New York: M. Chinsky, 1901.

[Frenkel]. *Frenkel's liebes-brief-bukh.* Warsaw: Kultur, 1912.

Fridman, Dov Arye [Baer Leib]. *Der nayer praktisher brifenshteller.* Berdichev: n.p., 1889. Reissued 1899. Other editions Berdichev: o.f.g, 1890. Berdichev: Yankev Sheftil, 1891, 1892, 1893.

Goldman, Yakov ben Mordekhai. *Tepukhey zohov* [*Tapuhe zahav*]. Warsaw: Yitskhok Goldman, 1887.

Goldshteyn, Em. *Yidishe shenshraybmethode, fershiedener origineller handshriften und briefmuster tsum gebroykh fir hoyz und shule.* Lodz: n.p., n.d.

Goldshteyn-Gershonovitsh, Tsvi Hirsh [I. G. Gershonovitsh, Yoysef Tsvi Gershonovitsh]. *Der praktisher brifenshteller.* Berdichev: n.p., 1890.

———. *Der praktisher zhargon-russish-daytsher briefenlehrer, un briefenshteller in zeks theyl.* Berdichev: n.p., 1904. Another edition Berdichev: Mayer Epshteyn, 1913.

———. *Yudish-daytsher morall brifenshteller.* Berdichev: Mayer Epshteyn, 1890. Other editions Berdichev: n.p., 1895. Berdichev: Yankev Sheftil, 1891, 1902.

Gorodinski, Yoysef [Yosif Grodinski; Yoysef Horodinski]. *Der hoyz-korrespondent, oder der berihmter zhargon-russisher briefenshteller.* Berdichev: Khayim Yankev Sheftil, 1901.

———. *Der nayer Berditshuver briefenshteller.* Warsaw: n.p., 1895.

———. *Der postalion.* Warsaw: Ha-akhim Shuldberg, 1895.

———. *Gorodinski's Korrespondent: Der nayer brifenshteller. Der postalion.* Berdichev: Yoysef Berman, 1910.

Harkavy, Alexander. *Der englisher brifenshteller.* New York: Sapirshtayn un Katsenelenbogen, 1890. Reissued 1892. Another edition New York: Aleksander Yosef Verbelovski, 1900.

————. *Harkavi's amerikanisher briefen-shteler: english un yudish.* New York: Hebrew Publishing Co., 1902. Reissued 1928.

————. *Harkavi's amerikanisher briefen-shteler un speller.* New York: Sapirshtayn un Katsenelenbogen, 1901. Another edition New York: Hebrew Publishing Co., 1902.

————. *Harkavi's english in Amerika.* New York: Hebrew Publishing Co., 1894. Another edition New York: Y. Sapirshteyn, 1894.

Inditski, Y. Y. [Yisroel Yekhiel]. *Ha-metargem.* Warsaw: n.p., 1896. Other editions Warsaw and Vilna: Yitshak Funk, 1899. Vilna: Yitshak Funk, 1902, 1912, 1913.

Khalifas igroys [*Halifat igrot*]: *Brif shteler.* Warsaw: J. M. Ehrenpreis, [1850?].

Kresin, B. *Der berihmter zhargohn loshn koydesh russisher brief korespondenter. Un zhargohn russishe khristomatye. Tsu zammen mit di tsvey zeltene brief fun Berditshever tsirk un Viener tehater.* Berdichev: Yoysef Berman, 1903.

Lion Dor, Avrom [Leondor, Leon d'or, Liondor, Liondor-Lewin]. *Eyn nayer kinstlikher brifen shteller.* Vilna: Romm, 1843. Reissued 1844, 1846, 1860, 1861, 1865, 1868, 1870, 1873, 1876, 1882.

————. *Mikhtovim* [*Mikhtavim*], *oder eyn nayer brifshteller.* Vilna: Romm, 1833. Reissued 1862, 1873, 1882, 1910.

Lion Dor, Hirsh. [Hirsch Leondor, Leon d'or, Liondor]. *Eyn nayer brifen shteller.* Vilna: Shmu'el/Yosef Fuenn and Avrom Tsvi Rozenkrants, 1865. Other editions Warsaw: Rozenkrants and Shriftzetser: 1876, 1879, 1887.

Mesader igeres [*Mesadar igeret*]: *oder eyn nayer shrayb lehrer un brifshteller fir yidishi kinder beyde geshlekhter.* Vilna and Horodno, n.p., 1825. Reissued 1827. Another edition Vilna: Menakhem Man and son, Borekh and Simkhe Zimel and son, Menachem Nokhem, 1830.

Mesader igeres [*Mesadar igeret*]: *oder eyn nayer shrayb-lehrer und brifn-formal fir yudisher kinder beyde geshlekhter.* [Same title as previous citation but completely different content.] Warsaw: Nosn Shriftgisser, 1858. Reprinted as *Misdar igeret: eyn nayer brief shteller* Lemberg: J. D. Süss, 1891.

Miller, Eliezer. *E. Miller's nayer brifenshteller in tsvey theyl.* Zhitomir: n.p., 1891. Other editions Warsaw: n.p., 1906. Piotrkow: Shloyme Belkhotovski, 1911, 1913.

Poliak-Gilman, H. *Der nayer obraztsover brifenshteller.* Berdichev: Yoysef Berman, 1904.

Shaykevitsh, Nokhem Meyer (Shomer). *Der nayer obrazhover Shomers brifenshteller.* Berdichev: n.p., n.d..

————. *Der nayer Shomer's briefenshteller.* 1908. Vilna: Farlag fun Kh. M. [This title, attributed to Shaykevitsh, is a plagiarization of Dov Arye Fridman's *Der nayer praktisher brifenshteller.*]

————. *Shaykevitsh'es nayer briefenshteler.* New York: Hebrew Publishing Co., 1905. Reissued 1909, 1915, 1923; 1925, 1927, 1928.

————. *Shomer's briefenshteler.* Vilna: Y. Reznikovski, 1898. Reissued 1901, 1910, 1911, 1912, 1914. Other editions Vilna: Romm, 1898, 1899, 1902, 1903, 1904, 1905, 1907. Vilna: n.p., 1913.

————. *Shomer's pinkas.* Vilna: Y Reznikovski, 1902.

Shnayder, Mordkhe Betsalel. *Koyvets sipurim u-mikhtovim* [*Kovets sipurim u-mikhtavim*]. Vilna: Avrom Tsvi Rozenkrants, 1901. Reissued 1914.

Steinberg, Abraham. *Shteynberg's brifenshteler.* New York: Star Hebrew Book Co., 1926.

Trubnik, Yoyne. *Zhargon-lehrer.* Warsaw: Yankev Smertenko, 1886. Reissued 1888.

Warne, Frederick. *Varn's folshtendiger englisher-yidisher briefenshteler und fershiedene gezetslikhe formen fun fershiedene kontrakten.* New York: Y. L. Verbelavski, 1899. Reissued 1900.

Y.K. *Shrayb lehrer oder brifen formal fir yudishe kinder beyde geshlekhter.* Warsaw: Nosn Shriftgisser, 1867. Reissued 1871, 1879.

Other Sources

Adler, Eliyana R. *In Her Hands: The Education of Jewish Girls in Tsarist Russia.* Detroit: Wayne State University Press, 2011.

———. "Women's Education in the Pages of the Russian Jewish Press." In *Jewish Women in Eastern Europe,* ed. ChaeRan Freeze, Paula Hyman, and Anthony Polonsky, 121–123. Polin: Studies in Polish Jewry 18. Oxford: Littman Library of Jewish Civilization, 2005.

Alroey, Gur. *Bread to Eat and Clothes to Wear: Letters from Jewish Migrants in the Early Twentieth Century.* Detroit: Wayne State University Press, 2011.

An-skii [An-ski], S. A. *Pionery.* In *Sobranie sochinenii,* 3:3–232. St. Petersburg: Aktison, 1909.

———. Diary fragment, 9–12 July 1912. Yiddish Literature and Language Collection, RG 3, 3260.1. YIVO Institute for Jewish Research, New York.

Babel', Isaak. "Istoriia moei golubiatiny." In *Sobranie sochinenii v dvukh tomakh,* 2:142–152. Moscow: Khudozhestvennaia literatura, 1990 (orig. pub. 1925).

Bannet, Eve Tavor. *Empire of Letters: Letter Manuals and Transatlantic Correspondence, 1680–1820.* Cambridge: Cambridge University Press, 2006.

Bar El, Joseph. "The Yiddish 'Briefenshteler' (Letter Writing Manual) of the 18th to the 20th Centuries." PhD diss. [in Yiddish], Jewish Teachers Seminary, 1970.

Bartal, Israel. *The Jews of Eastern Europe, 1772–1881.* Philadelphia: University of Pennsylvania Press, 2002.

Barton, David, and Nigel Hall. *Letter Writing as a Social Practice.* Amsterdam: John Benjamins, 1999.

Baumgarten, Jean. *Le peuple des livres.* Paris: Biblioteque Albin Michel, 2010.

———. "Prayer, Ritual and Practice in Ashkenazic Jewish Society: The Tradition of Yiddish Custom Books in the Fifteenth to Eighteenth Centuries." In *Speaking Jewish—Jewish Speak: Multilingualism in Western Ashkenazic Culture,* ed. Shlomo Berger et al., 121–146. Leuven: Peeters, 2003.

Baumgarten, Jean, and Jerold C. Frakes. *Introduction to Old Yiddish Literature.* Oxford: Oxford University Press, 2005.

Berkowitz, Joel, and Jeremy Asher Dauber. *Landmark Yiddish Plays: A Critical Anthology.* Albany: State University of New York, 2006.

Bernstein, Lina. "The First Published Russian Letter-Writing Manual: Priklady, kako pishutsia komplementy raznye." *Slavic and East European Journal* 46, no. 1 (2002): 98–103.

Biale, David. *Eros and the Jews from Biblical Israel to Contemporary America.* Berkeley: University of California Press, 1997.

Bielefeld, Otto Leopold. *Deutscher briefsteller: leitfaden der deutschen privat- und handelskorrespondenz.* Freiburg (Baden): J. Bielefelds Verlag, 1910.

Bilik, Dorothy. *Love in Sholem Aleykhem's Early Novels*. New York: YIVO Institute for Jewish Research, 1975.

Birnboym, Y. "Brivenshtelers." In *Dertsiungs-enstiklopedye*, vol. 1, ed. H. B. Bass. New York: Altveltlekhe yidishn kultur congres, 1957.

Blackman, Aylward M., and T. Eric Peet. "Papyrus Lansing: A Translation with Notes." *Journal of Egyptian Archaeology* 11 (1925): 3–4, 284–298. http://o-www.jstor.org .library.colgate.edu/stable/3854153.

Bray, Bernard Alain. *L'art de la lettre amoureuse: des manuels aux romans (1550–1700)*. La Haye, Paris: Mouton, 1967.

Brocke, Michael, and Christiane E. Mueller. "De Mortuis Nil Nisi Hebraice? The Language of Tombstone Inscriptions in Nineteenth-Century Germany." In *Speaking Jewish—Jewish Speak: Multilingualism in Western Ashkenazic Culture*, ed. Shlomo Berger et. al., 49–76. Leuven: Peeters, 2003.

Brown, Charles Walter, ed. *The Complete Letter Writer and Book of Social Forms: A Comprehensive and Practical Guide and Assistant to Letter Writing*. Chicago, Ill.: Frederick J. Drake, 1902.

Brushtein, Aleksandra. *Doroga ukhodit v dal'* . . . Moscow: Astrel'; Vladimir: VKT, 2012 (orig. pub. 1957).

Cahan, Abraham. *Bleter fun mayn leben*. 5 vols. New York: Forverts Asosieyshon, 1926.

Carlebach, Elisheva. "Letter into Text: Epistolarity, History, and Literature." In *Jewish Literature and History: An Interdisciplinary Conversation*, ed. Eliyana R Adler and Sheila E. Jelen, 113–133. Bethesda: University Press of Maryland, 2008.

———. *Palaces of Time: Jewish Calendar and Culture in Early Modern Europe*. Cambridge, Mass: Belknap Press of Harvard University Press, 2011.

Chambers, Alfred B. *The New Century Standard Letter-Writer: Business, Family and Social Correspondence, Love-Letters, Etiquette, Synonyms, Legal Forms, etc.* Chicago: Laird and Lee, 1900. http://www.archive.org/stream/newcenturystandaoochamrich.

Chekhov, A. P. "Ionych." In *Polnoe sobranie sochinenii i pisem v tridtsati tomakh*, vol. 10. Moscow: Nauka, 1977 (orig. pub. 1898).

Cohen, Jocelyn, and Daniel Soyer. *My Future Is in America: Autobiographies of Eastern European Jewish Immigrants*. New York: New York University Press, 2006.

Cohen, Tova. "The Maskilot: Feminine or Feminist Writing?" In *Jewish Women in Eastern Europe*, ed. ChaeRan Freeze, Paula Hyman, and Anthony Polonsky, 57–86. Polin: Studies in Polish Jewry 18. Oxford: Littman Library of Jewish Civilization, 2005.

———. "Reality and Its Refraction in Descriptions of Women in Haskalah Fiction." In *New Perspectives on the Haskalah*, ed. Shmuel Feiner and David Jan Sorkin, 144–165. London: Littman Library of Jewish Civilization, 2001.

"The Collected Writings of Rabbi B. Z. Eisenstadt.." *American Jewish Legacy* 8 (2009): 6.

Cooke, Thomas. *Universal Letter-Writer*. London: Printed for J. Cook and S. Hodgson, 1861 (orig. pub. 1771).

Dauphin, Cécile. "Letter-writing Correspondence Manuals in the Nineteenth Century." In Roger Chartier, Alain Boureau, and Cécile Dauphin, *Correspondence: Models of Letter-Writing from the Middle Ages to the Nineteenth Century*. Princeton, N.J.: Princeton University Press, 1997.

———. *Prête-moi ta plume: les manuels épistolaires au XIXe siècle*. Paris: Kimé, 2000.

Dick, William B. *Dick's Society Letter-Writer for Ladies, Containing More Than Five Hundred Entirely Original Letters and Notes, with Appropriate Answers.* New York: Fitzgerald Publishing, 1884.

Dik, Ayzik Meyer. *Di yuden in lite.* Vilna: Widow Romm and Brothers, 1871.

Dohrn, Verena. "Seminary." In *The YIVO Encyclopedia of Jews in Eastern Europe,* ed. Gershon Hundert, 2:1685–1688. New Haven, Conn.: Yale University Press, 2008.

El'iashevich, D. A. *Pravitsel'stvennaia politika i evreiskaia pechat' v Rossii 1797–1917.* St. Petersburg: Gesharim, 1999.

Elzet, Yehuda. *Shtudien in dem amoligenn inerlikhen idishen lebn: Mit hundert yor tsurik.* Montreal: n.p., 1927.

Estraikh, Gennady. "Changing Ideologies of Artisanal 'Productivisation': ORT in Late Imperial Russia." *East European Jewish Affairs* 39, no. 1 (2009): 3–18.

Feiner, Shmuel. "Towards a Historical Definition of the Haskalah," In *New Perspectives on the Haskalah,* ed. Shmuel Feiner and David Jan Sorkin, 184–219. London: Littman Library of Jewish Civilization, 2001.

Fishman, David E. *The Rise of Modern Yiddish Culture.* Pittsburgh: University of Pittsburgh Press, 2005.

Fishman, Joshua A. "Language: Planning and Standardization of Yiddish." In *The YIVO Encyclopedia of Jews in Eastern Europe,* ed. Gershon Hundert, 1:987–991. New Haven, Conn.: Yale University Press, 2008.

———. *Yiddish: Turning to Life.* Amsterdam: J. Benjamins, 1991.

Freeze, ChaeRan Y. *Jewish Marriage and Divorce in Imperial Russia.* Hanover: University Press of New England for Brandeis University Press, 2002.

Frieden, Ken. "Joseph Perl's Escape from Biblical Epogonism through Parody of Hasidic Writing." *AJS Review* 29, no. 2 (1988): 265–282.

Frishman, David, Abraham Paperna [Papirna], and Mrs. Hess. *Igron shalem.* Warsaw: L. Kontorovits, 1911.

Froment, Édouard, and L. Mueller. *Deutsch-französischer Briefsteller. Muster zu Briefen jeder Art. Mit der gegenübergedruckten französischen Ubersetzung,* Stuttgart: Paul Neff, 1867. http://books.google.com/books?id=c9MCAAAAYAAJ.

Fuchs, Paul. *Deutsch-russischer Briefsteller; Muster zu Briefen jeder Art mit der gegenubergedruckten russischen Ubersetzung, nach der eltfen Auflage des Deutsch-franzozischen Briefstellers von Froment und Muller.* Berlin: Schöneberg, 1907.

Fuks, P. [Paul Fuchs], and S. Mandel'kern. *Obraztsy pisem" vsiakago roda c" riadom" pomieshchennym" niemetskim" tekstom"* Berlin: Schöneberg, 1907.

Gitelman, Zvi. *A Century of Ambivalence: The Jews of Russia and the Soviet Union, 1881 to the Present.* Bloomington: Indiana University Press, 2001.

Glinert, Lewis. *Mamme Dear: A Turn-of-the-Century Collection of Model Yiddish Letters.* Northvale, N.J.: J. Aronson, 1997.

Goldsmith, Emanuel L. *Modern Yiddish Culture.* New York: Fordham University Press, 1997.

Gottheil, Richard, and Isaac Broydé. "Letter-Writing and Letter Writers." In *The Jewish Encyclopedia,* ed. Cyrus Adler et al. New York: Funk & Wagnalls, 1901–1906. http://www.jewishencyclopedia.com/articles/9790-letter-writing-and-letter-writers.

Grabherr, Eva. "Multilingualism among the Jews of Hohenems: A Micro-Historical Study." In *In Speaking Jewish—Jewish Speak: Multilingualism in Western Ashkenazic Culture,* ed. Shlomo Berger et al., 33–47. Leuven: Peeters, 2003.

Grace-Pollak, Sophie. "Shomer l'or Shomers mispet l'Sholom Aleikhem." *Khulyot: Journal of Yiddish Research* 5 (1998): 125–159.

———. "Shomer ha-publitsist." *Khulyot: Journal of Yiddish Research* 9 (2005): 161–195.

Gries, Zeev. "Printing and Publishing: Printing and Publishing before 1800." In *The YIVO Encyclopedia of Jews in Eastern Europe,* ed. Gershon Hundert, 2:1454–1458. New Haven, Conn.: Yale University Press, 2008.

ha-Kohen, Shalom. *Ksav yoysher [Ketav yosher].* Warsaw: N. Shriftgisser, 1859; Vilna: Romm, 1864 (orig. pub. 1819).

———. *Mikhtov meshulesh [Mikhtav meshulash].* Vilna: Feigensohn, 1882; Vilna: Feigensohn, 1884; Vilna: Feigensohn, 1889 (orig. pub. Vilna: Feigensohn, 1876).

Harkavy, Alexander. *Der englisher lehr bukh.* New York: Hebrew Publishing Company, 1900?

Harshav, Benjamin. *The Meaning of Yiddish.* Stanford, Calif.: Stanford University Press, 1990.

Hoffmann, Peter Friedrich Ludwig. *Allgemeiner Familien- und Geschäftsbriefsteller.* Leipzig: Friedrich Brandstetter, 1922 (preface says 1884).

Hurvitz, Nathan. "Courtship and Arranged Marriages among Eastern European Jews prior to World War I as Depicted in a Briefenshteller." *Journal of Marriage and the Family* 37, no. 2 (1975): 422–430. http://www.jstor.org/stable/350977.

Iuridicheskii fakul'tet Vysshikh Zhenskikh (Bestuzhevskikh) kursov. http://law.spbu.ru/ru/library/ExhibitionLib/ExhibitionLibTema/BectyKursi/WmanBectyKursi.aspx.

Ivanov, N. *Polnyi noveishii delovoi pis'movnik.* Moscow: tipo-litografiia Iakovlevoi i A. P. Poplavskogo, 1898–1899.

Joselit, Jenna Weissman. *The Wonders of America: Reinventing Jewish Culture, 1880–1950.* New York: Hill and Wang, 1994.

Kaplan, Marion A. "Based on Love: The Courtship of Hendele and Jochanan, 1803–1804." In Marion Kaplan, Beate Meyer, and Monika Richarz, *Jüdische Welten: Juden in Deutschland vom 18. Jahrhundert bis in die Gegenwart [Festschrift für Monika Richarz].* Göttingen: Wallstein, 2005.

———. *The Making of the Jewish Middle Class: Women, Family, and Identity in Imperial Germany.* New York: Oxford University Press, 1991.

Katz, Dovid. "Alexander Harkavy and His Trilingual Dictionary." In Alexander Harkavy, *Yiddish-English-Hebrew Dictionary,* vi–xxiii. New York: YIVO and Schocken Books, 1988.

———. "Language: Yiddish." In *The YIVO Encyclopedia of Jews in Eastern Europe,* ed. Gershon Hundert, 1: 979–987. New Haven, Conn.: Yale University Press, 2008.

———. "The Phonology of Ashkenazic. " In *Hebrew in Ashkenaz: A Language in Exile,* ed. Lewis Glinert, 46–87. Oxford: Oxford University Press, 1993.

Kaufmännischer Briefsteller und Haus-sekretar. Krakow: Aron Faust, ca. 1908.

Kazdan, Kh. Sh. *Fun kheyder un "shkoles" biz tsisho: dos ruslendishe yidentum in gerangl far shul, shprakh, kultur.* Mexico: Shloyme Mendelson Fond, 1956.

"Kazennye evreiskie uchilishcha." In *Kratkaia evreiskaia entsiklopediia,* ed. Y. Oren, M. I. Zand, and Samuel Ettinger, 4:31–33. Jerusalem: Keter, 1976.

Kellman, Ellen. "The Newspaper Novel in the Jewish Daily Forward (1900–1940): Fiction as Entertainment and Serious Literature." PhD diss., Columbia University, 2000.

The Writings: Kethubim: a New Translation of the Holy Scriptures according to the Masoretic Text: Third Section. Philadelphia: Jewish Publication Society of America, 1982.

Klier, John D. "1855–1894 Censorship of the Press in Russian and the Jewish Question." *Jewish Social Studies* 48, no. 3/4 (1986): 257–268.

Kotlerman, Boris. "Kol Mevaser." In *The YIVO Encyclopedia of Jews in Eastern Europe,* ed. Gershon Hundert, 1:916–918. New Haven, Conn.: Yale University Press, 2008.

Kramer, Samuel Noah. *The Sumerians: Their History, Culture, and Character.* Chicago: University of Chicago Press, 1963.

Kulbak, Moyshe. *Zelmenyaner.* Moscow: Farlag Sovetski pisatel, 1971 (orig. pub. 1931).

The Lady's Letter-Writer. New York: J. Ivers and Co., 1902.

Lederhendler, Eli. "America." In *The YIVO Encyclopedia of Jews in Eastern Europe,* ed. Gershon Hundert, 1:32–39. New Haven, Conn.: Yale University Press, 2008.

Leivick, H. "Sonaten ring." In *Ale verk,* vol. 1, 255–261. New York: H. Leyvik Yubiley-Komitet, 1940.

Lichtheim, Miriam. *Ancient Egyptian Literature: A Book of Readings,* vol. 2: *The New Kingdom.* Berkeley: University of California Press, 1976.

Litvak, Olga. *Haskalah: The Romantic Movement in Judaism.* New Jersey: Rutgers University Press, 2012.

Lovins, Daniel. "AJL 2004 Proposal to Rewrite Reference Structure for 'Judeo-German' in *MARC Code List of Languages.*" Paper presented at the AJL 2004 R&S Cataloging Committee Meeting, 2004.

Lowenstein, Steven. "The Complicated Language Situation of German Jewry, 1760–1914." In *Speaking Jewish—Jewish Speak: Multilingualism in Western Ashkenazic Culture,* ed. Shlomo Berger et al., 3–31. Leuven: Peeters, 2003.

———. "The Yiddish Written Word in Nineteenth-Century Germany." In *Leo Baeck Institute Year Book* 24, 179–192. London: Secker & Warburg, 1979.

Malherbe, Abraham J. *Ancient Epistolary Theorists.* Atlanta, Ga: Scholars Press, 1988.

Medvedeva (Gurevich), Doba-Mera. "Dnevnik moikh prozhitykh dnei." In Nataliia Vasil'evna Iukhneva, *Izrail': materialy ekspeditsii i komandirovok,* ed. Mikhail Beizer, 93–215. St. Petersburg: MAE RAN, 2010.

Miron, Dan. *A Traveler Disguised: The Rise of Modern Yiddish Fiction in the Nineteenth Century.* Syracuse, N.Y.: Syracuse University Press, 1996.

Mlotek, Chana. "Opruf afn lid vegn a brivnshteler." *Forverts,* April 15–28, 2011, 22.

Moss, Kenneth. "Printing and Publishing: Printing and Publishing after 1800." In *The YIVO Encyclopedia of Jews in Eastern Europe,* ed. Gershon Hundert, 2:1459–1468. New Haven, Conn.: Yale University Press, 2008.

Nakhimovsky, Isaac. *The Closed Commercial State: Perpetual Peace and Commercial Society from Rousseau to Fichte.* Princeton, N.J.: Princeton University Press, 2011.

Nathans, Benjamin. *Beyond the Pale: The Jewish Encounter with Late Imperial Russia.* Berkeley: University of California Press, 2002.

Neumann, Moshe Shmu'el, and ha-Kohen, Shalom. *Sefer Mikhtevey ivris* [*Mikhtave 'ivrit*] *oder ebraisher und daytsher briefshteller.* 1827. http://sammlungen.ub.uni-frankfurt.de/jd/content/titleinfo/1740282. (Orig. pub. 1815.)

A New Letter-Writer, for the Use of Ladies. Philadelphia: Porter & Coates, 1860–1869[?].

Newbold, W. Webster. "Letter Writing and Vernacular Literacy in Sixteenth-Century England." In *Letter-Writing Manuals and Instruction from Antiquity to the Present: Historical and Bibliographic Studies,* ed. Carol Poster and Linda C. Mitchell, 127–140. Columbia: University of South Carolina Press, 2007.

Niger, Shmuel. *Sholem-Aleichem—zayne vikhtikste verk, zayn humor, un zayn ort in der yidishe literatur.* New York: YKUF, 1928.

Nikolini. *Polnyi pis'movnik dlia vliublennykh i rukovodstvo k izucheniiu zhiteickoi mudrosti.* Moscow: E. Konovalova, 1915 (orig. pub. Moscow: Tip. I. Ia. Poliakova, 1898).

Novyi russkii pis'movnik v 5 otdelakh, spetsial'no poprisoblennyi dlia Russkikh, zhivushchikh v Amerike. New York? 1900s.

Paperna [Papirna], Avraham. "Iz Nikolaevskoi epokhi." In *Evrei v Rossii: XIX vek,* ed. Viktor Kel'ner, 27–176. Moscow: Novoe literaturnoe obozrenie, 2000 (orig. pub. in *Perezhitoe* [St. Petersburg, Brokgauz-Efron, 1910–1911]).

———. *Meyroyts igroys* [*Merots igrot*]. Warsaw: Yu. Levenson, 1874.

———. *Mikhtov meshulesh* [*Mikhtav meshulash*]. Warsaw: Yisroel Alapin, 1878.

———. *Mikhtov meshulesh* [*Mikhtav meshulash*]. Warsaw: n.p., 1889.

———. *Polnyi pis'movnik na russkom i evreisko-nemetskom iazykakh.* Warsaw, 1884.

Parush, Iris. "The Politics of Literacy: Women and Foreign Languages in Jewish Society of 19th Century Eastern Europe." *Modern Judaism* 15, no. 2 (1995): 183–206.

———. "Readers in Cameo: Women Readers in Jewish Society of Nineteenth-Century Eastern Europe." Trans. Ann Brener. *Prooftexts* 14, no. 1 (1994): 1–23.

———. *Reading Jewish Women: Marginality and Modernization in Nineteenth-Century Eastern European Jewish Society.* Waltham, Mass: Brandeis University Press, 2004.

Perlman, Joel. "Literacy among the Jews of Russia in 1897." Working Paper 182, Levy Economics Institute of Bard College, 1996. http://www.levyinstitute.org/publications /?docid=284.

"Pis'movniki." In *Kratkaia evreiskaia entsiklopediia,* ed. Y. Oren, M. I. Zand, and Samuel Ettinger, 6:512–16. Jerusalem: Keter, 1976.

Poletika, Nikolai Pavlovich. *Vidennoe i perezhitoe: iz vospominanii.* Ed. Felix Roziner. Tel-Aviv: Biblioteka-Aliia, 1982.

Poliakov, Aleksandr. "Serebrianyi samovar." In Zinaida Poliakova and Aleksandr Poliakov, *Sem'ia Poliakovykh,* 11–130. Moscow: Atlantida, 1995.

Poliakova, Zinaida. "Dnevniki." In Zinaida Poliakova and Aleksandr Poliakov, *Sem'ia Poliakovykh,* 133–202. Moscow: Atlantida, 1995.

Poplavski, Khayim. *Der nayer vegvayzer.* Warsaw, 1882.

———. *Nayer Shprakhfihrer.* Vilna: A. G. Rozenkrants and M. Shriftzetser, 1895.

Poster, Carol, and Linda C. Mitchell, eds. *Letter-Writing Manuals and Instruction from Antiquity to the Present: Historical and Bibliographic Studies.* Columbia: University of South Carolina Press, 2007.

"Protsentnaia norma." In *Kratkaia evreiskaia entsiklopediia,* ed. Y. Oren, M. I. Zand, and Samuel Ettinger, 6:851–859. Jerusalem: Keter, 1976.

Quint, Alyssa. "Yiddish Literature for the Masses? A Reconsideration of Who Read What in Jewish Eastern Europe." *AJS Review* 29, no. 1 (2005): 61–89.

Quint, Alyssa, and Eric Goldstein. "Pop'em in Yiddish: The Subterranean World of Jewish Pulp Fiction." *Guilt and Pleasure.* 2009. http://www.guiltandpleasure.com /index.php?site=rebootgp&page=gp_article&id=248.

"Rabbi Eisenstadt—Author of 40 Books." *New York Times,* September 1, 1951.

Rakovska, Puah. *My Life as a Radical Jewish Woman: Memoirs of a Zionist Feminist in Poland*. Trans. and ed. Paula Hyman. Bloomington: Indiana University Press, 2002 (orig. pub. 1951).

"Ravvinskie seminarii." In *Kratkaia evreiskaia entsiklopediia*, ed. Y. Oren, M. I. Zand, and Samuel Ettinger, 7:35–37. Jerusalem: Keter, 1976.

Reyzen, Zalmen. *Leksikon fun der Yidisher literatur, prese un filologye*. Wilno, Poland: B. Kletskin, 1927–1929.

Rischin, Moses. *The Promised City: New York's Jews, 1870–1914*. New York: Harper & Row, 1970.

Robertson, Jean. *The Art of Letter Writing: An Essay on the Handbooks Published in England during the Sixteenth and Seventeenth Centuries*. London: University Press of Liverpool, Hodder and Stoughton, 1942.

Rogger, Hans. *Jewish Policies and Right-Wing Politics in Imperial Russia*. Berkeley: University of California Press, 1986.

Roskies, David G. "Ayzik-Meyer Dik and the Rise of Yiddish Popular Literature." PhD diss., Brandeis University, 1975.

———. *A Bridge of Longing: The Lost Art of Yiddish Storytelling*. Cambridge, Mass: Harvard University Press, 1995.

———. "The Genres of Yiddish Popular Literature, 1790–1860." In *Working Papers in Yiddish and East European Jewish Studies*. New York: Max Weinreich Center for Advanced Jewish Studies of the YIVO Institute for Jewish Research, 1975.

———. "The Medium and Message of the Maskilic Chapbook." *Jewish Social Studies* 41, no. 3/4 (Summer/Fall 1979): 275.

———. "Sholem Aleichem: Mythologist of the Mundane," *AJS Review* 13, no. 1–2 (1988): 27–46.

———. "Vegn daytshn original fun 'A graf fun Ungarn.'" *Forverts*, August 6, 2004, 6.

———. "Yiddish Popular Literature and the Female Reader." *Journal of Popular Culture* 10, no. 4 (1977): 852–858. http://onlinelibrary.wiley.com/doi/10.1111/j.0022-3840 .1977.1004_852.x.

Sandrow, Nahma. *Vagabond Stars: A World History of Yiddish Theater*. New York: Harper & Row, 1977.

Sazonov and Bel'skii, *Polnyi russkii pis'movnik v piati chast'iakh*. St. Petersburg, 1887.

Schaechter, Mordkhe. *The Standardized Yiddish Orthography*. New York: YIVO and Yiddish Language Resource Center of the League for Yiddish, 1999.

Shandler, Jeffrey. *Awakening Lives: Autobiographies of Jewish Youth in Poland before the Holocaust*. New Haven, Conn.: Yale University Press, 2002.

Shargorodska, F. "Der shure grus." In *Landoy Bukh: Filologishe shriften fun yivo*, 1:67–68. Wilno, Poland: B. Kletskin, 1926.

Sheldon, L. W. *Sheldon's Twentieth Century Letter Writer; An Up-to-Date and Accurate Guide to Correct Modern Letter Writing*. Philadelphia: D. McKay, 1901. http://digital .library.pitt.edu/cgi-bin/t/text/text-idx?idno=00a138205m;view=toc;c=nietz.

Sholem Aleichem. "Di ibergekhapte briv af der post." In *Ale verk*, 1:54–155. Moscow: Melukhe-Farlag Der Emes, 1948 (orig. pub. 1883–1884).

———. "Mayn ershter roman." In *Ale verk*, 17:117–148. New York: Sholem Aleykhem folksfond oysgabbe, 1925 (orig. pub. 1917–1923).

———. *Menakhem Mendl*. In *Ale verk*, 10:1–219. New York: Sholem Aleykhem folksfond oysgabbe, 1925 (orig. pub. 1910).

———. *Motl, Peysi dem khazns.* In *Ale verk,* vols. 13–14. New York: Sholem Aleykhem folksfond oysgabbe, 1917.

Shvarts, Y. Y. *Yunge Yorn.* Mexico: Farlag Tsvi Kesel bey der kultur-komitete fun yidishn tsentral komitet in Meksike, 1952.

Singer, Isaac Bashevis. *Collected Stories: A Friend of Kafka to Passions.* New York: Library of America, 2004.

Sorin, Gerald. *A Time for Building: The Third Migration, 1880–1920.* Baltimore: Johns Hopkins University Press, 1992.

Stampfer, Shaul. *Families, Rabbis and Education: Traditional Jewish Society in Nineteenth-Century Eastern Europe.* Oxford: Littman Library of Jewish Civilization, 2010.

———. "Literacy among Eastern European Jews in the Modern Period: Context, Background, and Implications." In *Transition and Change in Modern Jewish History: Essays Presented in Honor of Shmuel Ettinger,* ed. Shmuel Almog et al., 459–483. Jerusalem: Historical Society of Israel, 1987.

———. "What Did 'Knowing Hebrew' Mean in Eastern Europe?" In *Hebrew in Ashkenaz: A Language in Exile,* ed. Lewis Glinert, 129–140. Oxford: Oxford University Press, 1993.

Stanislawski, Michael. "Kahal." In *The YIVO Encyclopedia of Jews in Eastern Europe,* ed. Gershon Hundert, 1:845–848. New Haven, Conn.: Yale University Press, 2008.

———. "Russia: Russian Empire." In *The YIVO Encyclopedia of Jews in Eastern Europe,* ed. Gershon Hundert, 2:1607–1615. New Haven, Conn.: Yale University Press, 2008.

———. *Tsar Nicholas I and the Jews: The Transformation of Jewish Society in Russia, 1825–1855.* Philadelphia: Jewish Publication Society of America, 1983.

Troinitskii, N. A. *Obshchii svod po imperii rezul'tatov razrabotki dannykh Pervoi vseobshchei perepisi naseleniia, proizvedennoi 28 ianvaria 1897 goda.* St. Petersburg: Tipo-lit. N. L. Nyrkina, 1905.

Trotskii, Lev (Trotsky, Leon). *Moia zhizn': opyt avtobiografii.* Berlin: Granit, 1930.

———. Letters Collection, RG 107 Box 6. YIVO Institute for Jewish Research, New York.

Vengerova, Polina. *Vospominaniia babushki: ocherki kul'turnoi istorii evreev Rossii v XIX veke.* Moscow: Gesharim, 2003.

Weinberg, Jaime. Letters. Private collection.

Weinreich, Max. *History of the Yiddish Language.* 2 vols. New Haven, Conn.: Yale University Press, 2008.

———. "Levin Lion Dor's brivn-shtelers." *YIVO Bleter* 18 (1941): 109–112.

Weiser, Kalman. "Nationalism." In *Critical Terms in Jewish Language Studies,* 36–38. Frankel Institute Annual. Ann Arbor, Mich.: Frankel Institute for Advanced Judaic Studies, 2011.

Weiser, Keith Ian, and Joshua A. Fogel. *Czernowitz at 100: The First Yiddish Language Conference in Historical Perspective.* Lanham, Md.: Lexington Books, 2010.

Wengeroff, Pauline. *Memoiren einer Grossmutter. Bilder aus der Kulturgeschichte der Juden Russlands im 19. Jahrhundert.* 2 vols. Berlin: M. Poppelauer, 1913.

———. *Memoirs of a Grandmother: Scenes from the Cultural History of the Jews of Russia in the Nineteenth Century.* Trans. Shulamit S. Magnus. Stanford, Calif.: Stanford University Press, 2010.

Werses, Shmuel. "Portrait of the Maskil as a Young Man." In *New Perspectives on the Haskalah,* ed. Shmuel Feiner and David Jan Sorkin, 128–143. London: Littman Library of Jewish Civilization, 2001.

Zabarenko, Judith. "The Negative Image of America in the Russian-Language Jewish Press, 1881–1910." *American Jewish History* 75, no. 3 (1986): 267–279.

Zeitlin, William. "Bibliographie der hebräischen Briefsteller." *Zeitschrifte fur Hebräische Bibliographie* 22 (1919): 32– 47.

Zimman Family. Letters. Private collection.

Zipperstein, Steven J. *Imagining Russian Jewry: Memory, History, Identity.* Seattle: University of Washington Press, 1999.

Zlatogor, Maksim. *Russkii semeinyi pis'movnik: obraztsy pisem na raznye sluchai zhizni, s prilozheniem pisem russkikh pisatelei.* London: Jaschke, 1920.

Zwick, Judith Halevi. *Toldot sifrut ha-igronim: (ha-brivenshtelers) ha-'Ivriyim (me'ah 16-me'ah 20).* Tel-Aviv: Papirus, 1990.

INDEX

Italicized page numbers refer to figures.

Fogelzohn, Y. (Yisroel Yekhiel Inditski),
59n69. See also *Ha-metargem*
fonts, 15, 19, 20, 34. See also *vayber-taytsh;
yidish-taytsh*
foreign-language acquisition, 2, 8, 26, 29,
71, 87–88, 94, 95, 174; *brivnshtelers*
used for, ix, 28, 32; employment and,
140, 144
Formelsammlungen, xiii
forms of address, 16, 45; Russian, 48, 168
formulaic greetings, 31, 192
Forverts, viii, 118
Frankel, Aaron H., 190n96
Frankfurt, 144
freedom, 170, 174, 186
Freeze, ChaeRan, xiv, 111
French letter manuals, 31, 48
Freynkel's English-yudisher brifenshteler,
190n96
Fridman, Dov Arye, 39, 53, 87, 94. See also
Der nayer praktisher brifenshteller
friendship, 32, 68, 69, 114, 117, 142
Frishman, David, 85
Froment, Éduard, 50
Frug, Shimen, 69
Fuenn, Shmu'el Yosef, 39

Galicia, 26, 37
German language, 8, 27–28, 34, 35. See also
foreign-language acquisition
German letter manuals. See *briefstellers*
Germanic spelling. See *daytshmerism*
Gintsburg, Horace, 5
Goethe, Johann Wolfgang von, 44, 48
Goffman, Erving, xiii
Gogol, Nikolai, 44
Goldfadn, Avrom, 4, 37, 111
Goldshteyn-Gershonovitsh, Tsvi Hirsh,
15, 139. See also *Der praktisher
zhargon-russish-daytsh Briefenlehrer;
Yudish-daytsher morall brifenshteller*
Gordon, Yehudah Leib, 44
Gorodinski, Yoysef, 40, 115–116. See also
*Der hoyz-korrespondent; Gorodinski's
Korrespondent*
*Gorodinski's Korrespondent. Der nayer
brienshteller. Der postalion*, 24, 62n115,

65n167; letters from, 73–75, 99, 147–
148; list of ethics, 195
Gottlober, Avraham Ber, 113
government schools: Russian, 39
Graetz, Heinrich, 35, 69, 78–79
grammar: Hebrew, 56n26, 78–79; Yiddish,
16, 35–36, 56n26
guides. See lists and guides

ha-Kohen, Shalom, 32, 59n64, 62n115,
85–86, 87–88. See also *Ksav yoysher;
Mikhtov meshulesh; Sefer Mikhtevey
ivris*
Hall, Nigel, xiii
Ha-metargem (The translator), 28, 68–69;
letters from, 78–79
handwriting. See penmanship; *shraybers*
Harkavi's amerikanisher briefen-shteler
(Harkavy's American brivnshteler),
28, 48, 64n147, 190n94; on business
and finance, 140, 141; on courtship
and marriage, 124, 127–128
*Harkavi's amerikanisher briefen-shteler
un speller* (Harkavy's American
brivnshteler and speller), ix, xivn6,
28, 47, 54
Harkavy, Alexander, 28, 54, 59n70,
65n166, 124, 190n94, 190n96. See
also *Der englisher lehr bukh; Harkavi's amerikanisher briefen-shteler;
Harkavi's amerikanisher briefenshteler un speller*
Hartmann, Moritz, 76
Ha-shakhar (*Razsvet; Dawn*), 161
Hasidism, 1, 35, 36–37, 68; Bratslaver, 75;
conflict with Zionism, 33
Haskalah (Jewish Enlightenment), xi, xiv,
1–2, 13, 37, 40, 58n48, 67; German,
36, 85; and study of Hebrew, 27, 35,
56n26. See also *maskilim*
haskamah (rabbinical endorsement), 32
Haynt, 41
Hebrew language, 8, 17, 26, 27–28, 36, 68–
69, 156; biblical and rabbinical, 35;
grammar, literacy, 11, 158; prose style
in, 143, 152. See also fonts; *shoreshim*;
grammar: Hebrew

Rhetorik, xiii
romance. *See* courtship; love letters
Romm press, 37
Rosenfeld, Morris, 69
Rosh Hashanah, 148–149, 156–157, 187n11
Roskies, David, 112
Rousseau, Jean-Jacques, 43
Russian Army, 89; draft, viii, 1, 2, 33, 169,
    170, 191n112
Russian Empire: courtship and marriage,
    111–124; emigration from, 168; as
    location of *brivnshteler* publication,
    xivn10; parents and children, 83–101
Russian language, 8, 14, 27–28. *See also*
    foreign-language acquisition
Russian letter manuals (*pis'movniki*), 48,
    64n145
Russian Social Democratic Labor Party, 7
Russification, 7, 56n21, 63n128, 153, 159–160
Russo-Japanese War, 89, 100

Sabbath: observance of, xi, 156, 165; viola-
    tion of, 49, 50
Saint Petersburg, 3, 6, 41; Jewish library
    use in, 112; restrictions on Jewish
    residence, 4; restrictions on Jewish
    students, 13
salutations, 31, 192
sarcasm, 141–142
Schiller, Friedrich, 48, 75, 112–113
schools: Russian government, 2–3. *See
    also besmedresh;* education; *kheyder;*
    yeshivas
scribes, 29–30.
secularization, 67. *See also* acculturation;
    modernity
sefer, use in titles, 33
*Sefer Mikhtevey ivris [Mikhtave 'ivrit] oder
    ebraisher und daytsher briefshteller*
    (Letters in Hebrew, or Hebrew and
    German letter-writer), 32, 33, 60n95
sermons, 35
shabes. See Sabbath
shadkhonim (marriage brokers), 45, 71,
    117; in America, 124–126, 130–132;
    satirized in Russian manuals, 116–117,
    121–122

Shakespeare, William, 44
Shapira press, 37
Shargorodska, Fayge, 14–15
Shaykevitsh, Nokhem Meyer. *See* Shomer
Shaykevitsh'es nayer brivnshteler (Shay-
    kevitsh's new brivnshteler), xii, 39;
    business, 142, 143; courtship and
    marriage, 125–126, 127, 128, 129,
    130–137; immigration to America,
    101–105, 108–109, 171–172, 180–182,
    183–186; Jewish tradition and
    identity, 154, 164–165; letters from,
    107–110, 130–137, 164–165, 180–182,
    183–186; parents and children,
    101–105, 107–110
Sheldon, L. W., 52
Shmaye der gut-yontev biter, 42
Shnayder, Mordkhe Betsalel, 7, 56n21
Sholem Aleichem (Shalom Rabinovitz), 6,
    11, 12, 18, 25, 39, 42, 43–45
Shomer (Nokhem Meyer Shaykevitsh),
    39, 40, 41, 43, 46–47, 63n140, 187n29,
    190n104; on courtship and marriage,
    124, 125–126, 127, 128–129; on finan-
    cial matters, 140–142; on immigra-
    tion to America, 101–104, 171–172;
    on Jewish tradition and identity,
    154–156; on parents and children,
    101–105. *See also Shaykevitsh'es nayer
    brivnshteler; Shomer's briefenshteler;
    Shomer's pinkas*
Shomer's briefenshteler, 39; foreword to,
    194–195; letters from, 97–98
Shomer's mishpet (Shomer's trial), 39
Shomer's pinkas, 187n18
shopping lists, xii
shoreshim (Hebrew root words), 17
shraybers (handwriting and spelling teach-
    ers), ix, 14–15, 45, 58n48, 58n50, 58n59
Shternshis, Anna, xiv
shtetlakh: vs. cities, 66–67, 69–70, 79, 80–
    81, 82–83; education in, 73–74; New
    York compared to, 180, 181–182
Shteynberg's brifenshteler (Steinberg's
    brivnshteler), 40
Shulkhan Arukh, 75
shund (trash), viii, 39

ALICE NAKHIMOVSKY is Professor of Russian and Eurasian Studies and Jewish Studies at Colgate University, where she directs the Program in Russian and Eurasian Studies. She has written extensively on Russian-Jewish literature and everyday life, and served on the editorial board of *The YIVO Encyclopedia of Jews in Eastern Europe.*

ROBERTA NEWMAN is an independent scholar living in New York City. She is Director of Digital Initiatives at the YIVO Institute for Jewish Research and was the illustrations editor and director of archival research for *The YIVO Encyclopedia of Jews in Eastern Europe.*